Small Business Made Simple

S-Corporation
Small Business
Start-Up Kit

S-Corporation
Small Business
Start-Up Kit

by Daniel Sitarz
Attorney-at-Law

Nova Publishing Company
Small Business and Consumer Legal Books and Software
Carbondale, Illinois

ISBN 1-892949-05-9   Book w/CD   ($29.95)
Library of Congress Catalog Card Number 99-28195

Library of Congress Cataloging-in-Publication Data
    Sitarz, Dan, 1948-
        S-Corporation : small business start-up kit / Daniel Sitarz
        P. cm-(The small business library)
        ISBN 01-892949-05-9
        1. Subchapter S corporations—Popular works.
        I. Title. II. Title: Small Business Start-up kit. III. Series
        KF1466.Z9 .S48 2000   346.73'0652-dc21   CIP 99-28195

Nova Publishing Company is dedicated to providing up-to-date and accurate legal information to the
public. All Nova publications are periodically revised to contain the latest available legal information.

2nd Edition; 1st Printing: August, 2004   1st Edition; 2nd Printing: October, 2001
1st Edition; 4th Printing: April, 2004   1st Edition; 1st Printing: January, 2000
1st Edition; 3rd Printing: June, 2003

This publication is designed to provide accurate and authoritative information in regard to the subject
matter covered. It is sold with the understanding that the publisher and author are not engaged in
rendering legal, accounting, or other professional services. If legal advice or other expert assistance is
required, the services of a competent professional person should be sought.
—From a Declaration of Principles jointly adopted by a Committee of
the American Bar Association and a Committee of Publishers

DISCLAIMER

Because of possible unanticipated changes in governing statutes and case law relating to the application of any information contained in this book, the author, publisher, and any and all persons or entities involved in any way in the preparation, publication, sale, or distribution of this book disclaim all responsibility
for the legal effects or consequences of any document prepared or action taken in reliance upon information contained in this book. No representations, either express or implied, are made or given regarding the legal consequences of the use of any information contained in this book. Purchasers and persons
intending to use this book for the preparation of any legal documents are advised to check specifically
on the current applicable laws in any jurisdiction in which they intend the documents to be effective.

Nova Publishing Company   Distributed by:
Small Business and Consumer Legal Books and Software   National Book Network
1103 West College St.   4501 Forbes Blvd., Suite 200
Carbondale, IL 62901   Lanham, MD 20706
Editorial: (800) 748-1175   Orders: (800) 462-6420

Nova Publishing Company Green Business Policies

Nova Publishing Company is committed to preserving ancient forests and natural resources. Our company's policy is to print all of our books on recycled paper, with no less than 30% post-consumer waste
de-inked in a chlorine-free process. As a result, for the printing of this book, we have saved:

   32.7 trees • 9,450 gallons of water • 5,535 kilowatt hours of electricity • 81 pounds of pollution

Nova Publishing Company is a member of Green Press Initiative, a nonprofit program dedicated to
supporting publishers in their efforts to reduce their use of fiber obtained from endangered forests. For
more information, go to www.greenpressinitiative.org. In addition, Nova uses all compact fluorescent
lighting; recycles all office paper products, aluminum and plastic beverage containers, and printer
cartridges; uses 100% post-consumer fiber, process-chlorine-free, acid-free paper for 95% of in-house
paper use; and, when possible, uses electronic equipment that is EPA Energy Star-certified. Finally, all
carbon emissions from office energy use are offset by the purchase of wind-energy credits that are
used to subsidize the building of wind turbines on the Rosebud Sioux Reservation in South Dakota (see
www.nativeenergy.com/coop).

Table of Contents

List of Forms-on-CD

Business Start-up Checklist
Business Start-up Checklist (text and PDF form)

Developing a Business Plan
Business Plan Worksheet (text and PDF form)
Executive Summary (text and PDF form)

Developing a Marketing Plan
Business Marketing Worksheet (text and PDF form)

Developing a Financial Plan
Business Financial Worksheet (text and PDF form)
Estimated Profit and Loss Statement (PDF form)
Current Balance Sheet (PDF form)

Operating an S-Corporation
S-Corporation Checklist (text and PDF form)

Corporate Paperwork
Corporate Paperwork Checklist (text and PDF form)

Pre-Incorporation Activities
Pre-Incorporation Worksheet (text and PDF form)
Pre-Incorporation Checklist (text and PDF form)
Document Filing Checklist (text and PDF form)
Application for Reservation of Corporate Name (text and PDF form)

Articles of Incorporation
Articles of Incorporation Checklist (text and PDF form)
Articles of Incorporation (text and PDF form)

Corporate Bylaws
Corporate Bylaws Checklist (text and PDF form)
Corporate Bylaws (text and PDF form)

Corporate Directors Meetings
First Board of Directors Meeting Checklist (text and PDF form)
Notice of First Board of Directors Meeting (text and PDF form)
Waiver of Notice of First Board of Directors Meeting (text and PDF form)
Minutes of First Board of Directors Meeting (text and PDF form)

Annual Board of Directors Meeting Checklist (text and PDF form)
Notice of Annual Board of Directors Meeting (text and PDF form)
Waiver of Notice of Annual Board of Directors Meeting (text and PDF form)
Minutes of Annual Board of Directors Meeting (text and PDF form)

Corporate Shareholders Meetings
First Shareholders Meeting Checklist (text and PDF form)
Notice of First Shareholders Meeting (text and PDF form)
Waiver of Notice of First Shareholders Meeting (text and PDF form)
Authorization to Vote Shares [PROXY] (text and PDF form)
Minutes of First Shareholders Meeting (text and PDF form)
Resolution of Shareholders Regarding S-Corporation Status (text and PDF form)
IRS Form 2553: *Election by a Small Business Corporation* (PDF form)
Annual Shareholders Meeting Checklist (text and PDF form)
Notice of Annual Shareholders Meeting (text and PDF form)
Waiver of Notice of Annual Shareholders Meeting (text and PDF form)
Minutes of Annual Shareholders Meeting (text and PDF form)

Corporate Resolutions
Corporate Resolutions Checklists (text and PDF form)
Resolution of Board of Directors (text and PDF form)
Resolution of Shareholders (text and PDF form)
Consent Resolution of Board of Directors (text and PDF form)

Corporate Stock
Corporate Stock Checklist (text and PDF form)
Corporate Stock Certificate (PDF form)
Corporate Stock Certificate [Front] (text form)
Corporate Stock Certificate [Back] (text form)
Corporate Stock Transfer Book (text and PDF form)
Receipt for Stock Certificate (text and PDF form

Employee Documents
General Employment Contract (text and PDF form)
Independent Contractor Agreement (text and PDF form)
Contractor/Subcontractor Agreement (text and PDF form)

Business Financial Recordkeeping
Financial Recordkeeping Checklist (text and PDF form)

Business Accounts
Income Chart of Accounts (PDF form)
Expense Chart of Accounts (PDF form)

Balance Sheet Chart of Accounts (PDF form)
Chart of Accounts (PDF form)
Current Asset Account (PDF form)
Physical Inventory Report (PDF form)
Periodic Inventory Record (PDF form)
Cost of Goods Sold Report (PDF form)
Fixed Asset Account (PDF form)
Accounts Payable Record (PDF form)
Long-Term Debt Record (PDF form)
Weekly Expense Report (PDF form)
Monthly Expense Summary (PDF form)
Annual Expense Summary (PDF form)
Weekly Cash Report (PDF form)
Monthly Cash Report Summary (PDF form)
Weekly Income Record (PDF form)
Monthly Income Summary (PDF form)
Annual Income Summary (PDF form)
Monthly Credit Sales Record (PDF form)
Credit Sales Aging Report (PDF form)
Invoice (PDF form)
Statement (PDF form)
Past Due Statement (PDF form)
Credit Memo (PDF form)

Business Payroll
Quarterly Payroll Time Sheet (PDF form)
Employee Payroll Record (PDF form)
Payroll Depository Record (PDF form)
Annual Payroll Summary (PDF form)
Payroll Checklist (PDF form)

Taxation of Corporations
S-Corporation Tax Forms Checklist (text and PDF form)
S-Corporation Tax Schedules (text and PDF form)

FORMS-ON-CD (Not included in book)
(All IRS forms are PDF forms)
IRS Form SS-4: *Application for Employer Identification Number*
IRS Form 1096: *Annual Summary and Transmittal of U.S. Information Returns*
IRS Form 1099-Misc: *Miscellaneous Income*
IRS Form 1120-S: *U.S. S-Corporation Income Tax Return*
IRS Form 1120-W: *Estimated Tax for Corporations*
IRS Form 940: *Employer's Annual Federal Unemployment (FUTA) Tax Return*

IRS Form 940-EZ: *Employer's Annual Federal Unemployment (FUTA) Tax Return*

IRS Form 941: *Employer's Quarterly Federal Tax Return*

IRS Form W-2: *Wage and Tax Statement*

IRS Form W-3: *Transmittal of Wage and Tax Statements*

IRS Form W-4: *Employee's Withholding Allowance Certificate*

Directors Resolution Authorizing Contract (text and PDF form)

Directors Resolution Authorizing Sale of Real Estate (text and PDF form)

Directors Resolution Authorizing Purchase of Real Estate (text and PDF form)

Directors Resolution Authorizing Borrowing Money (text and PDF form)

Directors Resolution Authorizing Lease (text and PDF form)

Directors Resolution Authorizing Commencement of Lawsuit (text and PDF form)

Directors Resolution Authorizing Appointing of Lawyer (text and PDF form)

Directors Resolution Authorizing Appointing of Accountant (text and PDF form)

Directors Resolution Authorizing Stock Dividend (text and PDF form)

Directors Resolution Authorizing Annual Dividend (text and PDF form)

Directors Resolution Authorizing Quarterly Dividend (text and PDF form)

Directors Resolution Authorizing Expense Reimbursement (text and PDF form)

Directors Resolution Authorizing Retention of Earnings (text and PDF form)

Directors Resolution Authorizing Employee Stock Option Plan (text and PDF form)

Directors Resolution Authorizing Pension Plan (text and PDF form)

Directors Resolution Authorizing Profit-Sharing Plan (text and PDF form)

Directors Resolution Authorizing Health Care Plan (text and PDF form)

Directors Resolution Authorizing Group Insurance Plan (text and PDF form)

Directors Resolution Authorizing Death Benefit Plan (text and PDF form)

Directors Resolution Authorizing Employee Benefit Plan (text and PDF form)

Directors Resolution Authorizing Rescinding Prior Resolution (text and PDF form)

Directors Resolution Authorizing Loan to Corporate Officer (text and PDF form)

Directors Resolution Authorizing Officer's Annual Salary (text and PDF form)

Directors Resolution Authorizing Stock Transfer (text and PDF form)

Directors Resolution Authorizing Change of Location of Registered Office (text and PDF form)

Directors Resolution Authorizing Bonus (text and PDF form)

Preface

This book is part of Nova Publishing Company's continuing Small Business Made Simple series. The various business guides in this series are prepared by business professionals who feel that small business owners deserve the clearest and most understandable information available to assist them in starting and running their businesses. The business references in this series are designed to provide concrete information to small business owners to allow them to understand and start their own businesses with a minimum of outside assistance.

With the proper information, the average person in today's world can easily understand and operate a small business and apply many areas of law. However, each year many thousands of small businesses fail because their owners have been unable to manage their financial, legal, or management affairs properly. This book and others in Nova's Small Business Made Simple series are intended to provide the necessary information to those members of the public who wish to both understand and operate their own businesses.

However, in an endeavor as complex as starting a business, it is not always prudent to attempt to handle every legal, financial, or accounting situation that arises without the aid of a competent professional. Although the information presented in this book will give readers a basic understanding of the areas of law, business, and accounting covered, it is not intended that this text entirely substitute for experienced assistance in all situations. Throughout this book there are references to those particular situations in which the aid of a lawyer or other professional is strongly recommended.

Regardless of whether or not a lawyer or accountant is ultimately retained in certain situations, the information in this handbook will enable the reader to understand the framework of starting a business in this country. To make that task as easy as possible, technical legal jargon has been eliminated whenever possible and plain English used instead. When it is necessary in this book to use a legal term which may be unfamiliar to most people, the word will be defined when first used. A glossary of legal, business, and accounting terms most often encountered is also included at the end of this book.

Introduction

How to Use This Book

This book is designed to be used as a workbook to start your own business as an S-corporation. You will work through various worksheets, complete various checklists, and prepare numerous forms. In each chapter of this book, you will find an introductory section that will give you an overview of the types of situations in which the worksheets, checklists, or forms in that chapter will generally be used. This explanation will, generally, include a listing of the information that must be compiled to complete the form. The forms are not designed to be torn out of this book (especially if this is a library's copy!). It is expected that the forms may be used on more than one occasion. By using the copies of the forms that are contained on the attached CD-ROM, it is possible to easily fill in the forms and prepare them for filing or use. If you do not have access to a computer, the preferable manner for using these forms is to make a photocopy of the form, fill in the information that is necessary, and then retype the form in its entirety on white letter-sized paper. The trend in the legal profession is to move entirely to letter-sized (8½" x 11") paper. In fact, many court systems (including the entire Federal court system) now refuse to accept documents on legal-sized paper.

It is recommended that you review the table of contents of this book in order to gain a broad overview of the range and type of legal, business, and accounting documents that are available. Then, before you prepare any of the forms for use, you should carefully read the introductory information and instructions in the chapter in which the particular form is contained. Try to be as detailed and specific as possible as you fill in these forms. The more precise the description, the less likely that later disputes might develop over what was actually intended by the language chosen. The forms can be carefully adapted to a particular situation that may confront your corporation. However, be very careful in altering the Articles of Incorporation and Corporate Bylaws. Certain clauses are mandatory in these documents and must be included.

The careful preparation and use of the legal, business, and accounting forms in this book should provide the typical business corporation with most of the documents necessary for day-to-day operations. If in doubt as to whether a particular form will work in a specific application, please consult a competent lawyer. It may also be wise to consult with an experienced accountant as you begin to organize the corporation. The tax laws regarding corporations are very complex and must be carefully complied with in order to obtain the maximum tax benefits. Understanding the use of the corporate business entity and the use of corporate forms will enable you to intelligently discuss your corporation with the professionals whom you choose to assist you in your business.

How to Use the Forms-on-CD

Over 100 of the worksheets, checklists, and legal, business, tax, and accounting forms from this book have been provided on the enclosed Forms-on-CD for your use if you have access to a computer. Please note that the Forms-on-CD also includes a number of forms that are not included in this book. The forms on the Forms-on-CD are provided in two separate formats. First, all of the legal and business forms are provided in text-only format. These files all have the file extension> .txt. In addition, all of the accounting and Internal Revenue Service tax forms and most of the business and legal forms are provided in Adobe® PDF format. These files all have the file extension> .pdf.

System Requirements

There are a few system requirements in order to use the Forms-on-CD:

- A PC with an i486 or Pentium processor
- Windows 95, Windows 98, Windows NT 4.0 with Service Pak 3.0 or later, Windows ME, Windows 2000, or Windows EX
- 8 MB RAM on Windows 95 or Windows 98 (16 recommended)
- 16 MB RAM on Windows NT (24 recommended)
- 20 MB of available hard-drive space to install the software

How to Install the Forms-on-CD
For PCs:

1. Insert the enclosed CD in your computer. The installation program should start in a few seconds. Follow the onscreen dialog boxes and make the appropriate choices.
2. If the CD installation does not start automatically, click on the Windows START box, then select RUN, then BROWSE, then select your computer's CD drive, then select the file "Install.exe." Finally, click OK to run the installation program.
3. Open the "Readme.doc" document (which should be visible on your Windows desktop). Print out and follow the instructions on this document.

For MACs:

1. Insert the enclosed CD in your computer and copy the folder "Forms for MACs" to your hard drive.
2. Open the folder and double-click the file: "Adobe Acrobat Install.exe" to install Adobe Acrobat Reader®.
3. Print out the "Readme.doc" document and follow the instructions on this document.

CHAPTER 1
Deciding to Start Business as an S-Corporation

One of the first decisions that potential business owners must confront is how their business should be structured and operated. This crucial decision must be made even before the business has actually begun operations. The legal documents that will generally accompany the formation of a business can follow many different patterns, depending on the particular situation and the type of business to be undertaken.

Initially, the type of business entity to be used must be selected. There are many basic forms of business operating entities. The five most common forms are:

- Sole proprietorship
- Partnership
- Limited liability company
- Corporation
- S-corporation

The choice of entity for a particular business depends on many factors. Which of these forms of business organization is chosen can have a great impact on the success of the business. The structure chosen will have an effect on how easy it is to obtain financing, how taxes are paid, how accounting records are kept, whether personal assets are at risk in the venture, the amount of control the "owner" has over the business, and many other aspects of the business. Keep in mind that the initial choice of business organization need not be the final choice. It is often wise to begin with the simplest form, the sole proprietorship, until the business progresses to a point where another form is clearly indicated. This allows the business to begin in the least complicated manner and allows the owner to retain total control in the important formative period of the business. As the business grows and the potential for liability and tax burdens increase, circumstances may dictate a re-examination of the business structure. The advantages and disadvantages of the five choices of business operation are detailed below.

Sole Proprietorship

A *sole proprietorship* is both the simplest and the most prevalent form of business organization. An important reason for this is that it is the least regulated of all types of business structures. Technically, the sole proprietorship is the traditional unincorporated one-person business. For legal and tax purposes, the business is the owner. It has no existence outside the owner. The liabilities of the business are personal to the owner and the business ends when the owner dies. On the other hand, all of the profits are also personal to the owner and the sole owner has full control of the business.

Disadvantages

Perhaps the most important factor to consider before choosing this type of business structure is that all of the personal and business assets of the sole owner are at risk in the sole proprietorship. If the demands of the creditors of the business exceed those assets which were formally placed in the name of the business, the creditors may reach the personal assets of the owner of the sole proprietorship. Legal judgments for damages arising from the operation of the business may also be enforced against the owner's personal assets. This unlimited liability is probably the greatest drawback to this type of business form. Of course, insurance coverage of various types can lessen the dangers inherent in having one's personal assets at risk in a business. However, as liability insurance premiums continue to skyrocket, it is unlikely that a fledgling small business can afford to insure against all manner of contingencies and at the maximum coverage levels necessary to guard against all risk to personal assets.

A second major disadvantage to the sole proprietorship as a form of business structure is the potential difficulty in obtaining business loans. Often in starting a small business, there is insufficient collateral to obtain a loan and the sole owner must mortgage his or her own house or other personal assets to obtain the loan. This, of course, puts the sole proprietor's personal assets in a direct position of risk should the business fail. Banks and other lending institutions are often reluctant to loan money for initial small business start-ups due to the high risk of failure for small businesses. Without a proven track record, it is quite difficult for a small business owner to adequately present a loan proposal based on a sufficiently stable cash flow to satisfy most banks.

A further disadvantage to a sole proprietorship is the lack of continuity that is inherent in the business form. If the owner dies, the business ceases to exist. Of course, the assets and liabilities of the business will pass to the heirs of the owner, but the expertise and knowledge of how the business was successfully carried on will often die with the owner. Small sole proprietorships are seldom carried on profitably after the death of the owner.

Advantages

The most appealing advantage of the sole proprietorship as a business structure is the total control the owner has over the business. Subject only to economic considerations and certain legal restrictions, there is total freedom to operate the business however one chooses. Many people feel that this factor alone is enough to overcome the inherent disadvantages in this form of business.

Related to this is the simplicity of organization of the sole proprietorship. Other than maintenance of sufficient records for tax purposes, there are no legal requirements on how the business is operated. Of course, the prudent businessperson will keep adequate records and sufficiently organize the business for its most efficient operation. But there are no outside forces dictating how such internal decisions are made in the sole proprietorship. The sole owner makes all decisions in this type of business.

As was mentioned earlier, the sole proprietorship is the least regulated of all businesses. Normally, the only license necessary is a local business license, usually obtained by simply paying a fee to a local registration authority. In addition, it may be necessary to file an affidavit with local authorities and publish a notice in a local newspaper if the business is operated under an assumed or fictitious name. This is necessary to allow creditors to have access to the actual identity of the true owner of the business, since it is the owner who will be personally liable for the debts and obligations of the business.

Finally, it may be necessary to register with local, state, and federal tax bodies for I.D. numbers and for the purpose of collection of sales and other taxes. Other than these few simple registrations, from a legal standpoint little else is required to start up a business as a sole proprietorship.

A final and important advantage to the sole proprietorship is the various tax benefits available to an individual. The losses or profits of the sole proprietorship are considered personal to the owner. The losses are directly deductible against any other income the owner may have and the profits are taxed only once at the marginal rate of the owner. In many instances, this may have distinct advantages over the method by which partnerships are taxed or the double taxation of corporations, particularly in the early stages of the business.

Partnership

A *partnership* is a relationship existing between two or more persons who join together to carry on a trade or business. Each partner contributes money, property, labor, and/or skill to the partnership and, in return, expects to share in the profits or losses of the business. A partnership is usually based on a partnership agreement of some type, although the agreement need not be a formal document. It may even simply be an oral understanding between the partners, although this is not recommended.

A simple joint undertaking to share expenses is not considered a partnership, nor is a mere co-ownership of property that is maintained and leased or rented. To be considered a partnership for legal and tax purposes, the following factors are usually considered:

- The partners' conduct in carrying out provisions of the partnership agreement
- The relationship of the parties
- The abilities and contributions of each party to the partnership
- The control each partner has over the partnership income and the purposes for which the income is used

Disadvantages

The disadvantages of the partnership form of business begin with the potential for conflict between partners. Of all forms of business organization, the partnership has spawned more disagreements than any other. This is generally traceable to the lack of a decisive initial partnership agreement that clearly outlines the rights and duties of the partners. This disadvantage can be partially overcome with a comprehensive partnership agreement. However, there is still the seemingly inherent difficulty many people have in working within the framework of a partnership, regardless of the initial agreement between the partners.

A further disadvantage to the partnership structure is that each partner is subject to unlimited personal liability for the debts of the partnership. The potential liability in a partnership is even greater than that encountered in a sole proprietorship. This is due to the fact that in a partnership the personal risk for which one may be liable is partially out of one's direct control and may be accrued due to actions on the part of another person. Each partner is liable for all of the debts of the partnership, regardless of which partner may have been responsible for their accumulation.

Related to the business risks of personal financial liability is the potential personal legal liability for the negligence of another partner. In addition, each partner may even be liable for the negligence of an employee of the partnership if such negligence takes place during the usual course of business of the partnership. Again, the attendant risks are broadened by the potential for liability based on the acts of other persons. Of course, general liability insurance can counteract this drawback to some extent to protect the personal and partnership assets of each partner.

Again, as with the sole proprietorship, the partnership lacks the advantage of continuity. A partnership is usually automatically terminated upon the death of any partner. A final accounting and a division of assets and liabilities is generally necessary in such an instance unless specific methods under which the partnership may be continued have been outlined in the partnership agreement.

Finally, certain benefits of corporate organization are not available to a partnership. Since a partnership cannot obtain financing through public stock offerings, large infusions of capital are more difficult for a partnership to raise than for a corporation. In addition, many of the fringe benefit programs that are available to corporations (such as certain pension and profit-sharing arrangements) are not available to partnerships.

Advantages

A partnership, by virtue of combining the credit potential of the various partners, has an inherently greater opportunity for business credit than is generally available to a sole proprietorship. In addition, the assets which are placed in the name of the partnership may often be used directly as collateral for business loans. The pooling of the personal capital of the partners generally provides the partnership with an advantage over the sole proprietorship in the area of cash availability. However, as noted above, the partnership does not have as great a potential for financing as does a corporation.

As with the sole proprietorship, there may be certain tax advantages to operation of a business as a partnership, as opposed to a corporation. The profits generated by a partnership may be distributed directly to the partners without incurring any "double" tax liability, as is the case with the distribution of corporate profits in the form of dividends to the shareholders. Income from a partnership is taxed at personal income tax rates. Note, however, that depending on the individual tax situation of each partner, this aspect could prove to be a disadvantage.

For a business in which two or more people desire to share in the work and in the profits, a partnership is often the structure chosen. It is, potentially, a much simpler form of business organization than the corporate form. Less start-up costs are necessary and there is limited regulation of partnerships. However, the simplicity of this form of business can be deceiving. A sole proprietor knows that his or her actions will determine how the business will prosper, and that he or she is, ultimately, personally responsible for the success or failure of the enterprise. In a partnership, however, the duties, obligations, and commitments of each partner are often ill-defined. This lack of definition of the status of each partner can lead to serious difficulties and disagreements. In order to clarify the rights and responsibilities of each partner and to be certain of the tax status of the partnership, it is good business procedure to have a written partnership agreement. All states have adopted a version of the *Uniform Partnership Act*, which provides an outline of partnership law. Although state law will supply the general boundaries of partnerships and even specific partnership agreement terms if they are not addressed by a written partnership agreement, it is better for a clear understanding of the business structure if the partner's agreements are put in writing.

Limited Liability Company

The limited liability company is a hybrid type of business structure. It contains elements of both a traditional partnership and a corporation. The limited liability company form of business structure is relatively new. Only in the last few years has it become available as a form of business in all 50 states and Washington D.C. Its uniqueness is that it offers the limited personal liability of a corporation and the tax benefits of a partnership. A limited liability company consists of one or more members/owners who actively manage the business of the limited liability company. There may also be nonmember managers employed to handle the business.

Disadvantages

In as much as the business form is still similar to a partnership in operation, there is still a potential for conflict among the members/owners of a limited liability company. Limited liability companies are formed according to individual state law, generally by filing formal Articles of Organization of a Limited Liability Company with the proper state authorities in the state of formation. Limited liability companies are, generally, a more complex form of business operation than either the sole proprietorship or the standard partnership. They are subject to more paperwork requirements than a simple partnership but somewhat less than a corporation. Limited liability companies are also subject to far more state regulations regarding both their formation and their operation than either a sole proprietorship or a partnership. In all states, they are also required to pay fees for beginning the company, and in some states, annual franchise fees of often hundreds of dollars are assessed for the right to operate as a limited liability company.

Similar to traditional partnerships, the limited liability company has an inherent lack of continuity. In recent years, however, an increasing number of states have allowed limited liability companies to exist for a perpetual duration, as may corporations. Even if the duration of a limited liability company is perpetual, however, there may be difficulties if the sole member of a one-member limited liability company becomes disabled or dies. These problems can be overcome to some extent by providing, in the Articles of Organization of the limited liability company, for an immediate reorganization of the limited liability company with the deceased member's heirs or estate becoming members of the company. In addition, similar to partnerships, it may be difficult to sell or transfer ownership interests in a limited liability company.

Advantages

The members/owners in such a business enjoy a limited liability, similar to that of a shareholder in a corporation. In general, their risk is limited to the amount of their investment in the limited liability company. Since none of the members will have personal liability and may not necessarily be required to personally perform any tasks of management, it is easier to attract investors to the limited liability company form of business than to a traditional partnership. The members will share in the potential profits and in the tax deductions of the limited liability company, but in fewer of the financial risks involved. Since the limited liability company is generally taxed as a partnership, the profits and losses of the company pass directly to each member and are taxed only at the individual level.

A further advantage of this type of business structure is that it offers a relatively flexible management structure. The company may be managed either by members (owners) themselves or by managers who may or may not be members. Thus, depending on needs or desires, the limited liability company can be a hands-on, owner-managed company or a relatively hands-off operation for its members/owners where hired managers actually operate the company.

A final advantage is that limited liability companies are allowed more flexibility than corporations in how profits and losses are actually allocated to the members/owners. Thus, one member/owner may be allocated 50 percent of the profits (or losses) even though that member/owner only contributed 10 percent of the capital to start the company.

Corporation

Corporations are the focus of this book. A corporation is a creation of law. It is governed by the laws of the state where it was incorporated and of the state or states in which it does business. In recent years it has become the business structure of choice for many small businesses. Corporations are, generally, a more complex form of business operation than either a sole proprietorship or partnership. Corporations are also subject to far more state regulations regarding both their formation and operation. The following discussion is provided in order to allow the potential business owner an understanding of this type of business operation.

The corporation is an artificial entity. It is created by filing Articles of Incorporation with the proper state authorities. This gives the corporation its legal existence and the right to carry on business. The Articles of Incorporation act as a public record of certain formalities of corporate existence. Preparation of Articles of Incorporation is explained in detail in Chapter 9. Adoption of corporate *bylaws*, or internal rules of operation, is often the first business of the corporation, after it has been given the authority to conduct business by the state. The bylaws of the corporation outline the actual mechanics of the operation and management of the corporation. The preparation of corporate bylaws is explained in Chapter 10.

There are two basic types of corporations: C-corporations and S-corporations. These prefixes refer to the particular chapter in the U.S. Tax Codes that specify the tax consequences of either type of corporate organization. In general, both of these two types of corporations are organized and operated in similar fashion. There are specific rules that apply to the ability to be recognized by the U.S. Internal Revenue Service as an S-corporation. In addition, there are significant differences in the tax treatment of these two types of corporations. These differences will be clarified later in this chapter under the heading "S-Corporations." The basic structure and organizational rules below apply to both types of corporations, unless noted.

C-Corporation

In its simplest form, the corporate organizational structure consists of the following levels:

- **Shareholders:** who own shares of the business but do not contribute to the direct management of the corporation, other than by electing the directors of the corporation and voting on major corporate issues

- **Directors:** who may be shareholders, but as directors do not own any of the business. They are responsible, jointly as members of the board of directors of the corporation, for making the major business decisions of the corporation, including appointing the officers of the corporation

- **Officers:** who may be shareholders and/or directors, but, as officers, do not own any of the business. Officers (generally the president, vice president, secretary, and treasurer) are responsible for day-to-day operation of the corporate business

Disadvantages

Due to the nature of the organizational structure in a corporation, a certain degree of individual control is necessarily lost by incorporation. The officers, as appointees of the board of directors, are answerable to the board for management decisions. The board of directors, on the other hand, is not entirely free from restraint, since it is responsible to the shareholders for the prudent business management of the corporation.

The technical formalities of corporation formation and operation must be strictly observed in order for a business to reap the benefits of corporate existence. For this reason, there is an additional burden and expense to the corporation of detailed recordkeeping that is seldom present in other forms of business organization. Corporate decisions are, in general, more complicated due to the various levels of control and all such decisions must be carefully documented. Corporate meetings, both at the shareholder and director levels, are more formal and more frequent. In addition, the actual formation of the corporation is more expensive than the formation of either a sole proprietorship or partnership. The initial state fees that must be paid for registration of a corporation with a state can run as high as $900.00 for a minimally capitalized corporation. Corporations are also subject to a greater level of governmental regulation than any other type of business entity. These complications have the potential to overburden a small business struggling to survive. The forms and instructions in this book are all designed to lessen the burden and expense of operating a business corporation.

Finally, the profits of a corporation, when distributed to the shareholders in the form of dividends, are subject to being taxed twice. The first tax comes at the corporate level.

The distribution of any corporate profits to the investors in the form of dividends is not a deductible business expense for the corporation. Thus, any dividends that are distributed to shareholders have already been subject to corporate income tax. The second level of tax is imposed at the personal level. The receipt of corporate dividends is considered income to the individual shareholder and is taxed as such. This potential for higher taxes due to a corporate business structure can be moderated by many factors, however. Forms dealing with taxation of corporations are contained in Chapter 19.

Advantages

One of the most important advantages to the corporate form of business structure is the potential limited liability of the founders of and investors in the corporation. The liability for corporate debts is limited, in general, to the amount of money each owner has contributed to the corporation. Unless the corporation is essentially a shell for a one-person business or unless the corporation is grossly under-capitalized or under-insured, the personal assets of the owners are not at risk if the corporation fails. The shareholders stand to lose only what they invested. This factor is very important in attracting investors as the business grows.

A corporation can have a perpetual existence. Theoretically, a corporation can last forever. This may be a great advantage if there are potential future changes in ownership of the business in the offing. Changes that would cause a partnership to be dissolved or terminated will often not affect the corporation. This continuity can be an important factor in establishing a stable business image and a permanent relationship with others in the industry.

Unlike a partnership, in which no one may become a partner without the consent of the other partners, a shareholder of corporate stock may freely sell, trade, or give away his or her stock unless this right is formally restricted by reasonable corporate decisions. The new owner of such stock is then a new owner of the business in the proportionate share of stock obtained. This freedom offers potential investors a liquidity to shift assets that is not present in the partnership form of business. The sale of shares by the corporation is also an attractive method by which to raise needed capital. The sale of shares of a corporation, however, is subject to many governmental regulations on both the state and federal levels.

Taxation is listed both as an advantage and as a disadvantage for the corporation. Depending on many factors, the use of a corporation can increase or decrease the actual income tax paid in operating a corporate business. In addition, corporations may set aside surplus earnings (up to certain levels) without any negative tax consequences. Finally, corporations are able to offer a much greater variety of fringe benefit programs to employees and officers than any other type of business entity. Various retirement, stock option, and profit-sharing plans are only open to corporate participation.

S-Corporation

The S-corporation is a certain type of corporation that is available for specific tax purposes. It is a creation of the Internal Revenue Service. S-corporation status is not relevant to state corporation laws. Its purpose is to allow small corporations to choose to be taxed, at the Federal level, like a partnership, but to also enjoy many of the benefits of a corporation. It is, in many respects, similar to a limited liability company. The main difference lies in the rules that a company needs to meet in order to qualify as an S-corporation under Federal law.

In general, to qualify as an S-corporation under current IRS rules, a corporation must meet certain requirements:

- It must not have more than 75 shareholders
- All of the shareholders must, generally, be individuals and U.S. citizens
- It must only have one class of stock
- Shareholders must consent to S-corporation status
- An election of S-corporation status must be filed with the IRS

The S-corporation retains all of the advantages and disadvantages of the traditional corporation except in the area of taxation. For tax purposes, S-corporation shareholders are treated similarly to partners in a partnership. The income, losses, and deductions generated by an S-corporation are "passed through" the corporate entity to the individual shareholders. Thus, there is no "double" taxation of an S-corporation. In addition, unlike a standard corporation, shareholders of S-corporations can personally deduct any corporate losses. Forms dealing with taxation of S-corporations are contained in Chapter 19.

The decision of which business entity to choose depends upon many factors and should be carefully studied. If the choice is to operate a business as a S-corporation, this book will provide an array of easy-to-use legal forms that will, in most cases, allow the business owner to start and operate the corporation with minimal difficulty while meeting all of the legal paperwork requirements.

CHAPTER 2

Business Start-up Checklist

Following is the first of many checklists that are provided in this book in order to help you organize your preparation for starting a business. This initial checklist provides an overview of the entire process of starting a business and, in many ways, is your blueprint for your personal business start-up. It incorporates references to many other forms, worksheets, and checklists from throughout this book. Keep this list handy as you proceed through the process of starting your own S-corporation.

Business Start-up Checklist

❏ Read through this entire book to understand the process of starting a S-corporation

❏ Install the software and forms from the Forms-on-CD if you will be using a computer to complete the forms (Introduction)

❏ Complete the Business Plan Worksheet (Chapter 3)

  ❏ Prepare your written Business Plan

❏ Complete the Business Marketing Worksheet (Chapter 4)

  ❏ Prepare your written Marketing Plan

❏ Prepare the Business Financial Worksheet (Chapter 5)

  ❏ Prepare your written Financial Plan

❏ Prepare your written Executive Summary (Chapter 3)

❏ Compile your final Business Plan package (Chapter 3)

❏ Review the Corporate Paperwork Checklist (Chapter 7)

❏ Complete the Pre-Incorporation Worksheet (Chapter 8)

❏ Review the Pre-Incorporation and Document Filing Checklists (Chapter 8)

❏ Prepare and file your Application for Reservation of Corporate Name (if desired)

❏ Prepare and file your Articles of Incorporation (Chapter 9)

❏ Prepare your Corporate Bylaws (Chapter 10)

❏ Hold first directors meeting using First Board of Directors Meeting Checklist (Chapter 11)

❏ Hold first shareholders meeting using First Shareholders Meeting Checklist (Chapter 12)

❏ Prepare and file IRS Form 2553: *Election by a Small Business Corporation* (Chapter 12)

❏ Prepare any necessary Corporate Resolutions (Chapter 13)

❏ Prepare and issue any Corporate Stock (Chapter 14)

❏ Prepare Employment Contracts for officers and employees of corporation (Chapter 15)

❏ Set up Business Accounting System Chart of Accounts (Chapter 17)

❏ Prepare Income/Expense/Asset/Liability Accounts (Chapter 17)

❏ Open Corporate Business Bank Account

❏ Set up Business Payroll (Chapter 18)

❏ Set up Corporate Tax Payment Schedules (Chapter 19)

CHAPTER 3
Developing a Business Plan

One of the most important and often overlooked aspects of starting a business is the process of preparing a Business Plan. It is through preparation of a formal business plan than you begin the process of refining what your business will actually be and, more importantly, how you can make it successful from the start. To develop a useful plan, you will need to research your business idea and determine how it can be developed into a feasible and successful business. You will use your business plan for many purposes: for your own use to continually fine-tune your actual business start-up; for obtaining financing, even it is only from family members; and for presenting your business ideas to potential shareholders, employees, investors, suppliers, and anyone else with whom you may be doing business. Your plan needs to be dynamic and detailed. If you prepare your plan with care and attention, it will help guide you through the process of starting a successful business. If you take shortcuts in researching, thinking about, and preparing your plan, your path to business success will become an everyday struggle.

This book has divided the preparation of your business plan into three separate parts. In this chapter, you will develop your overall plan. However, in the two following chapters, you will also develop plans that will become an integral part of your business plan. Chapter 4 concentrates on the plans to market your business service or product. Chapter 5 provides a worksheet and instructions for preparing and implementing a strategy for financing your business. Together, the three plans that you create will comprise your total Business Plan package. Finally, after completing all three sections, you will prepare an Executive Summary. The instructions for preparing the summary are at the end of this chapter. With the information you will have gathered and set down in your plan, starting a successful business will be simplified and streamlined. Each of these three chapters has a similar format. A worksheet is presented into which you will enter information that you have gathered or researched. Crucial business decisions will need to be made, even at this early stage, in order for you to honestly assess your chances for success. After completing the worksheet, you will use the compiled information to complete a written (typed or printed) plan. This process will take some time to do correctly, but time spent at this stage of your business start-up will save you many times the effort and headaches later in your business' evolution. If you are using a computer, all three of the Business Plan Worksheets are included on the Forms-on-CD. You may enter your answers to the questions directly on the forms which you can open in your own word-processing program. This will allow you to quickly and easily compile the answers that you have written out into the final Business Plan. Following this first worksheet are more detailed instructions for preparing your Business Plan.

Business Plan Worksheet

Preliminary Business Concept Analysis

In one sentence, describe your business concept: _____
_____

What is your business service or product? _____
_____
_____

How long do you estimate that it will take to develop this service or product to the point of being ready for the public? _____
_____

What are the estimated costs of development of this product or service? _____
_____

Why do you think that this business concept will succeed? _____
_____
_____

Who is your target market? _____
_____

Is this market readily identifiable? _____
_____

What are the buying patterns of this market? _____
_____

Is there sufficient advance interest in this type of product or service? _____
_____

What are your expected annual sales/revenue volumes?
    Year one: $ _____
    Year two: $ _____
    Year three: $ _____
    Year four: $ _____
    Year five: $ _____

Company Description

What is your company's mission? _____

_____

What is the type of business entity of your company?   *S-Corporation*

Who will be the directors of the company? _____

_____

Who will serve as the officers of the company?
President: _____
Vice President: _____
Treasurer: _____
Secretary: _____

What will the physical location of your company be? _____

_____

Where will be the company's main place of doing business? _____

Will there be any additional locations for the company? _____

_____

What geographic areas will your company serve? _____

What are the long-term plans for the business? (Expand, go public, sell to competitor, etc.)

_____

_____

Industry Analysis

In what industry will your company operate? _____

What is the overall size of the industry? _____

What is the growth rate of the industry? _____

What are any seasonal or business cycles in the industry? _____

_____

What have been the main technological advances in the past five years? _____

_____

What are projected technological advances in the industry for the next five years? _____
_____

Do any industry standards apply to your business? _____
_____

Are there any government regulatory approvals or requirements? _____
_____

Are there any local or state licenses necessary for the service or product? _____
_____

What are the main trade or business associations in your industry? _____
_____

To which associations do you currently belong? _____
_____

Product or Service Analysis

Description of product or service: _____
_____

What is the main purpose of the product or service? _____
_____

Is it a luxury item or a necessity? _____

What are the unique features of your product or service? (Cost, design, quality, capabilities, etc.) _____
_____
_____

What is the life of the product or service? _____

How does this product/service compare with the state-of-the-art for the industry? _____
_____

In what stage is the development of the product? (Idea, model, prototype, full production, etc.) _____

Describe the company's facilities: _____
_____

How will the product be produced or the service provided? _____

_____

Is it labor- or material-intensive to produce or supply? _____

What components or supplies are necessary to produce or supply this product? _____

_____

Has the service or product been the subject of any engineering or design tests? _____

_____

What types of quality control will be in place in the business? _____

_____

Are there any special technical considerations? _____

_____

What are the maintenance or updating requirements for the product/service? _____

_____

Can the product be copyrighted, patented, or trade- or service-marked? _____

_____

Are there other products, services, or spin-offs that will be developed and marketed in future
years? _____

_____

Are there any known dangers associated with the manufacture, supply, or use of the product/
service? _____

What types of liabilities are posed by the product, service, or any other business operations?
    To employees: _____
    To customers: _____
    To suppliers: _____
    To distributors: _____
    To the public: _____

Are there any litigation threats posed by this business? _____

Are there any other problems or risks inherent in this type of business? _____

_____

What types of insurance coverage will be necessary for the business? _____

_____

What are the costs of the needed insurance coverage? _____

What steps will be taken to minimize any potential liabilities, dangers, or risks? _____
_____
_____

Business Operations

Describe the type of facilities that your business will need to operate: _____
_____

Estimate the cost of acquiring and maintaining the facilities for two years: _____
_____

Describe your production plan or service plan: _____
_____
_____

How will orders be filled and your product or service delivered? _____
_____

Will you work through any wholesalers or distributors? _____
_____

Who will be the main wholesalers/distributors? _____
_____

Describe the equipment or machinery that you will need for your business: _____
_____
_____

Who will be the main suppliers of this equipment? _____
_____

What are the estimated costs of obtaining this equipment? _____

What type of inventory will you need? _____

Who will be the main suppliers of the inventory? _____
_____

Estimate the costs of obtaining sufficient inventory for the first two years of operation:
_____

Management Analysis

What will be the organizational structure of the company? (Include an organizational chart)

_____

Who will manage the day-to-day affairs of the company? _____

Describe the management style of the central manager: _____

_____

What are the qualifications of the main management? _____

What type of workforce will be necessary for your business? _____

_____

How many employees will be needed?
- Initially: _____
- First year: _____
- Second year: _____
- Third year: _____
- Fourth year: _____
- Fifth year: _____

What are the job descriptions of the employees? _____

What job skills will the employees need? _____

Are employment and hiring/firing procedures and guidelines in place? _____

What will be the hourly wages or salaries of the employees?
- Salaried: _____
- Full-time: _____
- Part-time: _____

Will any fringe benefits be provided to employees?
- Sick pay: _____
- Vacation pay: _____
- Bonuses: _____
- Health insurance or benefits: _____
- Profit-sharing or stock options: _____
- Other benefits: _____

Estimate the annual cost for employee compensation for the first two years of operations:

_____

Will you need to contract with lawyers, accountants, consultants, designers, or specialists?

_____

Who will be the outside contractors you will use? _____

_____

Estimate the annual cost of outside contractors for the first two years of operations:

_____

Is the business bookkeeping system set up and working? _____

Are business bank accounts set up? _____

Are there administrative policies set up for billings, payments, accounts, etc.? _____

Supporting Documentation

Do you have any professional photos of the product, equipment, or facilities? _____

_____

What contracts have already been signed? _____

Does the company hold any patents, trademarks, or copyrights? _____

_____

Have the company's incorporation papers been filed with the state and received? _____

_____

Do you have any samples of advertising or marketing materials? _____

Do you have references and resumés from each of the principals in the business? _____

_____

Do you have personal financial statements from each of the principals in the business?

_____

Have you prepared a time line chart for the company's development for the first five years?

_____

Have you prepared a list of the necessary equipment, with a description, supplier, and cost of each item noted? _____

Have you prepared current and projected balance sheets and profit/loss statements? _____

Preparing Your Business Plan

Once you have completed the previous worksheet and the worksheets in the next two chapters (relating to marketing and financial plans), you will need to prepare your final Business Plan and complete the Executive Summary. The Executive Summary is, perhaps, the most important document in the entire Business Plan, for it is in this short document that you will distill your entire vision of your company. Do not attempt to prepare the Executive Summary until you have completed all of the other worksheets and plans, for they will provide you with the insight that you will need to craft an honest and enthusiastic Executive Summary for your company.

To prepare your Business Plan, carefully read through the answers you have prepared for the Business Plan Worksheet to obtain a complete overview of your proposed business. Your task will be to carefully put the answers to the questions on the worksheet into a narrative format. If you have taken the time to fully answer the questions, this will not be a difficult task. If you have supplied the answers to the worksheet questions on the computer file version of the worksheet, you should be able to easily cut and paste your Business Plan sections together, adding only sentence and paragraph structure and connecting information. Keep the plan to the point but try to convey both a broad outline of the industry that you will be operating in and a clear picture of how your particular company will fit into that industry and succeed. Emphasize the uniqueness of your company, product, or service, but don't intentionally avoid the potential problems that your business will face. An honest appraisal of your company's risks and potential problems at this stage of the development of your company will convey to investors and bankers that you have thoroughly and carefully investigated the potential for your company to succeed.

For each subsection of the Business Plan Worksheet, use the answers to the questions to prepare your written plan. You may rearrange the answers within each section if you feel that it will present a clearer picture to those who will be reading your Business Plan. Try, however, to keep the information for each section in its own discreet portion of the Business Plan. You will use this same technique to prepare the written Marketing and Financial Plans in the following two chapters. Once you have prepared your written Business, Marketing, and Financial Plans, you are ready to prepare your Executive Summary.

Preparing Your Executive Summary

It is in the Executive Summary that you will need to convey your vision of the company and its potential for success. It is with this document that you will convince investors, suppliers, bankers, and others to take the risks necessary to back your dreams and help you to make them a reality. The Executive Summary portion of your Business Plan should be about one to three pages long. It should be concise, straightforward, and clearly written. Don't use any terms or technical jargon that the average person cannot understand. You may go into more detail in the body of the Business Plan itself, but keep the Executive Summary short and to the point. This document will be a distillation of the key points in your entire Business Plan. It is in the Executive Summary that you will need to infuse your potential backers with your enthusiasm and commitment to success. However, you will need to remain honest and forthright in the picture that you paint of your business and its competition. Use the following outline as a guide to assist you in preparing your Executive Summary. You will, of course, be using the information that you have included in your written Business, Marketing, and Financial Plans to prepare the Executive Summary. After completing your Executive Summary, there are some brief instructions to assist you in compiling your entire Business Plan package.

Executive Summary

Business Plan of _____

Executive Summary

In the year _____ , _____ was incorporated as a corporation in the State of _____ .

The purpose of the company is to: _____
_____
_____ .

Our mission statement is as follows: This company is dedicated to providing the highest quality _____ to a target market of _____ . Our long-term goals are to: _____
_____ .

Industry Analysis

The industry in which this company will operate is: _____
_____ .

The annual gross sales of the _____ industry are approximately $ _____ .

Continue with a brief explanation of how your company will fit into this industry: _____
_____

Product or Service Analysis

The product/service that this company will provide is: _____ .

It is unique in its field because: _____ .

Continue with a brief explanation of product/service: _____
_____
_____ .

Business Operations

Prepare a brief explanation of how the business will operate to obtain and deliver the product/service to the market. Include short explanations of strategies you will use to beat the competition: _____

_____
_____ .

Management of the Company

The company will be managed by: _____

_____ .

Include a brief summary of the management structure and the qualifications of the key management personnel and how their expertise will be the key to the success of the company:

_____
_____
_____ .

Market Strategy

The target market for this product/service is: _____

_____ .

Prepare a brief analysis of your market research and marketing plans and why your product/service is better than any competitors: _____

_____
_____
_____ .

Financial Plans

In this section, briefly review the data on your Current Balance Sheet and Estimated Profit and Loss Statements and describe both the annual revenue projections and the company's immediate and long-term needs for financing: _____

_____
_____
_____ .

Compiling Your Business Plan

1. Prepare a Title page filling in the necessary information:

> Business Plan of (*name of corporation*),
> Incorporated in the State of (*name of state*)
> Address:
> Phone:
> Fax:
> Internet:
> E-mail:
> Date:
> Prepared by (*name of preparer*)

2. Include a Table of Contents listing the following items that you have:

- Executive Summary
- Business Plan
    Business Concept and Objectives
    Industry Analysis
    Product/Service Analysis
    Business Operations
    Management Analysis
- Marketing Plan
    Target Market Analysis
    Competitive Analysis
    Sales and Pricing Analysis
    Marketing Strategy
        Advertising and Promotion
        Publicity and Public Relations
- Financial Plan
    Financial Analysis
    Estimated Profit/Loss Statement
    Current Balance Sheet
- Appendix
    Photos of Product/Service/Facilities
    Contracts
    Incorporation Documents
    Bank Account Statements
    Personal Financial Statements of Principals
    Proposed List of Equipment/Supplies/Inventory
    Proposed Time Line for Corporate Growth

3. Neatly print or type the necessary Business/Marketing/Financial Plans.

4. Compile all of the parts of your Plan and have multiple photocopies made.

5. Assemble all of the parts into a neat and professional folder or notebook.

Congratulations! Your completed Business Plan will serve as an essential guide to understanding your business and will allow potential backers, investors, bankers, and others to quickly see the reality behind your business goals.

CHAPTER 4
Developing a Marketing Plan

An integral part of the process of starting a business is preparing a Marketing Plan. Whether the business will provide a service or sell a product, it will need customers in some form. Who those customers are, how they will be identified and located, and how they will be attracted to the business are crucial to the success of any small business. Unfortunately, it is also one part of a business start-up that is given less than its due in terms of time and effort spent to fully investigate the possibilities. In this chapter, a Business Marketing Worksheet is provided to assist you in thinking about your business in terms of who the customers may be and how to reach them. In many ways, looking honestly at who your customers may be and how to attract them may be the most crucial part of starting your business, for if your understanding of this issue is ill-defined or unclear, your business will have a difficult time succeeding.

In order to create your written Marketing Plan, simply follow the same process that you used in creating your Business Plan in Chapter 3. Take the answers that you have supplied on the following worksheet and edit them into a narrative for each of the four sections of the worksheet:

- Target Market Analysis
- Competitive Analysis
- Sales and Pricing Analysis
- Marketing Strategy

By following this process, you should be able to create a clear and straightforward description of your own business's marketing objectives and methods.

Business Marketing Worksheet

Target Market Analysis

What is the target market for your product/service? _____
_____

What types of market research have you conducted to understand your market? _____
_____

What is the geographic market area you will serve? _____

Describe a typical customer:
    Sex: _____
    Marital status: _____
    Age: _____
    Income: _____
    Geographic location: _____
    Education: _____
    Employment: _____

Estimate the number of potential people in the market in your area of service: _____
_____

What is the growth potential for this market? _____

How will you satisfy the customers' needs with your product/service? _____
_____

Will your product/service make your customers' life more comfortable? _____

Will your product/service save your customers' time or money or stress? _____

Competitive Analysis

Who are your main competitors? _____

Are there competitors in the same geographic area as your proposed business? _____
_____

Are the competitors successful and what is their market share? _____

How long have they been in business? _____

Describe your research into your competitors' business operations: _____
_____

Are there any foreseeable new competitors? _____

What are the strengths and/or weaknesses of your competitor's product/service? _____
_____

Why is your product/service different or better than that of your competitors? _____
_____
_____

What is the main way that you will compete with your competitors (price, quality, technology, advertising, etc.)? _____
_____

How will your customers know that your product/service is available? _____
_____

What is the main message that you want your potential customers to receive? _____
_____

Why is your product/service unique? _____
_____

How will you be able to expand your customer base over time? _____
_____

Sales and Pricing Analysis

What are your competitors' prices for similar products/services? _____

Are your prices higher or lower, and why? _____

Will you offer any discounts for quantity or other factors? _____

Will you accept checks for payment? _____

Will you accept credit cards for payment? _____

Will you have a sales force? Describe: _____

What skills or education will the sales force need? _____

Will there be sales quotas? _____

Will the sales force be paid by salary, wages, or commission? _____

Are there any geographic areas or limitations on your sales or distribution? _____
_____

Will you sell through distributors or wholesalers? Describe: _____

Will there be dealer margins or wholesale discounts? _____

Do you have any plans to monitor customer feedback? Describe: _____
_____

Do you have warranty, guarantee, and customer return policies? Describe: _____
_____

Will any customer service be provided? Describe: _____
_____

What is your expected sales volume for the first five years?
    Year one: _____
    Year two: _____
    Year three: _____
    Year four: _____
    Year five: _____

Marketing Strategy

What is your annual projected marketing budget? _____

Have your company's logo, letterhead, and business cards already been designed?
_____

Do you have a company slogan or descriptive phrase? _____

Has packaging for your product/service been designed? _____

Has signage for your facility been designed? _____

Describe your advertising plans:

Signs: _____

Brochures: _____

Catalogs: _____

Yellow Pages: _____

Magazines: _____

Trade journals: _____

Radio: _____

Television: _____

Newspapers: _____

Internet: _____

Trade shows: _____

Videos: _____

Billboards: _____

Newsletters: _____

Have advertisements already been designed? _____

Have you prepared a media kit for publicity? _____

Describe your plans to receive free publicity in the media via news releases or new product/ service releases:

Radio: _____

Television: _____

Newspapers: _____

Magazines: _____

Internet: _____

Have you requested inclusion in any directories, catalogs, or other marketing vehicles for your industry? _____

Describe any planned direct mail campaigns: _____

Describe any planned telemarketing campaigns: _____

Describe any internet-based marketing plans:

E-mail account: _____

Website: _____

Will there be any special or seasonal promotions of your product/service? _____
_____

How will your customers actually receive the product/service? _____
_____

CHAPTER 5
Developing a Financial Plan

The third crucial part of your initial Business Plan entails how your business will obtain enough money to actually survive until it is successful. The failure of many small businesses relates directly to underestimating the amount of money needed to start *and* continue the business. Most business owners can, with relative ease, estimate the amount of money needed to start a business. The problem comes with arriving at a clear estimate of how much money will be necessary to keep the business operating until it is able to realistically support itself. If you can honestly determine how much is actually necessary to allow the business time to thrive before you can take out profits or pay, the next challenge is to figure out where to get that amount of money. To help you arrive at a clear picture of your business's finances, a Business Financial Worksheet follows. This worksheet will lead you through a number of questions to help you determine the amount of money needed and where it might be obtained. Following the worksheet are instructions on preparing both a Estimated Profit and Loss Statement and a Current Balance Sheet. Both of these financial forms will help you actually put some real numbers into your plans.

When you have completed the Business Financial Worksheet and your two financial forms, you will again need to prepare a written Financial Plan from your worksheet answers and the data that you have compiled on your Profit and Loss Statement and Balance Sheet. Use the same technique that you used in Chapters 3 and 4 to convert your answers to a narrative. After your written Financial Plan is completed, you will need to return to the instructions at the end of Chapter 3, complete your Executive Summary, and compile your completed parts into your entire final Business Plan package. You may then use your formal plan for presentations to prospective investors, bankers, family, or friends as you go in search of the assistance you will need to make your business a success. You will also need to develop a financial recordkeeping system. This and other accounting-related details are explained in Chapters 16 through 18.

Business Financial Worksheet

Describe the current financial status of your company: _____
_____
_____

Income and Expenses

Estimate the annual expenses for the first year in the following categories:

Advertising expenses: _____

Auto expenses: _____

Cleaning and maintenance expenses: _____

Charitable contributions: _____

Dues and publications: _____

Office equipment expenses: _____

Freight and shipping expenses: _____

Business insurance expenses: _____

Business interest expenses: _____

Legal and accounting expenses: _____

Business meals and lodging: _____

Miscellaneous expenses: _____

Postage expenses: _____

Office rent/mortgage expenses: _____

Repair expenses: _____

Office supplies: _____

Sales taxes: _____

Federal unemployment taxes: _____

State unemployment taxes: _____

Telephone/internet expenses: _____

Utility expenses: _____

Wages and commissions: _____

Estimate the first year's annual income from the following sources:

Sales income: _____

Service income: _____

Miscellaneous income: _____

Estimate the amount of inventory necessary for the first year: _____
_____

Estimate the amount of inventory that will be sold during the first year: _____

_____

Estimate the Cost of Goods Sold for the first year: _____

Using the above information, complete the Estimated Profit and Loss Statement as explained later.

Assets and Liabilities

What forms of credit have already been used by the business? _____

_____

How much cash is available to the business? _____

What are the sources of the cash? _____

What types of bank accounts are in place for the business and what are the balances?

_____

_____

What types of assets are currently owned by the business?
    Current assets: _____
    Inventory: _____
        Cash in bank: _____
        Cash on hand: _____
    Accounts receivable: _____
    Fixed and depreciable: _____
    Autos/trucks: _____
        Buildings: _____
        Equipment: _____
        Amount of depreciation taken on any of above: _____
    Fixed non-depreciable: _____
        Land: _____
    Miscellaneous: _____
        Stocks/bonds: _____

What types of debts does the business currently have?
    Current liabilities: _____
        Taxes due: _____
        Accounts payable: _____
        Short-term loans/notes payable: _____
        Payroll accrued: _____
        Miscellaneous: _____

Long-term liabilities: _____
    Mortgage: _____
    Other loans/notes payable: _____

Financial Needs

Based on the estimated profits and losses of the business, how much credit will be necessary for the business?

    Initially: _____
    First year: _____
    Second year: _____
    Third year: _____
    Fourth year: _____
    Fifth year: _____

Estimate the cash flow for the business for the first five years:

    First year: _____
    Second year: _____
    Third year: _____
    Fourth year: _____
    Fifth year: _____

From what sources are the necessary funds expected to be raised?

    Cash on hand: _____
    Personal funds: _____
    Family: _____
    Friends: _____
    Conventional bank financing: _____
    Finance companies: _____
    Equipment manufacturers: _____
    Leasing companies: _____
    Venture capital: _____
    U.S. Small Business Administration: _____
    Equity financing (*check with current Securities and Exchange rules on sales of shares*): _____

Preparing a Profit and Loss Statement

A Profit and Loss Statement is the key financial statement for presenting how your business is performing over a period of time. The Profit and Loss Statement illuminates both the amounts of money that your business has spent on expenses and the amounts of money that your business has taken in over a specific period of time. Along with the Balance Sheet, which is discussed later in this chapter, the Profit and Loss Statement should become an integral part of both your short- and long-range business planning.

This section will explain how to prepare an Estimated Profit and Loss Statement for use in your Business Plan. The Estimated Profit and Loss Statement can serve a valuable business planning service by allowing you to project estimated changes in your business over various time periods and examine what the results may be. Projections of various business plans can be examined in detail and decisions can then be made on the basis of clear pictures of future scenarios. Your estimates of your business profits and losses can take into account industry changes, economic factors, and personal business decisions. Your estimates are primarily for internal business planning purposes, although it may be useful to use an Estimated Profit and Loss Statement to convey your future Business Plans to others. As a trial exercise, you should prepare an Estimated Profit and Loss Statement using your best estimates before you even begin business. You may wish to prepare such pre-business statements for monthly, quarterly, and annual time periods. You may also desire to prepare Estimated Profit and Loss Statements for the first several years of your business's existence.

The Estimated Profit and Loss Statement differs from the other type of Profit and Loss Statements in that the figures that you will use are projections based on expected business income and expenses for a time period in the future. The value of this type of financial planning tool is to allow you to see how various scenarios will affect your business. You may prepare this form as either a monthly, quarterly, or annual projection. To prepare this form, use the data that you have collected for the above Business Financial Worksheet. For more information on Profit and Loss Statements, please see Chapter 16.

1. The first figure that you will need will be your Estimated Gross Sales Income. If your business is a pure service business, put your estimated income on the *Estimated Service Income Total* line. If your business income comes from part sales and part service, place the appropriate figures on the correct lines.

2. If your business will sell items from inventory, you will need to calculate your Estimated Cost of Goods Sold. In order to have the necessary figures to make this computation, you will need to prepare a projection of your inventory costs and how many items you expect to sell. Fill in the *Estimated Cost of Goods Sold* figure on the Estimated Profit and Loss Statement. If your business is a pure service business,

skip this line. Determine your Estimated Net Sales Income Total by subtracting your Estimated Cost of Goods Sold from your Estimated Gross Sales Income.

3. Calculate your Estimated Total Income for the period by adding your Estimated Net Sales Income Total and your Estimated Service Income Total and any Estimated Miscellaneous Income (for example: interest earned on a checking account).

4. Fill in the appropriate Estimated Expense account categories on the Estimated Profit and Loss Statement. If you have a large number of categories, you may need to prepare a second sheet. Based on your future projections, fill in the totals for each of your separate expense accounts. Add in any Estimated Miscellaneous Expenses.

5. Total all of your expenses and subtract your Estimated Total Expenses figure from your Estimated Total Income figure to determine your Estimated Pre-Tax Profit for the time period.

Estimated Profit and Loss Statement

For the period of:

ESTIMATED INCOME			
Income	Estimated Gross Sales Income		
	Less Estimated Cost of Goods Sold		
	Estimated Net Sales Income Total		
	Estimated Service Income Total		
	Estimated Miscellaneous Income Total		
	Estimated Total Income		
ESTIMATED EXPENSES			
Expenses	Advertising expenses		
	Auto expenses		
	Cleaning and maintenance expenses		
	Charitable contributions		
	Dues and publications		
	Office equipment expenses		
	Freight and shipping expenses		
	Business insurance expenses		
	Business interest expenses		
	Legal and accounting expenses		
	Business meals and lodging		
	Miscellaneous expenses		
	Postage expenses		
	Office rent/mortgage expenses		
	Repair expenses		
	Office supplies		
	Sales taxes		

Federal unemployment taxes	
State unemployment taxes	
Telephone/Internet expenses	
Utility expenses	
Wages and commissions	
Estimated General Expenses Total	
Estimated Miscellaneous Expenses	
Estimated Total Expenses	

Estimated Pre-Tax Profit (Income less Expenses)	

Preparing a Balance Sheet

A Profit and Loss Statement provides a view of business operations over a particular period of time. It allows a look at the income and expenses and profits or losses of the business during the time period. In contrast, a Balance Sheet is designed to be a look at the financial position of a company on a specific date. It shows what the business owns and owes on a fixed date. Its purpose is to depict the financial strength of a company as shown by its assets and liabilities. It is merely a visual representation of the basic business financial equation: assets – liabilities = equity (or *net worth*). Essentially, the Balance Sheet shows what the company would be worth if all of the assets were sold and all the liabilities were paid off. A value is placed on each asset and on each liability. These figures are then balanced by adjusting the value of the owner's equity figure in the equation. Your Balance Sheet will total your current and fixed assets and your current and long-term liabilities. Even if your business is very new, you will need to prepare a Balance Sheet of where the business currently stands financially. Use the figures that you have gathered for the previous Business Financial Worksheet to complete your Current Balance Sheet. For further information on Balance Sheets, please refer to Chapter 16. Please follow the instructions below to prepare your Current Balance Sheet for your Business Financial Plan:

1. Your Current Assets consist of the following items:

    - Cash in Bank (from your business bank account balance)
    - Cash on Hand
    - Accounts Receivable (if you have any yet)
    - Inventory (if you have any yet)
    - Prepaid Expenses (these may be rent, insurance, prepaid supplies, or similar items that have been paid for prior to their actual use)

2. Total all of your Current Assets on your Current Balance Sheet.

3. Your Fixed Assets consist of the following items, which should be valued at your actual cost:

    - Equipment
    - Autos and Trucks
    - Buildings

4. Total your Fixed Assets (except land) on your Current Balance Sheet. Total all of the depreciation that you have previously deducted for all of your fixed assets (except land). Include in this figure any business deductions that you have taken for Section 179 write-offs on business equipment. *Note*: If you are just starting a business, you will not have any depreciation or Section 179 deductions as yet. En-

ter this total depreciation figure under "Less Depreciation" and subtract this figure from the figure for Total Fixed Assets (except land).

5. Enter the value for any land that your business owns. Land may not be depreciated. Add Total Fixed Assets (except land) amount, minus the (less depreciation) figure, and the value of the land. This is your Total Fixed Assets value.

6. Add any Miscellaneous Assets not yet included. These may consist of stocks, bonds, or other business investments. Total your Current, Fixed, and Miscellaneous Assets to arrive at your Total Assets figure.

7. Your Current Liabilities consist of the following items:

   - Accounts Payable (if you have any yet)
   - Miscellaneous Payable (include here the principal due on any short-term notes payable. Also include any interest on credit purchases, notes, or loans that has accrued but not been paid. Also list the current amounts due on any long-term liabilities. Finally, list any payroll or taxes that have accrued but not yet been paid)

8. Your Fixed Liabilities consist of Loans Payable (the principal of any long-term note, loan, or mortgage due). Any current amounts due should be listed as "Current Liabilities."

9. Total your Current and Fixed Liabilities to arrive at Total Liabilities.

10. Subtract your Total Liabilities from your Total Assets to arrive at your Owner's Equity. For a corporation, this figure represents the total of contributions by the owners or stockholders plus earnings after paying any dividends. Total Liabilities and Owner's Equity will always equal Total Assets.

Current Balance Sheet

As of:

ASSETS			
Current Assets	Cash in Bank		
	Cash on Hand		
	Accounts Receivable		
	Inventory		
	Prepaid Expenses		
	Total Current Assets		
Fixed Assets	Equipment (actual cost)		
	Autos and Trucks (actual cost)		
	Buildings (actual cost)		
	Total Fixed Assets (except land)		
	(less depreciation)		
	Net Total		
	Add Land (actual cost)		
	Total Fixed Assets		
	Total Miscellaneous Assets		
	Total Assets		
LIABILITIES			
Current Liabilities	Accounts Payable		
	Miscellaneous Payable		
	Total Current Liabilities		
Fixed Liabilities	Loans Payable (long-term)		
	Total Fixed Liabilities		
	Total Liabilities		
Owner's Equity	Net Worth or Capital Surplus + Stock Value		

CHAPTER 6
Operating an S-Corporation

Having completed your Business Plan, including the Marketing and Financial Plans, you are ready to begin to understand, in detail, the type of business entity that you have chosen. An S-corporation is a type of corporation that is recognized by the U.S. Internal Revenue Service and is treated differently than other corporations in terms of Federal taxation. Some states also recognize S-corporation status for state income taxation purposes; some states do not. The only reason for becoming an S-corporation is to obtain a different method of taxation than other corporations.

For standard corporations, the corporation pays a Federal and, perhaps, state corporate tax on the business profits. If the after-tax profit is distributed to the shareholders as dividends, the shareholders then pay an additional personal income tax on the dividends. The amount distributed to the shareholders as dividends is not a deduction for the corporation. S-corporations, on the other hand, are taxed similarly to partnerships. They act merely as a conduit for passing the income and deductions of the corporation directly to the individual shareholders in much the same manner as partnerships, or even sole proprietorships. The S-corporation does not pay a corporate tax and files a different type of tax form than does a standard corporation (please see Chapter 19 for more information on taxation of S-corporations). Taxation of the profits of the S-corporation falls to the individuals who own shares in the corporation. This also allows for each individual shareholder to personally deduct their share of any corporate losses.

There are, however, certain basic requirements for qualifying a corporation with the IRS for S-corporation status. Every requirement must be met before the IRS will recognize S-corporation status and allow for the different tax treatment.

- The corporation must have no more than 75 shareholders. (Wives and husbands, even if they own stock separately, are considered as only one shareholder)

- Each of the corporation's shareholders must be a natural person or the estate of a natural person. Corporations and partnerships may not hold shares in the corporation. Each shareholder must also be a citizen or resident of the United States

- The corporation must have only one class of stock that is issued and outstanding. The corporation may have other classes of stock that are authorized, providing no shares are issued. Different voting rights within a class of stock (ie., voting and nonvoting) do not disqualify the corporation

- The corporation must already be incorporated in the United States or one of its possessions. Financial institutions, foreign corporations, and certain other very specialized corporations are not eligible

- The corporation must not have been qualified as an S-corporation within the previous five years. This restriction prevents abrupt shifting from one type of corporation to another in order to obtain the maximum tax benefits

- The corporation has a calendar tax year or has been approved by the IRS to have a tax year ending other than on December 31

- All shareholders consent to the election of S-corporation status on IRS Form 2553: *Election by a Small Business Corporation* which must then be filed with the IRS

If your corporation meets all of these requirements, S-corporation status may be elected. It may be prudent to obtain the advice of a competent accountant prior to making the election, however. The actual steps in electing S-corporation status are detailed at the end of this chapter in the S-Corporation Checklist. Please note that IRS Form 2553: *Election by a Small Business Corporation* is provided on the enclosed Forms-on-CD, as well as in Chapter 12. These forms and all other IRS forms can easily be downloaded from the IRS website:

www.irs.gov/formspubs/index.html

The corporate business structure has three levels: shareholders, directors, and officers. In order to understand the requirements for corporate recordkeeping, it is necessary to understand how a corporation actually functions. Each level has different rights and responsibilities. Each level also generates different types of paperwork. Although all three levels of corporate management may often work together and may even be the same individual, the levels must be treated as separate parts of the corporate structure.

Shareholders

The *shareholders* are the persons or other business entities who actually own the corporation. The corporation ownership is divided into shares of stock in the corporation. Each share may be sold to shareholders who are then issued a stock certificate that represents their ownership of a percentage of the corporation, represented by numbers of shares of stock. Although many different levels and classes of stock ownership may be designated, the forms and discussions in this book will deal with only one class of stock: common stock. Each share of stock is, generally, provided one vote in shareholder decisions. Although it is perfectly acceptable to provide for non-voting classes of stock, the forms and discussion in this book will only relate to voting shares of stock.

The ownership of stock certificates of the corporation is recorded in the *corporate stock transfer book*. This "book" can simply consist of a few pages in the corporate record book with places to note the issuance and transfer of certificates. Stock and stock transfer records are detailed in Chapter 14. The *corporate record book* that will contain all of the corporate records (except the accounting records) can consist of a simple three-ring binder in which the records are organized. It is possible to purchase fancy corporate record books, but they are not a legal requirement.

Ownership of shares of stock in a corporation brings with it both benefits and responsibilities. The benefits stem from the right to a share of ownership in the assets of the corporation. The business profits of the corporation may also be shared with the shareholders in the form of dividends. The decision of the corporation to issue dividends on stock, however, is within the realm of the board of directors. The main responsibility of the shareholders is to elect the directors of the corporation. The shareholders also have the authority to vote on extraordinary business actions of the corporation. These actions are generally limited to decisive activities of the corporation, such as the sale of all of the assets of the corporation, the merger of the corporation, or the dissolution of the corporation. Shareholders, finally, generally have the right to approve any amendments to the Articles of Incorporation. Shareholders' authority to direct the business only comes from the right to undertake these few actions. Their power must also always be exercised as a group. An individual shareholder has no power to direct the management of the corporation in any way, other than to buy or sell shares of stock.

The election of the directors of the corporation takes place at the annual meeting of the shareholders, although directors can be elected for terms that last for more than one year. At the annual meeting, the president and treasurer of the corporation (both officers of the corporation) will present their annual reports on the activities and financial state of the corporation. The shareholders will then elect (generally by secret ballot majority vote) the directors for the following year. If there are any major business decisions, these may also be addressed. The minutes of this meeting and any shareholders resolutions are typically the only shareholder records to be maintained, other than the stock transfer book. Shareholders meetings and paperwork are generally contained in Chapter 12. Shareholder resolutions are contained in Chapter 13.

Directors

As explained, the directors are elected by the shareholders at their annual meetings. Please note, however, that in the forms contained in this book, the initial board of directors is specified in the Articles of Incorporation which are prepared and filed with the state. This listing of the directors is to comply with many states' requirements. The directors who are selected in the articles may then be approved by the shareholders at their first meeting, or may be rejected and new directors elected.

The directors of the corporation must act as members of the board of directors. Individual directors, acting alone, have no authority to bind the corporation or, for example, to enter into contracts or leases for the corporation. The directors must act as a board of directors. Most states, however, allow corporations to have only a single director. This sole director must, however, continue to act as a board of directors. Please check the appendix for the specific requirements in your state. The board of directors of a corporation has two main responsibilities. The first is to appoint and oversee the officers who will handle the day-to-day actions of actually running the business. The second responsibility is for setting out the corporate policies and making most major decisions on corporate financial and business matters. The policies of the corporation are first contained in the corporate bylaws that will be prepared by the board of directors. Subsequent corporate policies can be outlined in board of directors resolutions, unless they conflict with the bylaws. In such a case, the bylaws must be formally amended by the board of directors, with the consent and approval of the shareholders. Thus, it is the directors who have the actual central authority and responsibility in a corporation.

This differentiation of responsibilities in corporate management is crucial and often difficult to grasp. The shareholders only have the right to elect the directors and vote on major extraordinary business of the corporation (for example, on a merger, complete sale of the corporation, dissolution, or amendments of the Articles of Incorporation). The directors' role is much wider. They have the power to authorize the corporation to enter into contracts, purchase property, open bank accounts, borrow or loan money, and other such significant actions. The board can also delegate this authority to its officers, but, and this is crucial, it must do so in writing with a specific board of directors resolution. In many corporations, in fact, much of the actual operations are handled by the officers. However, all of the officers' authority to operate on behalf of the corporation stems directly from the board of directors.

The bulk of the records of the corporation will consist of matters within the province of the board of directors. The directors will hold annual meetings for the purpose of appointing corporate officers and conducting any other business. They may also hold, with proper notice, special meetings to transact other corporate business that may develop from time to time. The minutes of all directors meetings are very important in establishing that a separate corporate entity has been respected by the persons involved with the corporate management. These minutes must be detailed, complete, and up-to-date. The various actions of the directors must be documented in formal resolutions. These resolutions are often required by banks and other businesses with which the corporation does business in order to verify that the corporation has authorized the particular transaction. The details of directors meetings and resolutions are outlined in Chapters 11 and 13. It should be noted that a few states have chosen to allow the shareholders of a corporation to actively participate in the management of the corporation. Although this may allow for ease of management in certain instances, it will not lessen the requirement for corporate recordkeeping. The forms in this book are all designed for use in traditional three-tiered corporate management with shareholders, directors, and officers.

Officers

To the officers of a corporation fall the responsibilities of running the business. Their powers, however, are dictated solely by the board of directors. Officers can be given very broad powers to transact virtually all business for the corporation, or they can be tightly limited in their authority. A single shareholder can act as both the sole director and the sole officer of a corporation in most states. The officers, however, even in this circumstance, still derive their authority from resolutions of the board of directors. Prudent businesses often require copies of the authorizing resolutions in the course of large transactions.

There may be many levels of corporate officers. Traditionally, there are four main officers: president, vice-president, treasurer, and secretary. Their specific powers should be outlined by the directors in the Corporate Bylaws and their authority to transact individual business deals should be detailed in board of directors resolutions. In general, the president acts as the corporation's general manager, handling the day-to-day operations. The vice-president normally acts only in the absence of the president, although this officer can be given specific responsibilities. The treasurer handles the corporate funds and is responsible for the accounting books. The secretary handles the corporate records (minutes, resolutions, etc.) and is also generally responsible for the corporate stock and stock transfer book.

The officers are appointed by the board of directors at annual meetings, although special meetings can be called for this purpose. The officers may be required to report individually to the board. Often the president will be called upon to present an annual report regarding the overall condition of the corporation. The treasurer will present an annual financial report at the directors meeting. The secretary will handle all of the records, including copies of these annual reports. In many corporations, the president keeps in contact with the board of directors on a much more continual basis. However, any major decisions that affect the corporation should be carefully documented and, if necessary, a special meeting of the board of directors should be called and a formal resolution adopted.

The formalities of corporate structure may seem complex for small businesses and even foolish for corporations with a single owner/director/officer. It is important to understand that it is the recognition of this structure and the documentation of corporate actions taken within this structure that afford the corporation its limited liability protection and taxation benefits. The specific formalities for preparing Articles of Incorporation are contained in Chapter 9; for adopting bylaws, Chapter 10; for board of directors meetings, Chapter 11; and for shareholders meetings, Chapter 12.

S-Corporation Checklist

❏ Determine that the corporation has fewer than 75 shareholders

❏ Determine that all shareholders are natural persons or estates

❏ Determine that the corporation has only one class of stock issued and outstanding

❏ Determine that the corporation is already incorporated in the U.S or in one of its possessions

❏ Determine that the corporation hasn't had "S" status within the past five years

❏ All shareholders must consent to the election to be treated as an S-corporation

❏ Notice of a special shareholders meeting for the purpose of consenting to the election as an S-corporation should be provided to all shareholders of record

❏ A special shareholders meeting should be held at which all shareholders of the corporation consent to the election by the corporation to be treated as an S-corporation

❏ A shareholders resolution consenting to the election to be treated as an S-corporation should be signed by all shareholders of record

❏ The secretary of the corporation should complete IRS Form 2553: *Election by a Small Business Corporation*

❏ All shareholders of record must sign IRS Form 2553: *Election by a Small Business Corporation*

❏ The secretary of the corporation should file IRS Form 2553: *Election by a Small Business Corporation*

CHAPTER 7
Corporate Paperwork

The business arena in America operates on a daily assortment of legal forms. There are more legal forms in use in American business than are used in the operations and government of many foreign countries. The business corporation is not immune to this flood of legal forms. Indeed the operation of a corporation, in general, requires more legal documents than does any other form of business. While large corporations are able to obtain and pay expensive lawyers to deal with their legal problems and paperwork, most small businesses cannot afford such a course of action. The small business corporation must deal with a variety of legal documents, usually without the aid of an attorney.

Unfortunately, many businesspeople who are confronted with such forms do not understand the legal ramifications of the use of them. They simply sign the forms with the expectation that it is a fairly standard document, without any unusual legal provisions. They trust that the details of the particular document will fall within what is generally accepted within the industry or trade. In most cases, this may be true. In many situations, however, it is not. Our court system is clogged with cases in which two businesses are battling over what was really intended by the incomprehensible legal language in a certain legal document.

Much of the confusion over corporate paperwork comes from two areas: First, there is a general lack of understanding among many in business regarding the framework of law; and second, many corporate documents are written in antiquated legal jargon that is difficult for even most lawyers to understand and nearly impossible for a lay person to comprehend.

The various legal documents that are used in this book are, however, written in plain English. Standard legal jargon, as used in most lawyer-prepared documents, is totally incomprehensible for most people. Despite the lofty arguments by attorneys regarding the need for such strained and difficult language, the vast majority of legalese is absolutely unnecessary. As with any form of communication, clarity, simplicity, and readability should be the goal in legal documents.

Unfortunately, in some specific instances, certain obscure legal terms are the only words that accurately and precisely describe some things in certain legal contexts. In those few cases, the unfamiliar legal term will be defined when first used. Generally, however, simple terms are used throughout this book. In most cases, masculine and feminine terms have been eliminated and the generic "it" or "them" used instead. In the few situations in which this leads to awkward sentence construction, "his or her" or "he or she" may be used instead.

All of the legal documents contained in this book have been prepared in essentially the same manner by which attorneys create legal forms. Many people believe that lawyers compose each legal document that they prepare entirely from scratch. Nothing could be further from the truth. Invariably, lawyers begin their preparation of a legal document with a standardized legal form book. Every law library has multi-volume sets of these encyclopedic texts which contain blank forms for virtually every conceivable legal situation. Armed with these pre-prepared legal forms, lawyers, in many cases, simply fill in the blanks and have their secretaries retype the form for the client. Of course, the client is generally unaware of this process. As the lawyers begin to specialize in a certain area of legal expertise, they compile their own files containing such blank forms.

This book provides to those businesspersons who wish to form a corporation a set of legal forms that has been prepared with the problems and normal legal requirements of the small business corporation in mind. These forms are intended to be used in those situations that are clearly described by the specific language of each particular form. Of course, while most corporate document use will fall within the bounds of standard business practices, some legal circumstances will present non-standard situations. The forms in this book are designed to be readily adaptable to most usual business situations. They may be carefully altered to conform to the particular transaction that confronts your business. However, if you are faced with a complex or tangled business situation, the advice of a competent lawyer is highly recommended. If you wish, you may also create forms for certain standard situations for your corporation and have your lawyer check them for any local legal circumstances.

The proper and cautious use of the forms provided in this book will allow the typical corporation to save considerable money on legal costs over the course of the life of the business, while enabling the business to comply with legal and governmental regulations. Perhaps more importantly, these forms will provide a method by which the businessperson can avoid costly misunderstandings about what exactly was intended in a particular situation. By using the forms provided to clearly document the proceedings of everyday corporate operations, disputes over what was really meant can be avoided. This protection will allow the business to avoid many potential lawsuits and operate more efficiently in compliance with the law.

The Importance of Corporate Recordkeeping

The amount of paperwork and recordkeeping required by the use of the corporate form of business may often seem overwhelming. Sometimes, it may even seem senseless. However, there are some very important reasons why detailed records of corporate operations are necessary. A corporation is a fiction. It is a creation of the government to enable businesses to have a flexibility to function in a complex national and even international marketplace. This form of enterprise provides the most adaptable type of business entity in today's world. Through the use of a corporate entity, a business may respond quickly to the changing nature of modern business. Of course, the limited liability of corporate investors is also a great advantage over other forms of business organization.

A corporation is, in many cases, afforded the legal status of a person. It may sue or be sued in its own name. A corporation may own property in its own name. In most situations, a corporation is treated as if it has a life of its own. In a legal sense, it does have a life of its own. It was born by filing the Articles of Incorporation with a state and it may die upon filing Articles of Dissolution with the state. While a corporation is alive, it is said to "exist." During its existence, it can operate as a separate legal entity and enjoy the benefits of corporate status as long as certain corporate formalities are observed. The importance of following these basic corporate formalities cannot be overemphasized. All of the advantages of operating under the corporate form of business are directly dependent upon careful observance of a few basic paperwork and management requirements.

Each major action that a corporation undertakes must be carefully documented. Even if there are only a few, or even a single shareholder, complete records of corporate activities must be recorded. There must be *minutes*, which are records of shareholders meetings that outline the election of directors of the corporation. Directors meetings must also be documented and the actions of directors recorded in the form of resolutions. Stock certificates must be issued and the ownership of them must be carefully tracked. This is true regardless of the size of the corporation. In fact, as the size of the corporation decreases, the importance of careful recordkeeping actually increases.

Corporate existence can be challenged in court. This will most likely happen in circumstances where a creditor of the corporation or victim of some corporate disaster is left without compensation, due to the limited liability of the corporation. Despite the fact that the corporation has been accepted by the state as a legal entity, if the formalities of corporate existence have not been carefully followed, the owners of a corporation are at risk. The court may decide that a single shareholder corporation merely used the corporation as a shell to avoid liability. The court is then empowered to *pierce the corporate veil*, or declare that the corporation was actually merely the alter ego of the owner. In either outcome, the court can disregard the existence of the corporation and the creditors or victims can reach the personal assets of the owner. This most often will occur when a corporation is formed without sufficient capitalization to reasonably cover normal business affairs; when the corporation has not maintained sufficient insurance to cover standard contingencies; when the owner has mingled corporate funds with his or her own; and when there are no records to indicate that the corporation was actually operated as a separate entity. The results of such a lawsuit can be devastating. The loss of personal assets and the loss of corporate legal status for tax purposes can often lead to impoverishment and bankruptcy.

This difficulty is not a rarity. Each year, many corporations are found to be shams that were not operated as separate business entities. In a lawsuit against a small corporation, an attack on the use of corporate formalities is often the single most powerful weapon of the opposition. The best defense against an attack on the use of a corporate business form is to always have treated the corporation as a separate entity. This requires documenting each and every major business activity in minutes, records, and resolutions. When it is desired that the corporation undertake a particular activity, the directors should meet and adopt a resolution that clearly identifies the action and the reasons for the action. If major actions are undertaken, the shareholders may also need to meet and document their assent. This is true even if there is only one shareholder who is also the single director. With such records, it is an easy task to establish that the actions taken were done for the benefit of the corporation and not for the personal betterment of the individual owner or owners. As long as it can be clearly shown that the owners respected the corporate separateness, the corporate existence cannot be disregarded by the courts, even if there is only one shareholder who is also the sole director and only officer of the corporation. It is not the size of the corporation, but rather the existence of complete corporate records, that provides the protection from liability for the owners of the corporation. It is crucial to recognize this vital element in operating a corporation. Careful, detailed recordkeeping is the key to enjoying the tax benefits and limited liability of the corporate business structure.

Corporate Paperwork Checklist

The following checklist outlines the various corporate documents that should be prepared and maintained during the life of a corporation:

❏ Pre-Incorporation Checklist (see Chapter 8)

❏ Application for Reservation of Corporate Name (filed with state)

❏ Articles of Incorporation (filed with state)

❏ Amendments to Articles of Incorporation (filed with state)

❏ Certificate of Good Standing (requested from state)

❏ Bylaws of the corporation (in corporate record book)

❏ Amendments to the Bylaws of the corporation (in corporate record book)

❏ Minutes of the first meeting of the board of directors (in corporate record book)

❏ Minutes of the first meeting of the shareholders (in corporate record book)

❏ Minutes of the annual board of directors meetings (in corporate record book)

❏ Minutes of the annual meetings of the shareholders (in corporate record book)

❏ Minutes of any special board of directors meetings (in corporate record book)

❏ Minutes of any special shareholders meetings (in corporate record book)

- ❏ Shareholder proxies (in corporate record book)

- ❏ Shareholder voting agreements (in corporate record book)

- ❏ Resolutions of the board of directors (in corporate record book)

- ❏ Resolutions of the shareholders (in corporate record book)

- ❏ IRS Form 2553: *Election by a Small Business Corporation* (filed with IRS)

- ❏ Corporate loans to officers or directors (in corporate record book)

- ❏ Corporate pension or profit-sharing plans (in corporate record book)

- ❏ Corporate insurance or health benefit plans (in corporate record book)

- ❏ Form and content of stock certificates (in corporate record book)

- ❏ Stock Transfer Book (in corporate record book)

- ❏ Corporate accounting books

- ❏ Annual financial reports (in corporate record book)

- ❏ Annual reports (filed with state)

- ❏ Articles of Merger (filed with state)

- ❏ Articles of Dissolution (filed with state)

- ❏ Corporate tax records (filed with state and Federal tax authorities)

- ❏ Applications to qualify as foreign corporation (filed with other states in which the corporation desires to conduct active business)

CHAPTER 8
Pre-Incorporation Activities

The planning stage of incorporation is vital to the success of any corporation. The structure of a new corporation, including the number of directors, number of shares of stock, and other matters, must be carefully tailored to the specific needs of the business. Attorneys typically use a pre-incorporation worksheet to assemble all of the necessary information needed to plan the incorporation process.

By filling out a Pre-Incorporation Worksheet, potential business owners will be able to have before them all of the basic data to use in preparing the necessary incorporation paperwork. The process of preparing this worksheet will also help uncover any potential differences of opinion among the persons who are desiring to form the corporation. Often, conflicts and demands are not known until the actual process of determining the corporate structure begins. Frank discussions regarding the questions of voting rights, number of directors, and other management decisions often will enable potential associates to resolve many of the difficult problems of corporate management in advance. The use of a written worksheet will also provide all persons involved with a clear and permanent record of the information. This may provide the principals of the corporation with vital support for later decisions that may be required.

All persons involved in the planned corporation should participate in the preparation of the following worksheet. Please take the time to carefully and completely fill in all the spaces. Following the worksheet, there is a Pre-Incorporation Checklist which provides a clear listing of all of the required actions necessary to incorporate a business. Follow this checklist carefully as the incorporation process proceeds. After the Pre-Incorporation Checklist, there is a Document Filing Checklist that provides a listing of the corporate documents that are normally required to be filed with the state corporation office. Finally, there is a discussion and form for reserving the corporate name with the state corporation department. If required, the name reservation form will be the first form filed with the state corporation department.

Unfamiliar terms relating to corporations are explained in the glossary of this book. As the Pre-Incorporation Worksheet is filled in, please refer to the following explanations:

Name/address of state corporation department: The appendix of this book provides this name and address. You should write to this department immediately, requesting all available information on incorporation of a for-profit business corporation in your state. Although the forms in this book are designed for use in all states and the appendix provides up-to-date information on state requirements, state laws and fees charged for incorporation are subject to change. Having the latest available information will save you time and trouble.

Proposed name of the corporation: The selection of a corporate name is often crucial to the success of a corporation. The name must not conflict with any existing company names, nor must it be deceptively similar to other names. It is often wise to clearly explain the business of the corporation through the choice of name. All states allow for a reservation of the corporate name in advance of actual incorporation. Check the appendix listing for your state.

Parties involved: This listing should provide the names, addresses, and phone numbers of all of the people who are involved in the planning stages of the corporation.

Principal place of business: This must be the address of the actual physical location of the main business. It may not be a post office box. If the corporation is home-based, this address should be the home address.

Purpose of corporation: Many states allow the use of an "all-purpose" business purpose clause in describing the main activity of the business; for example, "to conduct any lawful business." The Articles of Incorporation that are used in this book provide this type of form. However, a few states require a specific business purpose to be identified in the Articles of Incorporation. Please check in the appendix to see if this is a requirement in your state. If you must specify a purpose, be concise and specific, but broad enough to allow for flexibility in operating your business.

State/local licenses required: Here you should note any specific requirements for licenses to operate your type of business. Most states require obtaining a tax ID number and a retail, wholesale, or sales tax license. A federal tax ID (FEIN) number must be obtained by all corporations. Additionally, certain types of businesses will require health department approvals, state board licensing, or other forms of licenses. If necessary, check with a competent local attorney for details regarding the types of licenses required for your locality and business type.

Patents/copyrights/trademarks: If patents, copyrights, or trademarks will need to be transferred into the corporation, they should be noted here.

State of incorporation: In general, the corporation should be incorporated in the state in which it will conduct business. In the past, the state of Delaware was regarded as the best state in which to incorporate. This was due to the fact that Delaware was the first state to modernize its corporation laws to reflect the realities of present-day corporate business. This is no longer the case. Virtually all states have now enacted corporate laws very similar to those in Delaware. In the vast majority of situations, it is preferable to be incorporated in your home state.

Corporate existence: The choices here are *perpetual* (forever) or limited to a certain length. In virtually all cases, you should choose perpetual.

Proposed date to begin corporate business: This should be the date on which you expect the corporation to begin its legal existence. Until this date (actually, until the state formally accepts the Articles of Incorporation), the incorporators of your corporation will continue to be legally liable for any business conducted on behalf of the proposed corporation.

Incorporators: This should be the person (or persons) who will prepare and file the Articles of Incorporation. Most states allow for one incorporator. However, a few require more than one. Please check the appendix for the requirements in your particular state.

Proposed date of first directors meeting: This will be the date proposed for holding the first meeting of the board of directors, at which the corporate bylaws will be officially adopted.

Proposed bank for corporate bank account: In advance of incorporation, you should determine the bank which will handle the corporate accounts. Obtain from the bank the necessary bank resolution, which will be signed by the board of directors at the first directors meeting.

Cost of incorporation: The state fees for incorporation are listed in the appendix. This cost should also reflect the cost of obtaining professional assistance (legal or accounting); the cost of procuring the necessary supplies; and any other direct costs of the incorporation process.

Proposed number of directors: Most states allow a corporation to have a single director. A number of states require three directors unless there are fewer than three shareholders, in which case the state allows for the number of directors to equal the number of shareholders. Please check the appendix for the requirements in your particular state.

Proposed first board of directors: You should list the names and addresses of the proposed members of the first board of directors. Although not a requirement in every state, the Articles of Incorporation used in this book provide that these persons be listed. It is not possible to keep the names of the directors of a corporation secret.

Corporation's registered agent and office address: You should list the name and actual street address of the person who will act as the registered agent of the corporation. All states (except New York) require that a specific person be available as the agent of the corporation for the *service of process* (i.e., to accept subpoenas or summonses on behalf of the corporation). The person need not be a shareholder, director, or officer of the corporation. The registered agent need not be a lawyer. Normally, the main owner, chairperson of the board of directors, or president of the corporation is selected as the registered agent.

Proposed first officers: This information is not provided in the Articles of Incorporation and need not be made public. You should list here the persons who are proposed as the first officers of the business.

Qualification in other states: If the corporation desires to actively conduct business in a state other that the main state of incorporation, it is necessary to "qualify" the corporation in that state. This generally requires obtaining a Certificate of Authority to Transact Business from the other state. In this context, a corporation from another state is referred to as a "foreign" corporation. If you desire that your corporation qualify for activities in another state, you are advised to consult a competent business attorney.

Required quorum for shareholders meeting: This is the percentage of ownership of shares of issued stock in the corporation that must be represented at a shareholders meeting in order to officially transact any shareholder business. This is normally set at a "majority" (over 50 percent), although this figure can be set higher.

Annual shareholders meeting: The place, date, and time of the annual shareholders meeting should be specified.

Required vote for shareholders action: Once it is determined that a quorum of shareholders is present at a meeting, this is the percentage of ownership of shares of issued stock in the corporation that must vote in the affirmative in order to officially pass any shareholder business. This is normally set at a "majority" (over 50 percent), although this figure can be set higher and can be made to be unanimous.

Fiscal year and accounting type: For accounting purposes, the fiscal year and accounting type (cash or accrual) of the corporation should be chosen in advance. Please consult with a competent accounting professional.

Amendments to Articles of Incorporation: Under this item should be the determination of which bodies of the corporation will have the authority to amend the Articles of Incorporation. The forms in this book are designed to allow the articles of the corporation to be amended by the board of directors only upon approval by the shareholders.

Amendments to Bylaws: The determination of which bodies of the corporation will have the authority to amend the bylaws should be decided. The forms in this book are designed to allow the bylaws of the corporation to be amended by the board of directors only upon approval by the shareholders.

Annual directors meeting: The place, date, and time of the annual board of directors meeting should be specified.

Required quorum for directors meeting: This is the percentage of directors that must be present at a board of directors meeting in order to officially transact any directors business. This is normally set at a "majority" (over 50 percent), although this figure can be set higher.

Required vote for directors action: Once it is determined that a quorum of directors is present at a meeting, this is the percentage of directors who must vote in the affirmative in order to officially pass any board of directors business. This is normally set at a "majority" (over 50 percent), although this figure can be set higher and can be made to be unanimous.

Initial total investment: This figure is the total amount of money or property that will be transferred to the corporation upon its beginning business. This transfer will be in exchange for the issuance of shares of stock in the corporation. This is also referred to as "paid-in capital." A few states require a minimum amount of "paid-in-capital" before beginning corporate business. Please check your state's listing in the appendix.

Initial indebtedness: If there is to be any initial indebtedness for the corporation, please list here.

Initial authorized number of shares: This figure is required to be listed in the Articles of Incorporation. The number of shares of stock to be authorized should be listed. For small corporations, this number may be influenced by the incorporation fee structure of the state of incorporation. For example, some states allow for a minimum incorporation fee when only a certain minimum number of stock shares are authorized. Please see the appendix for the requirements in your state and check with your state corporation department.

Par value or no-par value: This refers to an arbitrary indication as to the value of the stock. The designation of stock as having a certain "par" value is not an indication of the actual value of the shares of stock. Shares must be sold for a price at or below par value. If no-par value is assigned, the shares are issued for the actual price paid per share. The choice of par or no-par value stock may affect the issuance of dividends and should be referred to the corporate accountant.

Proposed sales of shares of stock: Here should be listed the names, cash or property, and value of potential sales of shares of stock which may be approved by the board of directors once the corporation is officially authorized to issue stock.

Following the Pre-Incorporation Worksheet is a Pre-Incorporation Checklist and a Document Filing Checklist. Please use these checklists to be certain that you have completed all the necessary steps for incorporation. Once all the persons involved have completed the Pre-Incorporation Worksheet, agreed on all of the details, and reviewed the Pre-Incorporation and Document Filing Checklists, the actual process of incorporation may begin. If the choice for a corporate name may be similar to another business, or if the incorporators wish to insure that the name will be available, an Application for Reservation of Corporate Name may be filed. This is a simple form requesting that the state corporation department hold a chosen corporate name until the actual Articles of Incorporation are filed, at which time the name will become the official registered name of the corporation. Page 83 contains a sample of this form. There will be a fee required for the filing of this form and some states prefer that preprinted state forms be used. Please check in the appendix and with the specific state corporation department for information. In any event, the information required will be the same as is necessary for this sample form.

Pre-Incorporation Worksheet

Name/Address of State Corporation Department (from Appendix)

_____
_____
_____

Proposed Name of the Corporation

First choice: _____

Alternate choices: _____

_____

Parties Involved in Forming the Corporation

Name	Address	Phone
_____	_____	_____
_____	_____	_____
_____	_____	_____
_____	_____	_____
_____	_____	_____
_____	_____	_____

Location of Business

Address of principal place of business: _____

_____

Description of principal place of business: _____

_____

Ownership of principal place of business (own or lease?): _____

_____

Other places of business: _____

_____

Type of Business

Purpose of corporation: _____

State/local licenses required: _____

Patents/copyrights/trademarks: _____

Incorporation Matters

State of incorporation: _____

Corporate existence (limited or perpetual?): _____

Proposed date to begin corporate business: _____

Names and addresses of those who will act as incorporators:

Name	Address
_____	_____
_____	_____
_____	_____

Proposed date of first directors meeting: _____

Proposed bank for corporate bank account: _____

Cost of incorporation: _____

Corporate Management

Proposed number of directors: _____

Proposed first board of directors:

Name	Address
_____	_____
_____	_____
_____	_____
_____	_____
_____	_____
_____	_____

Corporation's registered agent and office address: _____
_____

Proposed first officers:

	Name	Address
President:	_____	_____
Vice President:	_____	_____
Secretary:	_____	_____
Treasurer:	_____	_____

Is qualification in other states necessary? _____

Corporate Bylaws

Required quorum for shareholders meeting: _____

Annual shareholders meeting:

Place	Date	Time
_____	_____	_____

Required vote for shareholders actions (majority/%/unanimous?): _____

Fiscal year: _____

Accounting type (cash or accrual?): _____

Authority to amend the following corporate documents:

Articles of Incorporation: _____ directors _____ shareholders _____ either

Bylaws: _____ directors _____ shareholders _____ either

Annual directors meeting:

Place	Date	Time
_____	_____	_____

Required quorum for directors meetings: _____

Required vote for directors actions (majority/%/unanimous?): _____

Corporate Stock

Initial total investment: $ _____

Initial indebtedness: $ _____

Initial authorized number of shares: _____

Par value or no-par value: _____

Proposed sales of shares of stock:

Name	*Cash/Property*	*Amount*
_____	_____	_____
_____	_____	_____
_____	_____	_____
_____	_____	_____
_____	_____	_____

Pre-Incorporation Checklist

❑ Write state corporation office for information (see appendix)

❑ Complete Pre-Incorporation Worksheet

❑ Check annual fees and filing requirements

❑ Prepare Articles of Incorporation (see appendix for state-specific name for "Articles")

❑ If desired, have attorney review Articles of Incorporation prior to filing

❑ Review tax impact of incorporation with an accountant

❑ Check state tax, employment, licensing, unemployment, and workers compensation requirements

❑ Check insurance requirements

❑ Procure corporate seal (if desired)

❑ Prepare stock certificates

❑ Prepare corporate accounting ledgers

❑ Prepare corporate record book (looseleaf binder)

Document Filing Checklist

❏ Application for Reservation of Corporate Name (if desired)

❏ Articles of Incorporation (mandatory, see appendix for state-specific name for "Articles")

❏ Amendments to Articles of Incorporation (mandatory, if applicable)

❏ IRS Form 2553: *Election by a Small Business Corporation* (mandatory)

❏ Annual Corporate Reports (mandatory)

❏ Change of Address of Registered Agent (mandatory)

❏ Articles of Merger (mandatory, if applicable)

❏ Articles of Dissolution (mandatory, if applicable)

❏ Any other required state forms (see appendix)

Application for Reservation
of Corporate Name

TO:

I, _____ , with an office located
at:

acting as an incorporator, apply for reservation of the following corporate name:
_____ .

This corporate name is intended to be used to incorporate a for-profit corporation in the State
of _____ , County of _____ .

I request that this corporate name be reserved for a period of _____ days.
Please issue a certificate of reservation of this corporate name.

Dated: _____ , 20 _____

_____
Signature of Incorporator

_____
Printed Name of Incorporator

CHAPTER 9
Articles of Incorporation

The central legal document for any corporation is the Articles of Incorporation. In some states, this document may be called a Certificate of Incorporation, Charter of Incorporation, or Articles of Organization. Please check the appendix for the requirements in your particular state. This form outlines the basic structure of the corporation and details those matters that are relevant to the public registration of the corporation. The name, purpose, owners, registered agent, address, and other vital facts relating to the existence of the corporation are filed with the state by using this form. Upon filing of the Articles of Incorporation, payment of the proper fee, and acceptance by the state corporation department, the corporation officially begins its legal existence. Until the state has accepted the articles, the incorporators are not shielded from liability by the corporate form. Some states have chosen to confuse matters slightly by referring to another form that may be issued by the state as a Certificate of Incorporation. Please check the appendix for the state requirements for the state of your potential incorporation. For clarity, however, this book will refer to the incorporator-prepared document as the Articles of Incorporation.

There are a number of items that are required to be noted in all Articles of Incorporation. The articles may also include many other details of the corporation's existence. Please check in the appendix and with your state incorporation department for specific details. Following is a checklist of items which are mandatory or optional for Articles of Incorporation.

Articles of Incorporation Checklist

The mandatory details for Articles of Incorporation under most state laws are:

❑ Title and introduction

❑ The name of the corporation

❑ The purpose and powers of the corporation

❑ The duration of the corporation

- ❏ The amount of initial capital of corporation (optional in some states)

- ❏ The number of shares of stock that the corporation is authorized to issue to shareholders

- ❏ Par value or no-par value for shares of stock (optional in some states)

- ❏ The name of the registered agent of the corporation

- ❏ The address of the office of the registered agent of the corporation

- ❏ The name, address, and age of each incorporator

- ❏ The number of directors (optional in some states)

- ❏ The names and addresses of the initial director or directors

- ❏ The signatures of the incorporators

- ❏ The signature of the registered agent

In addition, the following items may also be included at your option:

- ❏ The terms and qualifications for board members

- ❏ Provisions relating to the powers of the directors, officers, or shareholders

- ❏ Designation of different classes of stock

- ❏ Preemptive or cumulative voting rights

- ❏ Voting and other rights or restrictions on stock

- ❏ Additional articles

❑ Election to be a close corporation under state law

❑ Provisions indemnifying corporate officers and directors

The Articles of Incorporation for your corporation should include all of the required information. Since the articles are a public record, all of the information in them will be available for inspection. However, since the names of the directors will usually be required to be revealed in the annual reports that are filed with the state, there is no purpose in attempting to conceal identities of actual management of the corporation. Much of the information that is not required in the articles may instead be put into the bylaws of the corporation. In this manner, the actual management structure and details will remain unavailable for public inspection.

> *Note:* Some states provide preprinted Articles of Incorporation that are required to be used for filing. The information required, however, will be the same as is noted in the sample Articles of Incorporation in this chapter. Even if state-supplied forms are used, it will be helpful to read through this chapter and fill in the information as noted on the sample forms. Transferring it to the state form will then be a simple task. Please check the appendix listing for your state's requirement.

Articles of Incorporation can be amended at any time. However, this generally requires a formal filing with the state and the issuance of a Certificate of Amendment of Articles of Incorporation. It also normally requires the payment of a fee. For these reasons, it is often a good idea to put only those items in the original articles that are unlikely to require changes in the near future.

This chapter contains sample clauses for preparing Articles of Incorporation. The sample clauses in this chapter are labeled as either mandatory or optional. An explanation is also provided for each clause. You should check the appendix and any information that you have received from the state corporation department to be certain that you have included all of the necessary information for your state. A few states may require additional articles. Most of the information required for preparing the clauses for this form will be on your Pre-Incorporation Worksheet, which you prepared in Chapter 8. Once you have decided which of the clauses you will use, retype the Articles of Incorporation. (Type in the correct title for this document if your state has a different name for it; check the appendix). The articles should be typed in black ink, double-spaced, on one side of 8½" x 11" white paper. If state-supplied documents are used, fill them in with the information you have prepared in this book. Optional clauses may be added to state-supplied forms where necessary. If you use the forms on the enclosed CD, follow the instructions on the readme.doc file on the CD.

The articles must then be properly signed. Although not required by all states, the form in this book is designed to be notarized. A few states require that the articles be published as legal notices in newspapers. Please check the appendix for the requirements in your particular state. The signed Articles of Incorporation and the proper fee should be sent to the proper state office. Upon receipt, the state corporation department will check for duplication or confusing conflicts with the names of any other registered corporations. They will also check to be certain that all the statutory requirements have been fulfilled and that the proper fee has been paid. If there is a problem, the articles will be returned with an explanation of the difficulty. Correct the problem and refile the articles. If everything is in order, the business will officially be incorporated and will be able to begin to conduct business as a corporate entity. Some states have different procedures for indicating the beginning existence of a corporation. For example, you may need to request an official Certificate of Filing, Certificate of Good Standing, or other type of certificate and pay a fee for this record. Check with your state corporation department. A completed sample Articles of Incorporation is included at the end of this chapter.

Title and Introduction (*Mandatory*)

Check in the appendix and with your state corporation department for any changes to this clause. If your state has a different title for this document, please insert the proper title (for example, Certificate of Incorporation of _____). The name of the corporation should include the corporate designation (see below under "Name of the Corporation").

Articles of Incorporation of _____

The undersigned person(s), acting as incorporator(s) for the purpose of forming a stock business corporation under the laws of the State of _____ , adopt(s) the following Articles of Incorporation:

Name of the Corporation (*Mandatory*)

The name of the corporation should be unique. It should not be confusingly similar to any other business name in use within your state. In addition, it should not contain any terms which might lead people to believe that it is a governmental or financial institution.

Finally, it must generally contain an indication that the business is a corporation, such as "Inc.," "Incorporated," "Corporation," or "Limited." Some states allow the use of the word "Company" in the name of corporations. Others do not. If you wish to use a term of corporate designation other than "Corporation" or "Incorporated" (or abbreviations of these), please check in the appendix and with your state corporation department.

> **Article 1.** The name of the corporation is _____ .

Purpose and Powers of the Corporation (*Mandatory*)

Many states allow a general statement of purpose: "to transact any and all lawful business for which corporations may be incorporated under the Business Corporation Act of the State of _____ ." Others may require that you specifically state the purpose of your corporation, such as: "to operate a retail dry-cleaning business." Please check the appendix for the requirements in your particular state. If you are required to state a specific purpose, try to be broad enough to allow your business flexibility without the necessity of later amending the Articles of Incorporation to reflect a change in direction of your business. Choose the clause appropriate for your state and circumstances. (Please note that Kentucky and Massachusetts are referred to as "Commonwealths," rather than "States.")

> **Article 2.** The purpose for which this corporation is organized is to transact any and all lawful business for which corporations may be organized under the laws of the State of _____ , and to have all powers that are afforded to corporations under the laws of the State of _____ .

Or:

> **Article 2.** The purpose for which this corporation is organized is: _____ . This corporation shall have all powers under the laws of the State of _____ .

Duration of the Corporation (*Mandatory*)

All states allow for a *perpetual duration* for corporations, meaning that the corporation can continue in existence forever. Unless there is a specific business reason to indicate otherwise, this is generally the safest choice. A limited duration statement is not an acceptable method to dissolve a corporation.

> **Article 3.** The duration of this corporation shall be perpetual.

Minimum Capitalization (Usually *mandatory*)

This clause refers to the amount of capital which will form the initial basis for operating the corporation. Several states have specific dollar amounts of minimum capital that are required for a corporation to be incorporated, ranging from $500.00 to $1,000.00. All other states have no minimum and you may delete this clause. Please check in the appendix and check with your state corporation department.

> **Article 4.** The total amount of initial capitalization of this corporation is $ _____ .

Authorization to Issue Stock (*Mandatory*)

The number of shares of stock that will be issued is a business determination. There is no specific reason that the number of shares should be large. In fact, in some states the amount of fees charged for incorporation is based upon the number of shares that are authorized to be issued. Please check in the appendix for the requirements in your particular state.

> Article 5. The total number of shares of common capital stock that this corporation is authorized to issue is _____ .

Par or No-Par Value (*Mandatory*; may be *optional*)

This refers to the arbitrary value that has been assigned to your shares of stock. It does not refer to the actual purchase price required for the shares of stock. Please consult with the corporation's accountant if you have questions regarding this item. Choose the clause for Article 6 which is appropriate for your state and circumstances.

> **Article 6.** This stock shall have a par value of $ _____ .

Or:

Article 6. This stock shall have no-par value.

Name of the Registered Agent (*Mandatory*)

The registered agent for a corporation is the person upon whom *service of process* (summons, subpoena, etc.) can be served. This person must be an adult who is a resident of the state of incorporation. The usual choice is the main owner of the corporation. Residents of New York are required to have the Secretary of State be the authorized agent for service of process. Please see the appendix and check with your state corporation department. There is a place at the end of the Articles of Incorporation for the registered agent to sign.

Article 7. The initial registered agent of this corporation is _____ . By his or her signature at the end of this document, this person acknowledges acceptance of the responsibilities as registered agent of this corporation.

Address of the Registered Agent (*Mandatory*)

This address must be an actual place, usually the offices of the corporation. It may not be a post office box or other unmanned location.

Article 8. The initial address of the office of the registered agent of this corporation is _____ , City of _____ , in the County of _____ , State of _____ .

Name[s], Address[es], and Age[s] of Incorporator[s] (*Mandatory*)

This is the name and address of the person or persons who are filing for incorporation. The minimum age requirement for incorporating a business is generally 18. A few states allow corporations or partnerships to act as incorporators. Please check in the appendix or with your state corporation department.

```
┌─────────────────────────────────────────────────────────────────────┐
│  Article 9. The name[s], address[es], and age[s] of the incorporator[s] of │
│  this corporation is/are:                                              │
│                                                                         │
│         Name                    Address                    Age          │
│    _____    _____    _____        │
│    _____    _____    _____        │
│    _____    _____    _____        │
│                                                                         │
└─────────────────────────────────────────────────────────────────────┘
```

Number of Directors (Usually *mandatory*)

The minimum number of directors allowed is generally one. However, a few states require three directors if there are more than two shareholders. Thus, in those states, if there is only one shareholder, there may be one director. If there are two shareholders, there must be two directors. But if there are three shareholders or more, there must be three directors. Please check the appendix.

```
┌─────────────────────────────────────────────────────────────────────┐
│  Article 10. The number of directors of this corporation is _____ .│
└─────────────────────────────────────────────────────────────────────┘
```

Name[s] and Address[es] of Initial Director[s] (*Mandatory*)

This clause provides for the name and address of the initial director or directors of the corporation until the first meeting of the shareholders of the corporation either elect or replace these directors.

```
┌─────────────────────────────────────────────────────────────────────┐
│  Article 11. The name[s] and address[es] of the initial director[s] of this │
│  corporation is/are as follows:                                        │
│                                                                         │
│              Name                              Address                  │
│    _____    _____          │
│    _____    _____          │
│    _____    _____          │
│                                                                         │
└─────────────────────────────────────────────────────────────────────┘
```

Preemptive Rights (*Optional*)

Using this clause, you may include any preemptive stock rights in the articles, if desired. Preemptive rights are like a right of first refusal. If a corporation proposes to authorize new shares of stock, preemptive rights allow current shareholders the right to acquire an equivalent percentage of the new shares based on their current percentage of ownership. This prevents their ownership percentage from being watered down by the authorization and issuance of new shares of stock. Under the laws of some states, preemptive rights exist unless the Articles of Incorporation specifically state that they do not. In other states, preemptive rights *do not* exist unless the Articles of Incorporation specifically state that they do. The best method of dealing with this issue is to include one of the following clauses which fits your circumstances.

Article 12. This corporation shall have preemptive rights for all shareholders.

Or:

Article 12. This corporation shall have no preemptive rights for any shareholders.

Preferences and Limitations on Stock (*Optional*)

In this clause, any voting preferences or limitations on transfers or other rights or restrictions on stock can be listed. This information may instead be listed in the bylaws of the corporation, if preferred.

Article 13. The following are preferences and limitations on the common stock of this corporation:

_____

_____

_____

Additional Articles (*Optional*)

This clause may be used to adopt any additional articles which may be desired.

Article 14. This corporation adopts the following additional articles:

_____

_____

_____

Closing and Signatures (*Mandatory*)

This clause provides a statement certifying that the facts as stated in the Articles of Incorporation are true and correct. It also provides for the registered agent to sign acknowledging his acceptance of the responsibilities of this job. This should be signed in front of a notary public.

I certify that all of the facts stated in these Articles of Incorporation are true and correct and are made for the purpose of forming a business corporation under the laws of the State of _____ .

Dated: _____ , 20 _____

_____   _____
Signature of Incorporator   Printed Name of Incorporator

_____   _____
Signature of Incorporator   Printed Name of Incorporator

_____   _____
Signature of Incorporator   Printed Name of Incorporator

State of _____
County of _____

Before me, on _____ , 20 _____ , personally appeared
_____ , _____ , and
_____ , named as the incorporator(s), who is/are known to me to be the person(s) who subscribed his or her name(s) to this document, and acknowledged that he or she did so for the purposes stated.

_____
Signature of Notary Public

Notary Public, In and for the County of _____
State of _____

My commission expires: _____   Notary Seal

I acknowledge my appointment as registered agent of this corporation and accept the appointment.

Dated: _____ , 20 _____

_____   _____
Signature of Registered Agent   Printed Name of Registered Agent

Sample Articles of Incorporation

Articles of Incorporation of ABCXYZ Corporation

The undersigned person, acting as incorporator for the purpose of forming a stock business corporation under the laws of the State of Superior, adopts the following Articles of Incorporation:

Article 1. The name of the corporation is ABCXYZ Corporation.

Article 2. The purpose for which this corporation is organized is to transact any and all lawful business for which corporations may be organized under the laws of the State of Superior, and to have all powers that are afforded to corporations under the laws of the State of Superior.

Article 3. The duration of this corporation shall be perpetual.

Article 4. The total amount of initial capitalization of this corporation is $1,000.00.

Article 5. The total number of shares of common capital stock that this corporation is authorized to issue is 100.

Article 6. This stock shall have no-par value.

Article 7. The initial registered agent of this corporation is Mary Celeste. By her signature at the end of this document, this person acknowledges acceptance of the responsibilities as registered agent of this corporation.

Article 8. The initial address of the office of the registered agent of this corporation is 1234 Main Street, City of Capitol City, in the County of Inferior, State of Superior.

Article 9. The name, address, and age of the incorporator of this corporation is Mary Celeste, 1234 Main Street, Capitol City, Inferior, Superior, age 25 years.

Article 10. The number of directors of this corporation is two (2).

Article 11. The names and addresses of the initial directors of this corporation are as follows:

Name	Address
Mary Celeste	1234 Main Street, Capitol City, Superior
John Celeste	1234 Main Street, Capitol City, Superior

Article 12. This corporation shall have preemptive rights for all shareholders.

Article 13. The following are preferences and limitations on the common stock of this corporation: none.

Article 14. This corporation adopts the following additional articles: none.

I certify that all of the facts stated in these Articles of Incorporation are true and correct and are made for the purpose of forming a business corporation under the laws of the State of Superior.

Dated: June 4, 2005

Mary Celeste
_____
Signature of Incorporator

_____Mary Celeste_____
Printed Name of Incorporator

State of Superior
County of Inferior

Before me, on June 4, 2005, personally appeared Mary Celeste, named as the incorporator, who is known to me to be the person who subscribed her name to this document, and acknowledged that she did so for the purposes stated.

Andrea Doria
_____
Signature of Notary Public

Notary Public, In and for the County of Inferior
State of Superior

My commission expires: June 5, 2005   Notary Seal

I acknowledge my appointment as registered agent of this corporation and accept the appointment.

Dated: June 4, 2005

Mary Celeste
_____
Signature of Registered Agent

_____Mary Celeste_____
Printed Name of Registered Agent

CHAPTER 10
Corporate Bylaws

The bylaws of a corporation are the third part of the triangle that provides the framework for the management of the corporate business. Along with state law and the Articles of Incorporation, the bylaws provide a clear outline of the rights and responsibilities of all parties to a corporation. In particular, the bylaws provide the actual details of the operational framework for the business. The bylaws are the internal document that will contain the basic rules on how the corporation is to be run. Every corporation must have a set of bylaws. Many of the provisions cover relatively standard procedural questions, relating to quorums, voting, and stock. Other provisions may need to be specifically tailored to the type of business for which the bylaws are intended. They are generally able to be amended by vote of the board of directors, unless the Articles of Incorporation or the bylaws themselves have transferred that authority to the shareholders. The bylaws provided in this book specify that the power to amend them is vested in the board of directors, but that the shareholders have the power to approve or reject any amendment.

The bylaws can contain very specific or very general provisions for the internal management of the company. Typically, the bylaws cover five general areas:

- The rights and responsibilities of the shareholders
- The rights and responsibilities of the directors
- The rights and responsibilities of the officers
- Financial matters
- Methods for amending the bylaws

This chapter contains sample clauses for preparing your corporate bylaws. Once you have chosen which of the clauses you will use and have filled in any required information, retype the bylaws in black ink on one side of 8½" x 11" white paper, double-spaced, or use the forms on the enclosed CD. A completed sample set of Bylaws is included at the end of this chapter. Your completed bylaws should be both formally adopted at the first board of directors meeting and approved at the first shareholders meeting. The following is a checklist for use in preparing your bylaws:

Corporate Bylaws Checklist

❏ Power to designate the location of principal office of the corporation

❏ Power to designate the registered office and agent of the corporation

❏ Date, time, and place of annual shareholders meeting

❏ Procedures for special shareholders meetings

❏ Notice and waivers for shareholders meetings

❏ Voting eligibility requirements for shareholders

❏ Quorum and votes required for actions of shareholders

❏ Shareholders proxy requirements

❏ Shareholders consent resolutions

❏ Shareholders cumulative voting rights

❏ Powers of board of directors

❏ Number of directors and term of office

❏ Directors election procedures

❏ Date, time, and place of annual board of directors meeting

❏ Procedures for special board of directors meetings

❏ Notice and waivers for board of directors meetings

❏ Quorum and votes required for actions by board of directors

- ❏ Board of directors consent resolutions

- ❏ Removing and filling vacancies of directors

- ❏ Salaries of directors

- ❏ Fiduciary duty of directors

- ❏ Number of officers and appointment and terms of officers

- ❏ Removing and filling vacancies of officers

- ❏ Duties of officers

- ❏ Salaries of officers

- ❏ How stock certificates are to be handled

- ❏ Restrictions on the rights to transfer shares of stock (if any)

- ❏ How corporate financial matters are to be handled

- ❏ Whether officers or directors can borrow money from the corporation

- ❏ Bylaw amendment procedures

- ❏ Signatures of Secretary of Corporation and Chairperson of Board

Title

Bylaws of _____ ,

a corporation incorporated under the laws of the

State of _____

Corporate Office and Registered Agent

Corporate Office and Registered Agent. The board of directors has the power to determine the location of the corporation's principal place of business and registered office, that need not be the same location. The board of directors also has the power to designate the corporation's registered agent, who may be an officer or director.

Date, Time, and Place of Shareholders Annual Meeting

Date, Time, and Place of Shareholders Annual Meeting. The annual shareholders meeting will be held on the _____ of every year at the corporate offices of the corporation at _____ o'clock ___ . m. This meeting is for the purpose of electing directors and for transacting any other necessary business. If this day is a legal holiday, the meeting will be held on the next day.

Shareholders Special Meetings

Shareholders Special Meetings. Special meetings of the shareholders may be called at any time and for any purpose. These meetings may be called by either the president or the board of directors, or upon request of _____ percent of the shareholders of the corporation. The request for a special meeting must be made in writing that states the time, place, and purpose of the meeting. The request should be given to the secretary of the corporation who will prepare and send written notice to all shareholders of record who are entitled to vote at the meeting.

Place of Shareholders Meetings

Place of Shareholders Meetings. The board of directors has the power to designate the place for shareholders meetings, unless a waiver of notice of the meeting signed by all shareholders designates the place for the meeting. If no place is designated, either by the board of directors or all of the shareholders, then the place for the meeting will be the principal office of the corporation.

Notice and Waivers of Shareholders Meetings

Notice and Waivers of Shareholders Meetings. Written notice of shareholders meetings must be sent to each shareholder of record entitled to vote at the meeting. The notice must be sent no less than _____ days nor more than _____ days before the date of the meeting. The notice should be sent to the shareholder's address as shown in the corporate stock transfer book. The notice will include the place, date, and time of the meeting. Notices for special meetings must also include the purpose of the meeting. When notices are sent, the secretary of the corporation must prepare an Affidavit of Mailing of Notices. Shareholders may waive notice of meetings if done in writing, except that attendance at a meeting is considered a waiver of notice of the meeting.

Shareholders Entitled to Notice, to Vote, or to Dividends

Shareholders Entitled to Notice, to Vote, or to Dividends. For the purpose of determining which shareholders are entitled to notice, to vote at meetings, or to receive dividends, the board of directors may order that the corporate stock transfer book be closed for _____ days prior to a meeting or the issuance of a dividend. The shareholders entitled to receive notice, vote at meetings, or receive dividends are those who are recorded in the stock transfer book upon the closing of the book. Instead of closing the book, the board of directors may also set a Record Date. The shareholders recorded in the stock transfer book at the close of business on the Record Date will be entitled to receive notice, vote at meetings, or receive dividends. A list of shareholders entitled to receive notice, vote at meetings, or receive dividends will be prepared by the secretary when necessary and provided to the officers of the corporation. Every shareholder who is entitled to receive notice, vote, or receive dividends is also entitled to examine this list and the corporate stock transfer book.

Shareholders Quorum

Shareholders Quorum. A quorum for a shareholders meeting will be a majority of the outstanding shares that are entitled to vote at the meeting, whether in person or represented by proxy. Once a quorum is present, business may be conducted at the meeting, even if shareholders leave prior to adjournment.

Shareholders Voting

Voting. Each outstanding share of the corporation that is entitled to vote as shown on the stock transfer book will have one (1) vote. The vote of the holders of a majority of the shares entitled to vote will be sufficient to decide any matter, unless a greater number is required by the Articles of Incorporation or by state law. Adjournment shall be by majority vote of those shares entitled to vote.

Shareholders Proxies

Shareholders Proxies. At all meetings of shareholders, a shareholder may vote by signed proxy or by power of attorney. To be valid, a proxy must be filed with the secretary of the corporation prior to the stated time of the meeting. No proxy may be valid for over _____ months, unless the proxy specifically states otherwise. Proxies may always be revokable prior to the meeting for which they are intended. Attendance at the meeting by a shareholder for which a proxy has been authorized always revokes the proxy.

Shareholders Consent Resolutions

Shareholder Consent Resolutions. Any action that may be taken at a shareholders meeting may be taken instead without a meeting if a resolution is consented to, in writing, by all shareholders who would be entitled to vote on the matter.

Shareholders Cumulative Voting Rights

Shareholders Cumulative Voting Rights. For the election of directors, each shareholder may vote in a cumulative manner, if desired. Cumulative voting will mean that if each shareholder has one (1) vote per director to be elected, the shareholder may vote all votes for a single director or spread the votes among directors in any manner.

Powers of the Board of Directors

Powers of the Board of Directors. The affairs of the corporation will be managed by the board of directors. The board of directors will have all powers available under state law, including, but not limited to: the power to appoint and remove officers, agents, and employees; the power to change the offices, registered agent, and registered office of the corporation; the power to issue shares of stock; the power to borrow money on behalf of the corporation, including the power to execute any evidence of indebtedness on behalf of the corporation; and the power to enter into contracts on behalf of the corporation.

Number of Directors and Term of Office

Number of Directors and Term of Office. The number of directors will be as shown in the Articles of Incorporation and may be amended. The number is currently _____ . Each director will hold office for _____ year(s) and will be elected at the annual meeting of the shareholders.

Date and Time of Annual Meeting of the Board of Directors

Date and Time of Annual Meeting of the Board of Directors. The annual board of directors meeting will be held on the _____ of every year at the corporate offices at _____ o'clock ____ . m. This meeting is for the purpose of appointing officers and for transacting any other necessary business. If this day is a legal holiday, the meeting will be held on the next day.

Place of Board of Directors Meetings

Place of Board of Directors Meetings. The board of directors has the power to designate the place for directors meetings. If no place is designated, then the place for the meeting will be the principal office of the corporation.

Special Meetings of the Board of Directors

Special Meetings of the Board of Directors. Special meetings of the board of directors may be called at any time and for any purpose. These meetings may be called by either the president or the board of directors. The request for a special meeting must be made in writing that states the time, place, and purpose of the meeting. The request should be given to the secretary of the corporation who will prepare and send written notice to all directors.

Notice and Waivers of Board of Directors Meetings

Notice and Waivers of Board of Directors Meetings. Written notice of board of directors meetings must be sent to each director. The notice must be sent no less than _____ days nor more than _____ days before the date of the meeting. The notice should be sent to the director's address as shown in the corporate records. The notice will include the place, date, and time of the meeting, and for special meetings, the purpose of the meeting. When notices are sent, the secretary of the corporation must prepare an Affidavit of Mailing of Notices. Directors may waive notice of meetings if done in writing, except that attendance at a meeting is considered a waiver of notice of the meeting.

Board of Directors Quorum

Board of Directors Quorum. A quorum for directors meetings will be a majority of the directors. Once a quorum is present, business may be conducted at the meeting, even if directors leave prior to adjournment.

Board of Directors Voting

Board of Directors Voting. Each director will have one (1) vote. The vote of a majority of the directors will be sufficient to decide any matter, unless a greater number is required by the Articles of Incorporation or state law. Adjournment shall be by majority vote.

Board of Directors Consent Resolutions

Board of Directors Consent Resolutions. Any action that may be taken at a directors meeting may be taken instead without a meeting if a resolution is consented to, in writing, by all directors.

Removal of Directors

> **Removal of Directors.** A director may be removed from office, with or without cause, at a special meeting of the shareholders called for that purpose.

Filling Directors Vacancies

> **Filling Directors Vacancies.** A vacancy on the board of directors may be filled by majority vote of the remaining directors, even if technically less than a quorum. A director elected to fill a remaining term will hold office until the next annual shareholders meeting.

Salaries of Directors

> **Salaries of Directors.** The salaries of the directors will be fixed by the board of directors and may be altered at any time by the board. A director may receive a salary even if he or she receives a salary as an officer.

Fiduciary Duty of Directors

> **Fiduciary Duty of Directors.** Each director owes a a fiduciary duty of good faith and reasonable care with regard to all actions taken on behalf of the corporation. Each director must perform his or her duties in good faith in a manner that he or she reasonably believes to be in the best interests of the corporation, using ordinary care and prudence.

Number of Officers

Number of Officers. The officers of the corporation will include a president, vice-president, treasurer, and secretary. Any two (2) or more offices may be held by the same person.

Appointment and Terms of Officers

Appointment and Terms of Officers. The officers of the corporation will be appointed by the directors at the first meeting of the board of directors. Each officer will hold office until death, resignation, or removal by the board of directors.

Removal of Officers

Removal of Officers. Any officer may be removed by the board of directors, with or without cause. Appointment of an officer does not create any contract rights for the officer.

Filling Vacancies of Officers

Filling Vacancies of Officers. A vacancy in any office for any reason may be filled by the board of directors for the unexpired term.

Duties of the President

Duties of the President. The president is the principal executive officer of the corporation and is subject to control by the board of directors. The president will supervise and control all of the business and activities of the corporation. The president will preside at all shareholders and directors meetings, and perform any other duties as prescribed by the board of directors.

Duties of the Vice-President

> **Duties of the Vice-President.** If the president is absent, dies, or is incapacitated, the vice-president will perform the duties of the president. When acting for the president, the vice-president will have all of the powers and authority of the president. The vice-president will also perform any other duties as prescribed by the board of directors.

Duties of the Secretary

> **Duties of the Secretary.** The secretary will keep the minutes of all shareholders and directors meetings. The secretary will provide notices of all meetings as required by the bylaws. The secretary will be the custodian of the corporate records, corporate stock transfer book, and corporate seal. The secretary will keep a list of the addresses of all shareholders, directors, and officers. The secretary will sign, along with other officers, the corporation's stock certificates. The secretary will also perform any other duties as prescribed by the board of directors.

Duties of the Treasurer

> **Duties of the Treasurer.** The treasurer will be custodian of all corporate funds and securities. The treasurer will receive and pay out funds that are receivable or payable to the corporation from any source. The treasurer will deposit all corporate funds received into the corporate bank accounts as designated by the board of directors. The treasurer will also perform any other duties as prescribed by the board of directors.

Salaries of Officers

Salaries of Officers. The salaries of the officers will be fixed by the board of directors and may be altered at any time by the board. An officer may receive a salary even if he or she receives a salary as a director.

Stock Certificates

Stock Certificates. Certificates that represent shares of ownership in the corporation will be in the form designated by the board of directors. Certificates will be signed by all officers of the corporation. Certificates will be consecutively numbered. The name and address of the person receiving the issued shares, the certificate number, the number of shares, and the date of issue will be recorded by the secretary of the corporation in the corporate stock transfer book. Shares of the corporation's stock may only be transferred on the stock transfer book of the corporation by the holder of the shares in whose name they were issued as shown on the stock transfer book, or by his or her legal representative.

Financial Matters

Financial Matters. The board of directors will determine the accounting methods and fiscal year of the corporation. All checks, drafts, or other methods for payment shall be signed by an officer determined by resolution of the board of directors. All notes, mortgages, or other evidence of indebtedness shall be signed by an officer determined by resolution of the board of directors. No money will be borrowed or loaned by the corporation unless authorized by a resolution of the board of directors. No contracts will be entered into on behalf of the corporation unless authorized by a resolution of the board of directors. No documents may be executed on behalf of the corporation unless authorized by a resolution of the board of directors. A board of directors resolution may be for specific instances or a general authorization.

Loans to Officers or Directors

Loans to Officers or Directors. The corporation may not lend any money to an officer or director of the corporation unless the loan has been approved by a majority of the shares of all stock of the corporation, including those shares that do not have voting rights.

Amendments to the Bylaws

Amendments to the Bylaws. These bylaws may be amended in any manner by majority vote of the board of directors at any annual or special meeting. Any amendments by the board of directors are subject to approval by majority vote of the shareholders at any annual or special meeting.

Signatures Clause

Dated: _____ , 20 ___

_____
Signature of Secretary of Corporation

_____
Printed Name of Secretary of Corporation

Adopted by the Board of Directors on _____ , 20 ___

_____
Signature of Chairperson of Board

_____
Printed Name of Chairperson of Board

Approved by the Shareholders on _____ , 20 ___

_____
Signature of Secretary of Corporation

_____
Printed Name of Secretary of Corporation

Sample Corporate Bylaws

Corporate Bylaws of ABCXYZ Corporation, a corporation incorporated under the laws of the State of Superior

Corporate Office and Registered Agent. The board of directors has the power to determine the location of the corporation's principal place of business and registered office, that need not be the same location. The board of directors also has the power to designate the corporation's registered agent, who may be an officer or director.

Date, Time, and Place of Shareholders Annual Meeting. The annual shareholders meeting will be held on the First Tuesday in October of every year at the corporate offices of the corporation at 10:00 o'clock a.m. This meeting is for the purpose of electing directors and for transacting any other necessary business. If this day is a legal holiday, the meeting will be held on the next day.

Shareholders Special Meetings. Special meetings of the shareholders may be called at any time and for any purpose. These meetings may be called by either the president or the board of directors or upon request of 25 percent of the shareholders of the corporation. The request for a special meeting must be made in writing that states the time, place, and purpose of the meeting. The request should be given to the secretary of the corporation who will prepare and send written notice to all shareholders of record who are entitled to vote at the meeting.

Place of Shareholders Meetings. The board of directors has the power to designate the place for shareholders meetings, unless a waiver of notice of the meeting signed by all shareholders designates the place for the meeting. If no place is designated, either by the board of directors or all of the shareholders, then the place for the meeting will be the principal office of the corporation.

Notice and Waivers of Shareholders Meetings. Written notice of shareholders meetings must be sent to each shareholder of record entitled to vote at the meeting. The notice must be sent no less than seven (7) days nor more than 21 days before the date of the meeting. The notice should be sent to the shareholder's address as shown in the corporate stock transfer book. The notice will include the place, date, and time of the meeting. Notices for special meetings must also include the purpose of the meeting. When notices are sent, the secretary of the corporation must prepare an Affidavit of Mailing of Notices. Shareholders may waive notice of meetings if done in writing, except that attendance at a meeting is considered a waiver of notice of the meeting.

Shareholders Entitled to Notice, to Vote, or to Dividends. For the purpose of determining which shareholders are entitled to notice, to vote at meetings, or to receive dividends, the board of directors may order that the corporate stock transfer book be closed for 30 days prior to a meeting or the issuance of a dividend. The shareholders entitled to receive notice, vote at meetings, or receive dividends are those who are recorded in the stock transfer book upon the closing of the book. Instead of closing the book, the board of directors may also set a Record Date. The shareholders recorded in the stock transfer book at the close of business on the Record Date will be entitled to receive notice, vote at meetings, or receive dividends. A list of shareholders entitled to receive notice, vote at meetings, or receive dividends will be prepared by the secretary when necessary and provided to the officers of the corporation. Every shareholder who is entitled to receive notice, vote, or receive dividends is also entitled to examine this list and the corporate stock transfer book.

Shareholders Quorum. A quorum for a shareholders meeting will be a majority of the outstanding shares that are entitled to vote at the meeting, whether in person or represented by proxy. Once a quorum is present, business may be conducted at the meeting, even if shareholders leave prior to adjournment.

Shareholders Voting. Each outstanding share of the corporation that is entitled to vote as shown on the stock transfer book will have one (1) vote. The vote of the holders of a majority of the shares entitled to vote will be sufficient to decide any matter, unless a greater number is required by the Articles of Incorporation or by state law. Adjournment shall be by majority vote of those shares entitled to vote.

Shareholders Proxies. At all meetings of shareholders, a shareholder may vote by signed proxy or by power of attorney. To be valid, a proxy must be filed with the secretary of the corporation prior to the stated time of the meeting. No proxy may be valid for over 11 months, unless the proxy specifically states otherwise. Proxies may always be revocable prior to the meeting for which they are intended. Attendance at the meeting by a shareholder for which a proxy has been authorized always revokes the proxy.

Shareholders Consent Resolutions. Any action that may be taken at a shareholders meeting may be taken instead without a meeting if a resolution is consented to, in writing, by all shareholders who would be entitled to vote on the matter.

Shareholders Cumulative Voting Rights. For the election of directors, each shareholder may vote in a cumulative manner, if desired. Cumulative voting will mean that if each shareholder has one (1) vote per director to be elected, the shareholder may vote all votes for a single director or spread the votes among directors in any manner.

Powers of the Board of Directors. The affairs of the corporation will be managed by the board of directors. The board of directors will have all powers available under state law, including, but not limited to: the power to appoint and remove officers, agents, and employees; the power to change the offices, registered agent, and registered office of the corporation; the power to issue shares of stock; the power to borrow money on behalf of the corporation, including the power to execute any evidence of indebtedness on behalf of the corporation; and the power to enter into contracts on behalf of the corporation.

Number of Directors and Term of Office. The number of directors will be as shown in the Articles of Incorporation and may be amended. The number is currently three (3). Each director will hold office for one (1) year and will be elected at the annual meeting of the shareholders.

Date and Time of Annual Meeting of the Board of Directors. The annual board of directors meeting will be held on the First Tuesday of October of every year at the corporate offices at 11:00 o'clock p.m. This meeting is for the purpose of appointing officers and for transacting any other necessary business. If this day is a legal holiday, the meeting will be held on the next day.

Place of Board of Directors Meetings. The board of directors has the power to designate the place for directors meetings. If no place is designated, then the place for the meeting will be the principal office of the corporation.

Special Meetings of the Board of Directors. Special meetings of the board of directors may be called at any time and for any purpose. These meetings may be called by either the president or the board of directors. The request for a special meeting must be made in writing that states the time, place, and purpose of the meeting. The request should be given to the secretary of the corporation who will prepare and send written notice to all directors.

Notice and Waivers of Board of Directors Meetings. Written notice of board of directors meetings must be sent to each director. The notice must be sent no less than seven (7) days nor more than 21 days before the date of the meeting. The notice should be sent to the director's address as shown in the corporate records. The notice will include the place, date, and time of the meeting, and for special meetings, the purpose of the meeting. When notices are sent, the secretary of the corporation must prepare an Affidavit of Mailing of Notices. Directors may waive notice of meetings if done in writing, except that attendance at a meeting is considered a waiver of notice of the meeting.

Board of Directors Quorum. A quorum for directors meetings will be a majority of the directors. Once a quorum is present, business may be conducted at the meeting, even if directors leave prior to adjournment.

Board of Directors Voting. Each director will have one (1) vote. The vote of a majority of the directors will be sufficient to decide any matter, unless a greater number is required by the Articles of Incorporation or state law. Adjournment shall be by majority vote.

Board of Directors Consent Resolutions. Any action that may be taken at a directors meeting may be taken instead without a meeting if a resolution is consented to, in writing, by all directors.

Removal of Directors. A director may be removed from office, with or without cause, at a special meeting of the shareholders called for that purpose.

Filling Directors Vacancies. A vacancy on the board of directors may be filled by majority vote of the remaining directors, even if technically less than a quorum. A director elected to fill a remaining term will hold office until the next annual shareholders meeting.

Salaries of Directors. The salaries of the directors will be fixed by the board of directors and may be altered at any time by the board. A director may receive a salary even if he or she receives a salary as an officer.

Fiduciary Duty of Directors. Each director owes a a fiduciary duty of good faith and reasonable care with regard to all actions taken on behalf of the corporation. Each director must perform his or her duties in good faith in a manner that he or she reasonably believes to be in the best interests of the corporation, using ordinary care and prudence.

Number of Officers. The officers of the corporation will include a president, vice-president, treasurer, and secretary. Any two (2) or more offices may be held by the same person.

Appointment and Terms of Officers. The officers of the corporation will be appointed by the directors at the first meeting of the board of directors. Each officer will hold office until death, resignation, or removal by the board of directors.

Removal of Officers. Any officer may be removed by the board of directors, with or without cause. Appointment of an officer does not create any contract rights for the officer.

Filling Vacancies of Officers. A vacancy in any office for any reason may be filled by the board of directors for the unexpired term.

Duties of the President. The president is the principal executive officer of the corporation and is subject to control by the board of directors. The president will supervise and control all of the business and activities of the corporation. The president will preside at all shareholders and directors meetings, and perform any other duties as prescribed by the board of directors.

Duties of the Vice-President. If the president is absent, dies, or is incapacitated, the vice-president will perform the duties of the president. When acting for the president, the vice-president will have all of the powers and authority of the president. The vice-president will also perform any other duties as prescribed by the board of directors.

Duties of the Secretary. The secretary will keep the minutes of all shareholders and directors meetings. The secretary will provide notices of all meetings as required by the bylaws. The secretary will be the custodian of the corporate records, corporate stock transfer book, and corporate seal. The secretary will keep a list of the addresses of all shareholders, directors, and officers. The secretary will sign, along with other officers, the corporation's stock certificates. The secretary will also perform any other duties as prescribed by the board of directors.

Duties of the Treasurer. The treasurer will be custodian of all corporate funds and securities. The treasurer will receive and pay out funds that are receivable or payable to the corporation from any source. The treasurer will deposit all corporate funds received into the corporate bank accounts as designated by the board of directors. The treasurer will also perform any other duties as prescribed by the board of directors.

Salaries of Officers. The salaries of the officers will be fixed by the board of directors and may be altered at any time by the board. An officer may receive a salary even if he or she receives a salary as a director.

Stock Certificates. Certificates that represent shares of ownership in the corporation will be in the form designated by the board of directors. Certificates will be signed by all officers of the corporation. Certificates will be consecutively numbered. The name and address of the person receiving the issued shares, the certificate number, the number of shares, and the date of issue will be recorded by the secretary of the corporation in the corporate stock transfer book. Shares of the corporation's stock may only be transferred on the stock transfer book of the corporation by the holder of the shares in whose name they were issued as shown on the stock transfer book, or by his or her legal representative.

Financial Matters. The board of directors will determine the accounting methods and fiscal year of the corporation. All checks, drafts, or other methods for payment shall be signed by an officer determined by resolution of the board of directors. All notes, mortgages, or other evidence of indebtedness shall be signed by an officer determined by resolution of the board of directors. No money will be borrowed or loaned by the corporation unless authorized by a resolution of the board of directors. No contracts will be entered into on behalf of the corporation unless authorized by a resolution of the board of directors. No documents may be executed on behalf of the corporation unless authorized by a resolution of the board of directors. A board of directors resolution may be for specific instances or a general authorization.

Loans to Officers or Directors. The corporation may not lend any money to an officer or director of the corporation unless the loan has been approved by a majority of the shares of all stock of the corporation, including those shares that do not have voting rights.

Amendments to the Bylaws. These bylaws may be amended in any manner by majority vote of the board of directors at any annual or special meeting. Any amendments by the board of directors are subject to approval by majority vote of the shareholders at any annual or special meeting.

Dated: June 14, 2005

Mary Celeste
Signature of Secretary of Corporation

Mary Celeste
Printed Name of Secretary of Corporation

Approved by the Board of Directors on June 14, 2005

John Celeste
Signature of Chairperson of Board

John Celeste
Printed Name of Chairperson of Board

Approved by the Shareholders on June 14, 2005

Mary Celeste
Signature of Secretary of Corporation

Mary Celeste
Printed Name of Secretary of Corporation

CHAPTER 11
Corporate Directors Meetings

The board of directors of a corporation transacts business as a group. Each individual director has no authority to bind the corporation (unless the board of directors as a group has previously authorized him or her to exercise that power). Even in a corporation with a single director, there must be formal records of meetings and of the resolutions adopted by the board.

Corporate boards of directors must, at a minimum, hold an annual meeting to appoint the officers of the corporation for the coming year, decide if dividends will be declared for the year, and make any other annual decisions regarding the financial matters of the business. Typically, boards will hold special meetings for specific topics much more frequently. Whenever official corporate matters are discussed as a group, the board of directors should hold a meeting, keep minutes, and record the decisions made as corporate resolutions. This is not a difficult task and it will provide a clear record of the agreements made by the board for future reference. Prior to any annual or special meetings of the board, notice must be given to each board member according to the time limits set in the bylaws. If all board members are in agreement, an easier method to fulfill the notice requirement is to have the board sign waivers of notice. This document and all of the other documents necessary to conduct and record board meetings are contained in this chapter. Before each type of board meeting is a checklist of the information necessary to fill in the minutes and other forms. Follow the appropriate checklist for each meeting.

First Board of Directors Meeting Checklist

The following information should be covered and documented in the minutes of the first board of directors meeting:

- ❏ Name of corporation

- ❏ Date of meeting

- ❏ Location of meeting

- ❏ Officers present at meeting

- ❏ Others present at meeting

- ❏ Name of temporary chairperson presiding over meeting

- ❏ Name of temporary secretary acting at meeting

- ❏ Calling of meeting to order and quorum present

- ❏ Proper notification of meeting

  - ❏ Notices sent or waivers filed

- ❏ Articles of Incorporation filed with state

  - ❏ Date of filing

  - ❏ Effective date of incorporation

- ❏ Approve and ratify any acts of incorporators taken on behalf of corporation prior to effective date of incorporation

- ❏ Elect officers of corporation

- ❑ Decide on annual salaries of officers

- ❑ Direct that any organizational expenses be reimbursed to incorporators

- ❑ Authorize opening of corporate bank account

- ❑ Approve corporate seal, stock certificate, and stock transfer book

- ❑ Approve corporate bylaws

- ❑ Approve issuance of stock in exchange for transfers of property or money

- ❑ Designate fiscal year dates

- ❑ Designate accounting basis (cash or accrual basis)

- ❑ Document any other necessary business

- ❑ Adjournment of meeting

- ❑ Date and secretary signature on minutes

Notice of First Board of Directors Meeting of _____

TO:

In accordance with the bylaws of this corporation, the first organizational meeting of the board of directors will be held on _____ , 20 _____ , at _____ o'clock ___ . m. , at the offices of the corporation located at _____ .

Dated: _____ , 20 _____

_____
Signature of Incorporator

_____
Printed Name of Incorporator

_____
Signature of Incorporator

_____
Printed Name of Incorporator

_____
Signature of Incorporator

_____
Printed Name of Incorporator

Waiver of Notice of First Board of Directors Meeting of _____

We, the undersigned incorporators of this corporation, waive any required notice and consent to the holding of the first meeting of the board of directors of this corporation on _____ , 20 _____ , at _____ o'clock _____ . m., at the offices of the corporation, located at _____ .

Dated: _____ , 20 _____

Signature of Incorporator   _Printed Name of Incorporator_

_____   _____

_____   _____

_____   _____

_____   _____

_____   _____

_____   _____

_____   _____

Minutes of First Board of Directors Meeting of _____

The first meeting of the board of directors of this corporation was held on
_____ , 20 _____ , at _____ o'clock ____ . m., at the offices of
the corporation, located at _____ .

Present at the meeting were the following people: _____
_____
_____
all of whom are designated as directors of this corporation in the Articles of Incorporation.

The following other persons were also present: _____
_____
_____ .

1. _____ was elected as the temporary chairperson of the board.

   _____ was elected as the temporary secretary of the board.

2. The chairperson announced that the meeting had been duly called by the incorporators of the corporation, called the meeting to order, and determined that a quorum was present.

3. The secretary then presented an Affidavit of Mailing of Notice or a Waiver of Notice of the meeting which was signed by all directors.

   Upon motion made and carried, the secretary was ordered to attach the Affidavit of Notice or the Waiver of Notice to the minutes of this meeting.

4. The chairperson reported that the Articles of Incorporation had been duly filed with the State of _____ on _____ , 20 _____ , and that the incorporation was effective as of _____ , 20 _____ .

   Upon motion made and carried, a copy of the Articles of Incorporation was ordered to be attached to the minutes of this meeting.

5. Upon motion made and carried, the board of directors RESOLVED that:

   The joint and individual acts of _____ and
   _____ , the incorporators of this corporation, which were taken on behalf of the corporation, are approved, ratified, and adopted as acts of the corporation.

6. The following persons were elected as officers of the corporation to serve until the first annual board of directors meeting:

_____ , President

_____ , Vice-President

_____ , Treasurer

_____ , Secretary

7. Upon motion made and carried, the annual salaries of the officers were fixed at the following rates until the next annual meeting of the board of directors:

President $ _____

Vice-President $ _____

Secretary $ _____

Treasurer $ _____

8. Upon motion made and carried, the board of directors RESOLVED that:

The officers of this corporation are authorized and directed to pay all fees and expenses necessary for the organization of this corporation. The officers are also directed to procure and prepare the necessary books for corporate accounting.

9. Upon motion made and carried, the board of directors RESOLVED that:

The officers of this corporation be authorized and directed to open a bank account with _____ , located at _____ , and to deposit all funds of the corporation into this account, with checks payable upon the corporate signature of _____ only.

And further RESOLVED that:

The officers of this corporation are authorized to execute any formal Bank Resolutions and documents which may be necessary to open such an account. A copy of the formal Bank Resolution for opening this account is hereby adopted and ordered to be attached to the minutes of this meeting.

10. A proposed Corporate Seal, Corporate Stock Certificate, and Corporate Stock Transfer Book were presented.

Upon motion made and carried, the board of directors
RESOLVED that:

The Seal, Stock Certificates, and Stock Transfer Book presented at this meeting are adopted and approved as the Seal, Stock Certificates, and Stock Transfer Book of this corporation. A specimen copy of the Stock Certificate is ordered to be attached to the minutes of this meeting.

11. A copy of the proposed bylaws of the corporation was presented at the meeting and read by each director.

Upon motion made and carried, the board of directors
RESOLVED that:

The proposed bylaws of this corporation are approved and adopted. A copy of these by-laws are ordered to be attached to the minutes of this meeting.

12. The following persons have offered to transfer the property or money listed below to the corporation in exchange for the following number of shares of common capital stock in the corporation:

Name	Property or Money	Number of Shares
_____	_____	_____
_____	_____	_____
_____	_____	_____
_____	_____	_____
_____	_____	_____
_____	_____	_____

Upon motion made and carried, the board of directors
RESOLVED that:

The assets proposed for transfer are good and sufficient consideration and the officers are directed to accept the assets on behalf of the corporation and to issue and deliver the appropriate number of shares of stock in this corporation to the respective persons. The shares of stock issued shall be fully paid and non-assessable common capital stock of this corporation.

13. Upon motion made and carried, the board of directors
    RESOLVED that:

    The fiscal year of this corporation shall begin on _____ , 20 _____ , and end on _____ , 20 _____ . This corporation shall report its income and expenses on a(n) _____ basis.

14. The following other business was conducted:

There being no further business, upon motion made and carried, the meeting was adjourned.

Dated: _____ , 20 _____

Corporate Seal

_____
Signature of Secretary of Corporation

_____
Printed Name of Secretary of Corporation

Annual Board of Directors Meeting Checklist

The following information should be covered and documented in the minutes of the annual board of directors meeting:

- ❏ Name of corporation
- ❏ Date and time of meeting
- ❏ Location of meeting
- ❏ Notification of meeting
  - ❏ Notices sent or waivers filed
- ❏ Officers present at meeting
- ❏ Others present at meeting
- ❏ Officers presiding over meeting
- ❏ Calling of meeting to order and quorum present

Annual Matters

- ❏ Date last state corporate tax return filed
- ❏ Date last federal corporate tax return filed
- ❏ Date last state annual report filed
- ❏ Date any other required reports/returns filed
- ❏ Date of last financial statement
- ❏ Review current employment agreements
- ❏ Review current insurance coverage

- ❑ Review stock transfer ledger
- ❑ Review current financial statement
  - ❑ Review current year-to-date income and expenses
  - ❑ Review current salaries
  - ❑ Review current pension/profit-sharing plans
  - ❑ Review other employee fringe benefit plans
  - ❑ Review accounts receivable
    - ❑ Determine if collection procedures are warranted
  - ❑ Review status of any outstanding loans
  - ❑ Ascertain net profit
  - ❑ Determine if a stock dividend should be declared
- ❑ Discuss any major items requiring board action
  - ❑ Election and salaries of officers
  - ❑ Major purchases or leases (real estate or personal property)
  - ❑ Lawsuits
  - ❑ Loans
  - ❑ Other business
- ❑ Adjournment of meeting
- ❑ Date and secretary signature on minutes

Notice of Annual Board of Directors Meeting of _____

TO:

In accordance with the bylaws of this corporation, an annual meeting of the board of directors will be held on _____ , 20 _____ , at _____ o'clock ___ . m. , at the offices of the corporation located at _____ .

Dated: _____ , 20 _____

Corporate Seal

_____
Signature of Secretary of Corporation

_____
Printed Name of Secretary of Corporation

Waiver of Notice of Annual Board of Directors Meeting of _____

We, the undersigned directors of this corporation, waive any required notice and consent to the holding of the annual meeting of the board of directors of this corporation on _____ , 20 _____ , at _____ o'clock ____ . m., at the offices of the corporation located at _____ .

Dated: _____ , 20 _____

Signature of Director   *Printed Name of Director*

_____   _____

_____   _____

_____   _____

_____   _____

_____   _____

_____   _____

Minutes of Annual Board of Directors Meeting of _____

The annual meeting of the board of directors of this corporation was held on _____ , 20 _____ , at _____ o'clock ____ . m. , at the offices of the corporation located at _____ .

Present at the meeting were the following people: _____
_____
_____
all of whom are directors of this corporation.

The following persons were also present: _____
_____
_____ .

_____ , the president of the corporation, presided over the meeting.

_____ , the secretary of the corporation, served as secretary for the meeting.

1. The president called the meeting to order. The president determined that a quorum was present and that the meeting could conduct business.

2. The secretary reported that notice of the meeting had been properly given or waived by each director in accordance with the bylaws.

   Upon motion made and carried, the secretary was ordered to attach the appropriate Affidavit of Mailing of Notice or Waiver of Notice to the minutes of this meeting.

3. The secretary distributed copies of the minutes of the previous meeting of the board of directors which had been held on _____ , 20 _____ .

   Upon motion made and carried, these minutes were approved.

4. The president presented the annual President's Report.

   Upon motion made and carried, the President's Report was approved and the secretary was directed to attach a copy of the President's Report to these minutes.

5. The treasurer of the corporation presented the Treasurer's Report, which stated that as of _____ , 20 _____ , the corporation had a net profit of $ _____ .

Upon motion made and carried, the Treasurer's Report was approved and the secretary was directed to attach a copy of the Treasurer's Report to these minutes.

6. Upon motion made and carried, the board of directors
RESOLVED that:

A dividend of $ _____ per share of common stock is declared on the stock of this corporation. This dividend shall be paid to the shareholders of record as of
_____ , 20 _____ , and shall be paid on _____ ,
20 _____ . The officers of this corporation are directed to take all necessary actions to carry out this resolution.

7. Upon motion made and carried, the following persons were elected as officers of this corporation for a term of one (1) year:

_____ , President

_____ , Vice-President

_____ , Treasurer

_____ , Secretary

8. Upon motion made and carried, the salaries of the officers were fixed for the term of one (1) year at the following rates:

President $ _____

Vice-President $ _____

Secretary $ _____

Treasurer $ _____

9. The following other business was transacted:

There being no further business, upon motion made and carried, the meeting was adjourned.

Dated: _____ , 20 _____

                                        Corporate Seal

_____
Signature of Secretary of Corporation

_____
Printed Name of Secretary of Corporation

CHAPTER 12

Corporate Shareholders Meetings

The main responsibility of the shareholders of a corporation is to elect the directors of the business. This election is conducted at the annual meeting of the shareholders that is held on the date, time, and place as specified in the corporate bylaws. In addition, specific corporate business at other times of the year may occasionally need shareholder approval. For example, shareholders must vote on the dissolution of the corporation, on amendments to the Bylaws or Articles of Incorporation, and on any extraordinary business transactions, such as the sale of all of the assets of the corporation. For these purposes, a special meeting of the shareholders must be held.

The initial meeting of the shareholders also has a slightly different agenda. At this meeting, the shareholders approve and ratify the adoption of the corporate bylaws, and ratify the election or appointment of the initial board of directors who will serve until the first annual meeting of the shareholders. The shareholders also approve the election of the first officers of the corporation by the board of directors.

On the following pages, there are checklists and forms for the initial, annual, and special shareholders meetings. Please follow the checklists in preparing the forms. The notice requirements for shareholders meetings are identical to those for directors meetings. However, the forms are slightly different.

First Shareholders Meeting Checklist

The following information should be covered and documented in the minutes of the first shareholders meeting:

❏ Name of corporation

❏ Date of meeting

❏ Location of meeting

❏ Officers present at meeting

❑ Others present at meeting

❑ Calling of meeting to order and quorum present

❑ Shareholders present at meeting

❑ Shareholders represented by proxy at meeting

❑ Name of president acting at meeting

❑ Name of secretary acting at meeting

❑ Name of chairperson elected to preside over meeting

❑ Proper notification of meeting

❑ Notice sent and affidavit filed/or waivers filed

❑ Reading of minutes of first directors meeting

❑ Approval and ratification of minutes of first directors meeting

❑ Approval and ratification of election of officers and directors

❑ Approval and ratification of adoption of corporate bylaws

❑ Election of S-Corporation status resolution

❑ Any other business

❑ Meeting adjourned

❑ Dating and signing of minutes by secretary

Notice of First Shareholders Meeting
of _____

TO:

In accordance with the bylaws of this corporation, a first official meeting of the shareholders will be held on _____ , 20 _____ , at _____ o'clock ____ . m., at the offices of the corporation located at _____ .

The purpose of this meeting is to approve adoption of the bylaws of this corporation, approve election of the officers, approve continuation of the directors of this corporation, and to transact any other necessary business.

The Stock Transfer Book of this corporation will remain closed from _____ , 20 _____ , until _____ , 20 _____ .

Dated: _____ , 20 _____

Corporate Seal

_____
Signature of Secretary of Corporation

_____
Printed Name of Secretary of Corporation

Waiver of Notice of First Shareholders Meeting of _____

We, the undersigned shareholders of this corporation, waive any required notice and consent to the holding of the first meeting of the shareholders of this corporation on _____ , 20 _____ , at _____ o'clock ____ . m., at the offices of the corporation located at _____ .

Dated: _____ , 20 _____

Signature of Shareholder	*Printed Name of Shareholder*
_____	_____
_____	_____
_____	_____
_____	_____
_____	_____
_____	_____
_____	_____
_____	_____
_____	_____

Authorization to Vote Shares
(PROXY) _____

I, _____ , the record owner of this corporation's
stock certificate # _____ , which represents _____ shares in this corporation, authorize _____ to vote all of these shares at
the meeting of the shareholders of this corporation which is scheduled to be held on
_____ , 20 _____ , at _____ o'clock ___ . m., at the offices of this
corporation located at _____ .

Through the use of this proxy and authorization, _____
has the right to vote these shares at any business conducted at this meeting as if I personally
were present.

This proxy and authorization may be revoked by me at any time prior to the meeting and will
be void if I personally attend the meeting.

Dated: _____ , 20 _____

_____
Signature of Shareholder

_____
Printed Name of Shareholder

Minutes of First Shareholders Meeting of _____

The first meeting of the shareholders of this corporation was held on _____ , 20 _____ , at _____ o'clock ___ . m., at the offices of the corporation located at
_____ .

Present were:

_____ , President

_____ , Vice-President

_____ , Treasurer

_____ , Secretary

Other than shareholders of this corporation, the following persons were also present:
_____
_____
_____

1. The president of this corporation called the meeting to order. The president determined that a quorum was present, either in person or by proxy, and that the meeting could conduct business.

   The following shareholders were present in person:

Name of Shareholder	*Number of Shares*
_____	_____
_____	_____
_____	_____
_____	_____
_____	_____

The following shareholders were represented by proxy:

Name of Shareholder   *Number of Shares*

_____   _____

_____   _____

_____   _____

_____   _____

_____   _____

_____   _____

2. The secretary reported that notice of the meeting had been properly given or waived by each shareholder in accordance with the bylaws.

   Upon motion made and carried, the secretary was ordered to attach the appropriate Affidavit of Mailing of Notice or Waiver of Notice to the minutes of this meeting.

3. _____ was then elected chairperson of this meeting.

4. The secretary read the minutes of the first meeting of the board of directors of this corporation which was held on _____ , 20 _____ .

   Upon motion made and carried, the shareholders
   RESOLVED that:

   All acts taken and decisions made at the first meeting of the board of directors of this corporation are approved and ratified, specifically that the shareholders approve and ratify the adoption of the bylaws of this corporation and that the shareholders approve and ratify the election of the following persons as officers for the terms as stated in the minutes of the first meeting of the board of directors:

   _____ , President

   _____ , Vice-President

   _____ , Treasurer

   _____ , Secretary

5. Upon motion made and carried, the shareholders
   RESOLVED that:

   The following persons are designated as the initial directors of this corporation in the Articles of Incorporation and the shareholders approve and ratify this designation of the following persons as directors of this corporation until the first annual meeting of the shareholders of this corporation:

   _____ , Director

   _____ , Director

   _____ , Director

6. Upon motion made and carried, the following resolution was approved unanimously by the shareholders of all outstanding shares of the corporation:
   RESOLVED that:

   This corporation elects to be treated and taxed as an S-Corporation under IRS Code Section 1362.

   The president declared that this shareholders resolution was duly adopted.

7. The following other business was transacted:

There being no further business, upon motion made and carried, the meeting was adjourned.

Dated: _____ , 20 _____

                                            Corporate Seal

_____
Signature of Secretary of Corporation

_____
Printed Name of Secretary of Corporation

Resolution of Shareholders of _____ Regarding S-Corporation Status

A meeting of the shareholders of this corporation was duly called and held on
_____ , 20 _____ , at _____ o'clock ___ . m., at the offices of the
corporation located at _____ .
All of the shareholders of this corporation were present, in person or by proxy.

At the meeting it was decided, by unanimous vote, that it is in the best interests of the corporation that the corporation elect to be treated as an S-corporation under the provisions of IRS Code Section 1362.

Therefore, it is unanimously
RESOLVED, that this corporation elects to be treated as an S-corporation under the provisions of IRS Code Section 1362. The officers of this corporation are hereby authorized to perform all necessary acts to carry out this resolution.

The undersigned, _____ , certifies that he or she is the duly elected secretary of this corporation and that the above is a true and correct copy of the resolution that was duly adopted at a meeting of the shareholders that was held in accordance with state law and the bylaws of the corporation on _____ ,
20 _____ . I further certify that such resolution is now in full force and effect.

Dated: _____ , 20 _____

Corporate Seal

_____
Signature of Secretary of Corporation

_____
Printed Name of Secretary of Corporation

Signature of Shareholder   *Printed Name of Shareholder*

_____   _____

_____   _____

_____   _____

_____   _____

_____   _____

_____   _____

_____   _____

_____   _____

_____   _____

_____   _____

Being all of the shareholders of this corporation.

Form **2553**
(Rev. December 2002)
Department of the Treasury
Internal Revenue Service

Election by a Small Business Corporation
(Under section 1362 of the Internal Revenue Code)
▶ See Parts II and III on back and the separate instructions.
▶ The corporation may either send or fax this form to the IRS. See page 2 of the instructions.

OMB No. 1545-0146

Notes: 1. *Do not file Form 1120S, U.S. Income Tax Return for an S Corporation, for any tax year before the year the election takes effect.*

2. *This election to be an S corporation can be accepted only if all the tests are met under **Who May Elect** on page 1 of the instructions; all shareholders have signed the consent statement; and the exact name and address of the corporation and other required form information are provided.*

3. *If the corporation was in existence before the effective date of this election, see **Taxes an S Corporation May Owe** on page 1 of the instructions.*

Part I Election Information

Please Type or Print	Name of corporation (see instructions)	**A** Employer identification number
	Number, street, and room or suite no. (If a P.O. box, see instructions.)	**B** Date incorporated
	City or town, state, and ZIP code	**C** State of incorporation

D Check the applicable box(es) if the corporation, after applying for the EIN shown in **A** above, changed its name ☐ or address ☐

E Election is to be effective for tax year beginning (month, day, year) . . . . ▶ ___ / ___ / ___

F Name and title of officer or legal representative who the IRS may call for more information

G Telephone number of officer or legal representative ( )

H If this election takes effect for the first tax year the corporation exists, enter month, day, and year of the **earliest** of the following: (1) date the corporation first had shareholders, (2) date the corporation first had assets, or (3) date the corporation began doing business . . . . ▶ ___ / ___ / ___

I Selected tax year: Annual return will be filed for tax year ending (month and day) ▶ --------------------------

If the tax year ends on any date other than December 31, except for a 52–53-week tax year ending with reference to the month of December, you **must** complete Part II on the back. If the date you enter is the ending date of a 52–53-week tax year, write "52–53-week year" to the right of the date.

J Name and address of each shareholder; shareholder's spouse having a community property interest in the corporation's stock; and each tenant in common, joint tenant, and tenant by the entirety. (A husband and wife (and their estates) are counted as one shareholder in determining the number of shareholders without regard to the manner in which the stock is owned.)	K Shareholders' Consent Statement. Under penalties of perjury, we declare that we consent to the election of the above-named corporation to be an S corporation under section 1362(a) and that we have examined this consent statement, including accompanying schedules and statements, and to the best of our knowledge and belief, it is true, correct, and complete. We understand our consent is binding and may not be withdrawn after the corporation has made a valid election. (Shareholders sign and date below.)		L Stock owned		M Social security number or employer identification number (see instructions)	N Shareholder's tax year ends (month and day)
	Signature	Date	Number of shares	Dates acquired		

Under penalties of perjury, I declare that I have examined this election, including accompanying schedules and statements, and to the best of my knowledge and belief, it is true, correct, and complete.

Signature of officer ▶   Title ▶   Date ▶

For Paperwork Reduction Act Notice, see page 4 of the instructions.   Cat. No. 18629R   Form **2553** (Rev. 12-2002)

Part II   **Selection of Fiscal Tax Year** (All corporations using this part must complete item O and item P, Q, or R.)

O Check the applicable box to indicate whether the corporation is:

1. ☐ A new corporation adopting the tax year entered in item I, Part I.
2. ☐ An existing corporation retaining the tax year entered in item I, Part I.
3. ☐ An existing corporation changing to the tax year entered in item I, Part I.

P Complete item P if the corporation is using the automatic approval provisions of Rev. Proc. 2002-38, 2002-22 I.R.B. 1037, to request **(1)** a natural business year (as defined in section 5.05 of Rev. Proc. 2002-38) or **(2)** a year that satisfies the ownership tax year test (as defined in section 5.06 of Rev. Proc. 2002-38). Check the applicable box below to indicate the representation statement the corporation is making.

1. Natural Business Year ► ☐ I represent that the corporation is adopting, retaining, or changing to a tax year that qualifies as its natural business year as defined in section 5.05 of Rev. Proc. 2002-38 and has attached a statement verifying that it satisfies the 25% gross receipts test (see instructions for content of statement). I also represent that the corporation is not precluded by section 4.02 of Rev. Proc. 2002-38 from obtaining automatic approval of such adoption, retention, or change in tax year.

2. Ownership Tax Year ► ☐ I represent that shareholders (as described in section 5.06 of Rev. Proc. 2002-38) holding more than half of the shares of the stock (as of the first day of the tax year to which the request relates) of the corporation have the same tax year or are concurrently changing to the tax year that the corporation adopts, retains, or changes to per item I, Part I, and that such tax year satisfies the requirement of section 4.01(3) of Rev. Proc. 2002-38. I also represent that the corporation is not precluded by section 4.02 of Rev. Proc. 2002-38 from obtaining automatic approval of such adoption, retention, or change in tax year.

Note: *If you do not use item P and the corporation wants a fiscal tax year, complete either item Q or R below. Item Q is used to request a fiscal tax year based on a business purpose and to make a back-up section 444 election. Item R is used to make a regular section 444 election.*

Q Business Purpose—To request a fiscal tax year based on a business purpose, you must check box Q1. See instructions for details including payment of a user fee. You may also check box Q2 and/or box Q3.

1. Check here ► ☐ if the fiscal year entered in item I, Part I, is requested under the prior approval provisions of Rev. Proc. 2002-39, 2002-22 I.R.B. 1046. Attach to Form 2553 a statement describing the relevant facts and circumstances and, if applicable, the gross receipts from sales and services necessary to establish a business purpose. See the instructions for details regarding the gross receipts from sales and services. If the IRS proposes to disapprove the requested fiscal year, do you want a conference with the IRS National Office? ☐ Yes ☐ No

2. Check here ► ☐ to show that the corporation intends to make a back-up section 444 election in the event the corporation's business purpose request is not approved by the IRS. (See instructions for more information.)

3. Check here ► ☐ to show that the corporation agrees to adopt or change to a tax year ending December 31 if necessary for the IRS to accept this election for S corporation status in the event (1) the corporation's business purpose request is not approved and the corporation makes a back-up section 444 election, but is ultimately not qualified to make a section 444 election, or (2) the corporation's business purpose request is not approved and the corporation did not make a back-up section 444 election.

R Section 444 Election—To make a section 444 election, you must check box R1 and you may also check box R2.

1. Check here ► ☐ to show the corporation will make, if qualified, a section 444 election to have the fiscal tax year shown in item I, Part I. To make the election, you must complete **Form 8716,** Election To Have a Tax Year Other Than a Required Tax Year, and either attach it to Form 2553 or file it separately.

2. Check here ► ☐ to show that the corporation agrees to adopt or change to a tax year ending December 31 if necessary for the IRS to accept this election for S corporation status in the event the corporation is ultimately not qualified to make a section 444 election.

Part III   **Qualified Subchapter S Trust (QSST) Election Under Section 1361(d)(2)***

Income beneficiary's name and address	Social security number
Trust's name and address	Employer identification number

Date on which stock of the corporation was transferred to the trust (month, day, year) . . . . ►   / /

In order for the trust named above to be a QSST and thus a qualifying shareholder of the S corporation for which this Form 2553 is filed, I hereby make the election under section 1361(d)(2). Under penalties of perjury, I certify that the trust meets the definitional requirements of section 1361(d)(3) and that all other information provided in Part III is true, correct, and complete.

_____   _____
Signature of income beneficiary or signature and title of legal representative or other qualified person making the election   Date

*Use Part III to make the QSST election only if stock of the corporation has been transferred to the trust on or before the date on which the corporation makes its election to be an S corporation. The QSST election must be made and filed separately if stock of the corporation is transferred to the trust after the date on which the corporation makes the S election.

Annual Shareholders Meeting Checklist

The following information should be covered and documented in the minutes of the annual shareholders meetings:

- ❏ Name of corporation
- ❏ Date of meeting
- ❏ Location of meeting
- ❏ Officers present at meeting
- ❏ Others present at meeting
- ❏ Calling of meeting to order and quorum present
- ❏ Shareholders present at meeting
- ❏ Shareholders represented by proxy at meeting
- ❏ Name of president acting at meeting
- ❏ Name of secretary acting at meeting
- ❏ Name of chairperson elected to preside over meeting
- ❏ Proper notification of meeting
  - ❏ Notices sent and affidavit filed/or waivers filed
- ❏ Reading of minutes of previous shareholders meeting
- ❏ Approval of minutes of previous shareholders meeting

❑ Reading and approval of President's Report and direction that it be attached to minutes

❑ Reading and approval of Treasurer's Report and direction that it be attached to minutes

❑ Nomination of persons to serve as directors

❑ Election of directors

❑ Any other business

❑ Meeting adjournment

❑ Dating and signing of minutes by secretary

Notice of Annual Shareholders Meeting of _____

TO:

In accordance with the bylaws of this corporation, an official annual meeting of the shareholders will be held on _____ , 20 _____ , at _____ o'clock ____ . m., at the offices of the corporation located at _____ .

The purpose of this meeting is to elect directors of this corporation and to transact any other necessary business.

The Stock Transfer Book of this corporation will remain closed from _____ , 20 _____ , until _____ , 20 _____ .

Dated: _____ , 20 _____

Corporate Seal

_____
Signature of Secretary of Corporation

_____
Printed Name of Secretary of Corporation

Waiver of Notice of Annual Shareholders Meeting of _____

We, the undersigned shareholders of this corporation, waive any required notice and consent to the holding of the annual meeting of the shareholders of this corporation on _____ , 20 _____ , at _____ o'clock ____ . m., at the offices of the corporation located at _____ .

Dated: _____ , 20 _____

Signature of Shareholder	*Printed Name of Shareholder*
_____	_____
_____	_____
_____	_____
_____	_____
_____	_____
_____	_____
_____	_____
_____	_____
_____	_____
_____	_____

Minutes of Annual Shareholders Meeting of _____

The annual meeting of the shareholders of this corporation was held on
_____ , 20 _____ , at _____ o'clock ____ . m., at the offices of
the corporation located at _____ .

Present were:

_____ , President

_____ , Vice-President

_____ , Treasurer

_____ , Secretary

Other than shareholders of this corporation, the following persons were also present:
_____
_____
_____

1. The president of this corporation called the meeting to order. The president determined that a quorum was present, either in person or by proxy, and that the meeting could conduct business.

   The following shareholders were present in person:

   Name of Shareholder   *Number of Shares*

   _____   _____

   _____   _____

   _____   _____

   _____   _____

   _____   _____

The following shareholders were represented by proxy:

Name of Shareholder	Number of Shares
_____	_____
_____	_____
_____	_____
_____	_____
_____	_____
_____	_____

2. The secretary reported that notice of the meeting had been properly given or waived by each shareholder in accordance with the bylaws.

   Upon motion made and carried, the secretary was ordered to attach the appropriate Affidavit of Mailing of Notice or Waiver of Notice to the minutes of this meeting.

3. _____ was then elected chairperson of this meeting.

4. The secretary distributed copies of the minutes of the previous meeting of the shareholders which had been held on _____ , 20 _____ .

   Upon motion made and carried, these minutes were approved.

5. The president presented the annual President's Report.

   Upon motion made and carried, the President's Report was approved and the secretary was directed to attach a copy of the President's Report to these minutes.

6. The treasurer of the corporation presented the Treasurer's Report.

   Upon motion made and carried, the Treasurer's Report was approved and the secretary was directed to attach a copy of the Treasurer's Report to these minutes.

7. The following persons were nominated as directors of this corporation for a term of _____ year(s):

Name of Nominee   *Name of Nominee*

_____   _____

_____   _____

_____   _____

_____   _____

8. In accordance with the bylaws of this corporation, an election of directors was held, with each shareholder stating their choices for director by secret ballot and the number of shares held personally or by proxy.

9. The votes were tallied by the secretary and, by a majority vote of the outstanding shares entitled to vote in this election, the following persons were elected as directors of this corporation for a term of _____ year(s):

_____ , Director

_____ , Director

_____ , Director

10. On motion made and carried, it was directed that a report of the election be filed with the Clerk of _____ County, State of _____ , if required.

11. The following other business was transacted:

There being no further business, upon motion made and carried the meeting was adjourned.

Dated: _____ , 20 _____

                                        Corporate Seal

_____
Signature of Secretary of Corporation

_____
Printed Name of Secretary of Corporation

CHAPTER 13
Corporate Resolutions

Corporate resolutions are records of official acts of either the shareholders of the corporation or the board of directors. They are a permanent record of actions taken by either of these bodies as a group. In most situations and for most corporations, a majority vote of the directors or shareholders present at an official meeting (as long as the number present constitutes a quorum) is required to adopt a corporate resolution. The resolutions adopted should be kept permanently in the corporate record book. In some cases, a copy of the resolution will be required by a third party. For example, a financial institution will usually require a copy of the corporate resolution that authorizes an officer to bind the corporation in a loan transaction.

Two checklists follow that specify the general circumstances in which corporate resolutions are required. They are not required for all of the normal day-to-day transactions of a business. In general, directors resolutions are only necessary to document the major decisions or transactions of a corporation. Shareholders resolutions are even more rare, used only for extraordinary corporate matters. Note that many additional directors resolution forms for most situations that will arise in the general course of business have been included on the attached Forms-on-CD. This includes forms for all of the directors resolution situations that are included on the following Corporate Resolutions Checklist.

In recent years, the use of consent resolutions has increased among businesses. These resolutions are used in lieu of formal meetings and can simplify corporate management. They require, however, the written consent of all of the directors (or shareholders) of a corporation in order to be valid. Any of the resolutions in this chapter can be used as consent resolutions by adapting them using the consent resolution instructions located at the end of this chapter.

Corporate Resolutions Checklists

Directors Resolutions

Directors resolutions need to be adopted at official meetings of the board of directors of the corporation. The resolutions are necessary for the corporation or its officers to be specifically authorized to transact significant business transactions. The following items may be the subject of directors resolutions:

- ❏ Authorizing major contracts

- ❏ Authorizing the sale of corporate real estate

- ❏ Authorizing the purchase of real estate

- ❏ Authorizing the corporation to borrow money

- ❏ Authorizing the corporation to enter into a real estate lease

- ❏ Authorizing a lawsuit

- ❏ Authorizing the appointment of a lawyer

- ❏ Authorizing the appointment of an accountant

- ❏ Authorizing stock dividends

- ❏ Authorizing stock dividends to be declared and paid annually

- ❏ Authorizing stock dividends to be declared and paid quarterly

- ❏ Authorizing the reimbursement of expenses to an employee

- ❏ Authorizing the retention of corporate earnings

- ❏ Authorizing employee stock option plans

- ❏ Authorizing pension plans

- ❏ Authorizing profit-sharing plans

- ❏ Authorizing healthcare plans

- ❏ Authorizing group insurance plans

- ❏ Authorizing death benefit plans

- ❏ Authorizing other employee benefit plans

- ❏ Authorizing recision of prior resolutions

- ❏ Authorizing loans to directors or officers

- ❏ Authorizing the payment of officers' salaries

- ❏ Authorizing a restricted stock transfer

- ❏ Authorizing a registered office address change

- ❏ Authorizing the corporate president to make purchases

- ❏ Authorizing the payment of a bonus to employees

Shareholders Resolutions

Resolutions by shareholders are much rarer than those by directors. Shareholder resolutions are only necessary to approve major actions by the corporation, such as:

- ❏ Approving the sale of all the corporate assets

- ❏ Approving the sale of the corporation

- ❏ Approving the merger of the corporation with another company

- ❏ Approving the dissolution of the corporation

Resolution of Board of Directors
of _____

A meeting of the board of directors of this corporation was duly called and held on _____ , 20 _____ , at _____ o'clock ___ . m., at the offices of the corporation located at _____ .

A quorum of the board of directors was present and at the meeting it was decided, by majority vote, that it is necessary for the corporation to:

Therefore, it is
RESOLVED, that this corporation shall:

The officers of this corporation are hereby authorized to perform all necessary acts to carry out this resolution.

The undersigned, _____ , certifies that he or she is the duly elected secretary of this corporation and that the above is a true and correct copy of the resolution that was duly adopted at a meeting of the board of directors that was held in accordance with state law and the bylaws of the corporation on _____ , 20 _____ . I further certify that such resolution is now in full force and effect.

Dated: _____ , 20 _____

Corporate Seal

_____
Signature of Secretary of Corporation

_____
Printed Name of Secretary of Corporation

Resolution of Shareholders
of _____

A meeting of the shareholders of this corporation was duly called and held on
_____ , 20 _____ , at _____ o'clock ____ . m., at the offices of the
corporation located at _____ .

A quorum of the shareholders was present, in person or by proxy, and at the meeting it was
decided, by majority vote, that it is in the best interests of the corporation that:

Therefore, it is
RESOLVED that this corporation:

The officers of this corporation are hereby authorized to perform all necessary acts to carry
out this resolution.

The undersigned, _____ , certifies that he or she is
the duly elected secretary of this corporation and that the above is a true and correct copy
of the resolution that was duly adopted at a meeting of the shareholders that was held in
accordance with state law and the bylaws of the corporation on _____ ,
20 _____ . I further certify that such resolution is now in full force and effect.

Dated: _____ , 20 _____

                                              Corporate Seal

_____
Signature of Secretary of Corporation

_____
Printed Name of Secretary of Corporation

Consent Resolutions

Any of the resolution forms that are contained in this chapter can easily be adapted for use as consent resolutions. First, however, it must be verified that the bylaws of the corporation allow the use of consent resolutions for directors and shareholders. The bylaws that are presented in this book contain the following clauses which allow consent resolutions to be used:

[*For shareholders*]

Any action which may be taken at a shareholders meeting may be taken instead without a meeting if a resolution is consented to, in writing, by all shareholders who would be entitled to vote on the matter.

[*For directors*]

Any action which may be taken at a directors meeting may be taken instead without a meeting if a resolution is consented to, in writing, by all directors.

If you are operating under different bylaws, be certain that your bylaws contain a substantially similar authorization for consent resolutions.

The use of consent resolutions allows for a much greater flexibility in the management of corporations. Formal meetings are not necessary, although for many issues, meetings may be highly recommended as a method to record the remarks and positions of board members or shareholders who may oppose the action. Consent resolutions are most useful in those situations where the board of directors or number of shareholders is small and all of the directors or shareholders are in complete agreement regarding the action to be taken.

In order to adapt the standard resolutions in this and other chapters of this book for use as consent resolutions, simply alter the form in the following three ways (substitute "shareholders" where appropriate if you are preparing a shareholders consent resolution):

1. Add the word "Consent" to the title, for example:

Consent Resolution of the Board of Directors of the ABCXYZ Corporation

2. Substitute the following for the first paragraph of the resolution:

The undersigned, being all of the directors (or *shareholders*) of this corporation and acting in accordance with state law and the bylaws of this corporation, consent to the adoption of the following as if it was adopted at a duly called meeting of the board of directors (or *shareholders*) of this corporation. By unanimous consent of the board of directors (or *shareholders*) of this corporation, it is decided that:

3. Add signature lines for all of the directors (or shareholders) of the corporation. After all of the signatures, insert the following phrase:

    Being all of the directors (or *shareholders*) of the corporation.

4. Substitute the following for the last paragraph of the resolution:

    The undersigned, _____ , certifies that [*he* or *she*] is the duly elected secretary of this corporation and that the above is a true and correct copy of the resolution that was duly adopted by consent of the board of directors (or *shareholders*) in accordance with state law and the bylaws of the corporation on _____ , 20 ___ . I further certify that such resolution is now in full force and effect.

On the following page, you will find a general Consent Resolution of Board of Directors which has been adapted with these instructions from the general Resolution of Board of Directors form that was shown on page 155.

Consent Resolution of
Board of Directors of _____

The undersigned, being all of the directors of this corporation and acting in accordance with state law and the bylaws of this corporation, consent to the adoption of the following as if it was adopted at a duly called meeting of the board of directors of this corporation. By unanimous consent of the board of directors of this corporation, it is decided that:

Therefore, it is
RESOLVED, that the corporation shall:

The officers of this corporation are hereby authorized to perform all necessary acts to carry out such resolution.

Dated: _____ , 20 _____

Signature of Director of Corporation   *Printed Name of Director of Corporation*

_____   _____

_____   _____

_____   _____

_____   _____

_____   _____

Being all of the directors of the corporation.

The undersigned, _____ , certifies that he or she is the duly elected secretary of this corporation and that the above is a true and correct copy of the resolution that was duly adopted by consent of the board of directors in accordance with state law and the bylaws of the corporation on _____ , 20 _____ . I further certify that such resolution is now in full force and effect.

Dated: _____ , 20 _____

Corporate Seal

_____
Signature of Secretary of Corporation

_____
Printed Name of Secretary of Corporation

CHAPTER 14
Corporate Stock

Corporate stock represents the money or property that is invested in a corporation. It is a representation of the share of ownership in a corporate business. When a corporation files its Articles of Incorporation with the state, it states how many shares of stock it will be authorized to issue (for example, 500 shares). When the authorized shares are sold or transferred to a shareholder for something of value (money, property, or labor), the shares are said to be "issued and outstanding." All of the authorized shares need not be issued. The ownership of the shares in the corporation is then evidenced by a stock certificate describing the number of shares owned. The value of the shares can be a specific "par" value (for example, $1.00 per share) or they can be "no-par" value, which allows the board of directors to fix the value of the shares by resolution. If the shares are given a par value, the stock must be sold for at least the stated par value. The concept of par value is gradually being eliminated from modern business corporation acts, allowing board of directors discretion to fix the value of the shares. All states allow the use of no-par stock.

An example may best illustrate the use of stock: A corporation is formed and 500 shares of no-par value common stock are authorized in the Articles of Incorporation. Three people will form the initial shareholders of the corporation, with one desiring to own 50 percent of the shares and the other two desiring to own 25 percent each. All three comprise the board of directors. As a board, they decide to issue 300 shares of stock and they decide to fix the value per share at $10.00. Thus, the majority owner will pay the corporation $1,500.00 ($10.00 x 150 shares, or 50 percent of the issued and outstanding shares, *not* 50 percent of the authorized shares). The other two shareholders will pay $750.00 each for 75 shares apiece of the issued shares. The ownership of the shares that have been issued will be represented by stock certificates that will be delivered to each of the owners. The transactions will be recorded in the corporation's stock transfer book. At the close of these transactions, the corporation will have three shareholders: one with 150 shares of issued and outstanding stock and two with 75 shares each of issued and outstanding stock. The corporation will have $3,000.00 of paid-in capital. Two hundred shares will remain as authorized, but not issued or outstanding. At shareholder meetings, each share of issued and outstanding stock will represent one vote.

The above scenario presents stock ownership at its most basic. The shares described were no-par value common stock. There are many, many variable characteristics that can be given to stock. The forms in this book are based on basic single-class common stock with voting rights. Classes of stock may, however, be created with non-voting attributes, with preferences for dividends, and with many other different characteristics. Most small business corporations can operate efficiently with a single class of common stock with voting rights. There is no requirement that the stock certificate be in a particular format. The stock certificate for use in this book is a simple generic form. If you desire, you may obtain fancy blank stock certificates from most office supply stores, but these are not required. For the issuance of stock, follow the steps shown below in the Corporate Stock Checklist. Each of the steps taken at a meeting of the board of directors must be documented with a board resolution. Also included in this chapter is a page for use in the stock transfer book, which should be included in your basic corporate record book.

Corporate Stock Checklist

❏ Designate the number of authorized shares in the Articles of Incorporation and whether they are par or no-par value

❏ At the initial board of directors meeting, determine the number of shares to be issued

❏ If the shares are no-par, determine the value of the shares at the initial board of directors meeting

❏ At a board of directors meeting, determine who will purchase shares and how many will be sold to each person

❏ If necessary, at a board of directors meeting, the board of directors must fix the value of any property that will be accepted in exchange for shares of stock

❏ At a board of directors meeting, authorize officers to issue shares to persons designated

❏ The secretary will then prepare the appropriate stock certificates

❏ If there are restrictions on the transfer of stock, note the restrictions on the back of the certificate

❏ All of the officers of the corporation will sign the certificates

❏ The secretary will receive the money or property from the purchasers and deposit any funds in the corporate bank account

❏ The secretary will issue the certificates and receipts for money or property and record the transaction in the corporate stock transfer book

Corporate Stock Certificate
(Front)

Certificate Number: _____

Number of Shares: _____

Corporate Stock Certificate

_____
Name of Corporation

A business corporation incorporated under the laws of the State of: _____

Par Value of Shares: $ _____

Number of Shares Authorized: _____

This Certifies That

_____ is the owner of _____ shares

of common stock of this corporation. The shares represented are fully paid and are non-assessable. The shares represented by this certificate are only transferable on the official books of the corporation by the holder of this certificate, in person or by attorney. For transfer, this certificate must be properly endorsed on the back and surrendered to the corporation. This certificate is signed by all of the officers of this corporation.

Dated: _____ , 20 _____

_____
Signature of President

_____
Printed Name of President

_____
Signature of Treasurer

_____
Printed Name of Treasurer

_____
Signature of Vice-President

_____
Printed Name of Vice-President

_____
Signature of Secretary

_____
Printed Name of Secretary

For value received, I, _____, the owner of this certificate, transfer the number of shares represented by this certificate to _____, and I instruct the secretary of this corporation to record this transfer on the books of the corporation. Any restrictions on the transfer of these shares are shown below.

Dated: _____, 20 _____

_____
Signature of Shareholder

_____
Printed Name of Shareholder

Restrictions on Transfer:

Corporate Stock Transfer Book

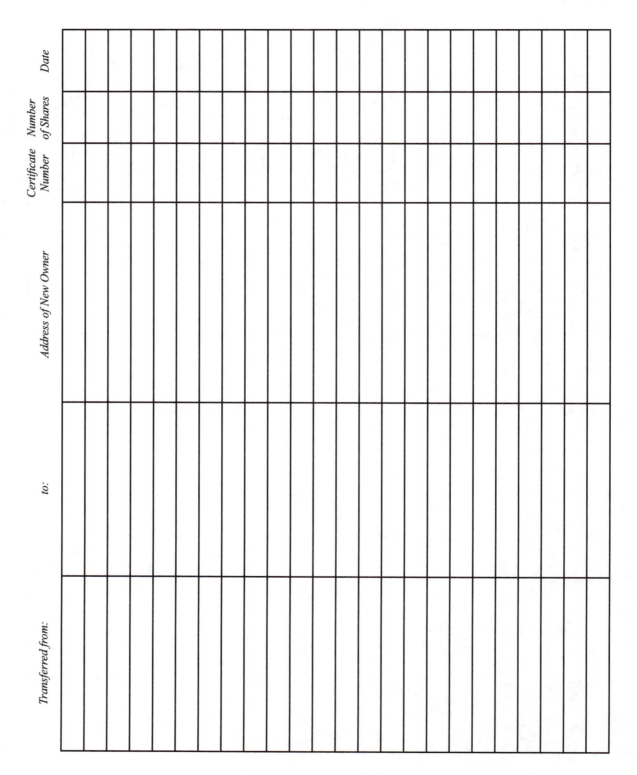

Date	Number of Shares	Certificate Number	Address of New Owner	to:	Transferred from:

Receipt for Stock Certificate of _____

On this date, _____ , 20 _____ , a shareholder in this corporation has purchased _____ shares of common stock in this corporation, represented by Stock Certificate Number _____ .

This certificate represents _____ percent (%) of ownership in this corporation.

The shareholder has transferred to the corporation the following assets, with a fair market value of $ _____ in consideration for the receipt of the shares of stock:

Payment in full has been received for these shares and the shares have been issued by the corporation, transferred to the shareholder, and received by the shareholder.

Record of this transaction has been recorded in the Stock Transfer Book of this corporation.

Dated: _____ , 20 _____

Corporate Seal

_____
Signature of Secretary of Corporation

_____
Printed Name of Secretary of Corporation

_____
Signature of Shareholder

_____
Printed Name of Shareholder

CHAPTER 15
Employee Documents

The legal forms in this chapter cover a variety of situations that arise in the area of employment. From hiring an employee to subcontracting work on a job, written documents that outline each person's responsibilities and duties are important for keeping an employment situation on an even keel. The employment contract contained in this chapter may be used and adapted for virtually any employment situation. Of course, it is perfectly legal to hire an employee without a contract at all. In many businesses, this is common practice. However, as job skills and salaries rise and employees are allowed access to sensitive and confidential business information, written employment contracts are often a prudent business practice. An independent contractor may also be hired to perform a particular task. As opposed to an employee, this type of worker is defined as one who maintains his or her own independent business, uses his or her own tools, and does not work under the direct supervision of the person who has hired him or her. A contract for hiring an independent contractor is provided in this chapter.

General Employment Contract: This form may be used for any situation in which an employee is hired for a specific job. The issues addressed by this contract are as follows:

- That the employee will perform a certain job and any incidental further duties
- That the employee will be hired for a certain period and for a certain salary
- That the employee will be given certain job benefits (for example: sick pay, vacations, etc.)
- That the employee agrees to abide by the employer's rules and regulations
- That the employee agrees to sign agreements regarding confidentiality and inventions
- That the employee agrees to submit any employment disputes to mediation and arbitration

The information necessary to complete this form is as follows:

- The names and addresses of the employer and employee
- A complete description of the job
- The date the job is to begin and the length of time that the job will last
- The amount of compensation and benefits for the employee (salary, sick pay, vacation, bonuses, and retirement and insurance benefits)
- Any additional documents to be signed

- Any additional terms
- The state whose laws will govern the contract
- Signatures of employer and employee

Independent Contractor Agreement: This form should be used when hiring an independent contractor. It provides a standard form for the hiring out of specific work to be performed within a set time period for a particular payment. It also provides a method for authorizing extra work under the contract. Finally, this document provides that the contractor agrees to *indemnify* (reimburse or compensate) the owner against any claims or liabilities arising from the performance of the work. To complete this form, fill in a detailed description of the work; dates by which certain portions of the job are to be completed; the pay for the job; the terms and dates of payment; and the state whose laws will govern the contract.

Contractor/Subcontractor Agreement: This form is intended to be used by an independent contractor to hire a subcontractor to perform certain work on a job that the contractor has agreed to perform. It provides for the "farming out" of specific work to be performed by the subcontractor within a set time period for a particular payment. It also provides a method for authorizing extra work under the contract. Finally, this document provides that the subcontractor agrees to indemnify the contractor against any claims or liabilities arising from the performance of the work. To complete this form, fill in a detailed description of the work; dates by which portions of the job are to be completed; the pay for the job; the terms and dates of payment; and the state whose laws will govern the contract.

General Employment Contract

This contract is made on _____ , 20 _____ , between
_____ , employer, of
_____ , City of _____ ,
State of _____ , and _____ ,
employee, of _____ , City of
_____ , State of _____ .

For valuable consideration, the employer and employee agree as follows:

1. The employee agrees to perform the following duties and job description:

   The employee also agrees to perform further duties incidental to the general job description. This is considered a full-time position.

2. The employee will begin work on _____ , 20 _____ . This position shall continue for a period of _____ .

3. The employee will be paid the following:

   Weekly salary: $ _____

   The employee will also be given the following benefits:

   Sick pay: $ _____
   Vacations: $ _____
   Bonuses: $ _____
   Retirement benefits: $ _____
   Insurance benefits: $ _____

4. The employee agrees to abide by all rules and regulations of the employer at all times while employed.

5. This contract may be terminated by:

   (a) Breach of this contract by the employee
   (b) The expiration of this contract without renewal
   (c) Death of the employee
   (d) Incapacitation of the employee for over _____ days in any one (1) year

170

6. The employee agrees to sign the following additional documents as a condition to obtaining employment:

7. Any dispute between the employer and employee related to this contract will be settled by voluntary mediation. If mediation is unsuccessful, the dispute will be settled by binding arbitration using an arbitrator of the American Arbitration Association.

8. Any additional terms of this contract:

9. No modification of this contract will be effective unless it is in writing and is signed by both the employer and employee. This contract binds and benefits both parties and any successors. Time is of the essence of this contract. This document is the entire agreement between the parties. This contract is governed by the laws of the State of _____ .

Dated: _____ , 20 _____

_____
Signature of Employer

_____
Printed Name of Employer

_____
Signature of Employee

_____
Printed Name of Employee

Independent Contractor Agreement

This agreement is made on _____ , 20 _____ , between
_____ , owner, of
_____ , City of _____ ,
State of _____ , and _____ ,
contractor, of _____ , City of
_____ , State of _____ .

For valuable consideration, the owner and contractor agree as follows:

1. The contractor agrees to furnish all of the labor and materials to do the following work for the owner as an independent contractor:

2. The contractor agrees that the following portions of the total work will be completed by the dates specified:

   Work:

   Dates: _____

3. The contractor agrees to perform this work in a workmanlike manner according to standard practices. If any plans or specifications are part of this job, they are attached to and are part of this agreement.

4. The owner agrees to pay the contractor as full payment $ _____ , for doing the work outlined above. This price will be paid to the contractor on satisfactory completion of the work in the following manner and on the following dates:

   Work:

   Dates: _____

172

5. The contractor and the owner may agree to extra services and work, but any such extras must be set out and agreed to in writing by both the contractor and the owner.

6. The contractor agrees to indemnify and hold the owner harmless from any claims or liability arising from the contractor's work under this agreement.

7. No modification of this agreement will be effective unless it is in writing and is signed by both parties. This agreement binds and benefits both parties and any successors. Time is of the essence of this agreement. This document, including any attachments, is the entire agreement between the parties. This agreement is governed by the laws of the State of

_____ .

Dated: _____ , 20 _____

_____
Signature of Owner

_____
Printed Name of Owner

_____
Signature of Contractor

_____
Printed Name of Contractor

Contractor/Subcontractor Agreement

This agreement is made on _____ , 20 _____ , between
_____ , contractor, of
_____ , City of _____ ,
State of _____ , and _____ ,
subcontractor, of _____ , City of
_____ , State of _____ .

1. The subcontractor, as an independent contractor, agrees to furnish all of the labor and materials to do the following portions of the work specified in the agreement between the contractor and the owner dated _____ , 20 _____ .

2. The subcontractor agrees that the following portions of the total work will be completed by the dates specified:

    Work:

    Dates: _____

3. The subcontractor agrees to perform this work in a workmanlike manner according to standard practices. If any plans or specifications are part of this job, they are attached to and are part of this agreement.

4. The contractor agrees to pay the subcontractor as full payment $ _____ , for doing the work outlined above. This price will be paid to the subcontractor on satisfactory completion of the work in the following manner and on the following dates:

    Work:

    Dates: _____

5. The contractor and subcontractor may agree to extra services and work, but any such extras must be set out and agreed to in writing by both the contractor and the subcontractor.

174

6. The subcontractor agrees to indemnify and hold the contractor harmless from any claims or liability arising from the subcontractor's work under this agreement.

7. No modification of this agreement will be effective unless it is in writing and is signed by both parties. This agreement binds and benefits both parties and any successors. Time is of the essence of this agreement. This document, including any attachments, is the entire agreement between the parties. This agreement is governed by the laws of the State of _____ .

Dated: _____ , 20 _____

_____
Signature of Contractor

_____
Printed Name of Contractor

_____
Signature of Subcontractor

_____
Printed Name of Subcontractor

CHAPTER 16
Business Financial Recordkeeping

Each year, thousands of small businesses fail because their owners have lost control of their finances. Many of these failures are brought on by the inability of the business owners to understand the complex accounting processes and systems that have become relatively standard in modern business. Accounting and bookkeeping have, in most businesses, been removed from the direct control and, therefore, understanding of the business owners themselves. If business owners cannot understand the financial situation of their own businesses, they have little chance of succeeding.

Keeping accurate and clear business financial records can, for many business owners, be the most difficult part of running a business. For most business owners, understanding those records is, at best, a struggle. And yet maintaining a set of clear and understandable financial records is perhaps the single most important factor that separates successful businesses from those that fail. The purpose of the next few chapters is to provide the small business owner with a clear understanding of how to develop a concise and easily-understood financial recordkeeping system, keep the books for a business, and, perhaps most importantly, actually understand those records.

Modern business practices have tended to complicate many areas of business when, in many cases, simplification is what most business owners need. In law, in management, and in accounting, many important business functions have been obscured from their owners by intricate systems and complex terminology. Business owners must then turn the handling of these affairs over to specialized professionals in a particular field. The result, in many cases, is that business owners lose crucial understanding of those portions of their business. With this loss of understanding comes the eventual and almost inevitable loss of control.

This is particularly true for small business owners and their financial records. It is absolutely vital that emerging small business owners intimately understand their financial position. Daily decisions must be made that can make or break a fledgling business. If the financial records of a small business are delegated to an outside accountant or bookkeeper, it is often difficult, if not impossible, for a novice business owner to understand the current financial position of the business on a day-to-day basis. Critical business decisions are then made on the basis of incomplete or often unknown financial information.

The basic aspects of the accounting outlined in this book have been used successfully by millions of businesses in the past. The system presented in this book is designed to be set up and initially used by the business owners themselves. This will insure that the system is both thoroughly understood by the owner and provides the type of information that the owner actually wants. As a business grows and becomes more complex, and a business owner becomes more comfortable with financial recordkeeping, other more sophisticated and complex accounting systems may become appropriate. There are numerous computer-based accounting programs on the market, such as QuickBooks, that can provide the framework for a company accounting system. However, in order to understand and use any of the computer accounting systems, it is necessary to first have an understanding of the basics of financial recordkeeping.

Understanding Financial Records

The purpose of any business financial recordkeeping system is to provide a clear vision of the relative health of the business, both on a day-to-day basis and periodically. Business owners themselves need to know whether they are making a profit, why they are making a profit, which parts of the business are profitable, and which are not. This information is only available if the business owner has a clear and straight-forward recordkeeping system. Business owners also need to be able to produce accurate financial statements for income tax purposes, for loan proposals, and for the purpose of selling the business. Clear, understandable, and accurate business records are vital to the success of any small business. In order to design a good recordkeeping system for a particular business, an understanding of certain fundamental ideas of accounting is necessary. For those unfamiliar with the terms and concepts of accounting, grasping these basic ideas may be the most difficult part of accounting, even simplified accounting.

First, let's get some of the terminology clarified. *Accounting* is the design of the recordkeeping system that a business uses and the preparation and interpretation of reports based on the information that is gathered and put into the system. *Bookkeeping* is the actual inputting of the financial information into the recordkeeping system. The purpose of any business recordkeeping system is to allow the business owner to easily understand and use the information gathered. Certain accounting principles and terms have been adopted as standard over the years to make it easier to understand a wide range of business transactions. In order to understand what a recordkeeping system is trying to accomplish, it is necessary to define some of the standard ways of looking at a business. There are two standard reports that are the main sources of business financial information: the *balance sheet* and the *profit-and-loss statement*.

The Balance Sheet

The purpose of the balance sheet is to look at what the business owns and owes on a specific date. By seeing what a business owns and owes, anyone looking at a balance sheet can tell the relative financial position of the business at that point in time. If the business owns more than it owes, it is in good shape financially. On the other hand, if it owes more than it owns, the business may be in trouble. The balance sheet is the universal financial document used to view this aspect of a business. It provides this information by laying out the value of the assets and the liabilities of a business. One of the most critical financial tasks that a small business owner must confront is keeping track of what the business owns and owes. Before the business buys or sells anything or makes a profit or loss, the business must have some assets.

The *assets* of a business are anything that the business owns. These can be cash on hand or in a bank account; personal property, like office equipment, vehicles, tools, or supplies; inventory, or material that will be sold to customers; real estate, buildings, and land; and money that is owed to the business. Money that is owed to a business is called its *accounts receivable*, basically the money that the business hopes to eventually receive. The total of all of these things that a business owns are the business's assets.

The *liabilities* of a business are anything that the business owes to others. These consist of long-term debts, such as a mortgage on real estate or a long-term loan. Liabilities also consist of any short-term debts, such as money owed for supplies or taxes. Money that a business owes to others is called its *accounts payable*, basically the money that the business hopes to eventually pay. In addition to money owed to others, the *equity* of a business is also considered a liability. The equity of a business is the value of the ownership of the business. It is the value that would be left over if all of the debts of the business were paid off. If the business is a partnership or a sole proprietorship, the business equity is referred to as the *net worth* of the business. If the business is a corporation, the owner's equity is called the *capital surplus* or *retained capital*. All of the debts of a business and its equity are together referred to as the business's liabilities.

The basic relationship between assets and liabilities is shown in a simple equation:

$$Assets = Liabilities$$

This simple equation is the basis of business accounting. When the books of a business are said to *balance*, it is this equation that is in balance: the assets of a business must equal the liabilities of a business. Since the liabilities of a business consist of both equity and debts, the equation can be expanded to read:

$$Assets = Debts + Equity$$

Rearranging the equation can provide a simple explanation of how to arrive at the value of a business to the owner, or its equity:

$$\text{Equity} = \text{Assets} - \text{Debts}$$

A basic tenet of recordkeeping is that both sides of this financial equation must always be equal. The formal statement of the assets and liabilities of a specific business on a specific date is called a *balance sheet*. A balance sheet is usually prepared on the last day of a month, quarter, or year. A balance sheet simply lists the amounts of the business's assets and liabilities in a standardized format.

On a balance sheet, the assets of a business are generally broken down into two groups: *current assets* and *fixed assets*. Current assets consist of cash, accounts receivable (remember, money that the business intends to receive; basically, bills owed to the business), and inventory. Current assets are generally considered anything that could be converted into cash within one year. Fixed assets are more permanent-type assets and include vehicles, equipment, machinery, land, and buildings owned by the business.

The liabilities of a business are broken down into three groups: *current liabilities, long-term liabilities*, and *owner's equity*. Current liabilities are short-term debts, generally those that a business must pay off within one year. This includes accounts payable (remember, money that the business intends to pay; basically, bills the business owes), and taxes that are due. Long-term liabilities are long-term debts such as mortgages or long-term business loans. Owner's equity is whatever is left after debts are deducted from assets. Thus, the owner's equity is what the owner would have left after all of the debts of the business were paid off. Owner's equity is the figure that is adjusted to make the equation of assets and liabilities balance.

Let's look at a simple example: a basic sales business.

Smith's Gourmet Foods has the following assets: Smith has $500.00 in a bank account, is owed $70.00 by customers who pay for their food monthly, has $200.00 worth of food supplies, and owns food preparation equipment worth $1,300.00.

These are the assets of Smith's Gourmet Foods and they are shown on a balance sheet as follows:

Cash	$ 500.00
+ Accounts owed to it	$ 70.00
+ Inventory	$ 200.00
+ Equipment	$ 1,300.00
= Total assets	$ 2,070.00

Smith also has the following debts: $100.00 owed to the supplier of the food, $200.00 owed to the person from whom she bought the food equipment, and $100.00 owed to the state for sales taxes that have been collected on food sales. Thus, the debts of Smith's Gourmet Foods are shown as follows:

Accounts it owes	$	100.00
+ Loans it owes	$	200.00
+ Taxes it owes	$	100.00
= Total debts	$	400.00

To find what Smith's equity in this business is, we need to subtract the amount of the debts from the amount of the assets. Remember: assets − debts = equity. Thus, the owner's equity in Smith's Gourmet Foods is as follows:

Total assets	$ 2,070.00
− Total debts	$ 400.00
= Owner's equity	$ 1,670.00

That's it. The business of Smith's Gourmet Foods has a net worth of $1,670.00. If Smith paid off all of the debts of the business, there would be $1,670.00 left. This basic method is used to determine the net worth of businesses worldwide, from the smallest to the largest: assets = debts + equity, or assets − debts = equity. Remember, both sides of the equation always have to be equal.

The Profit and Loss Statement

The other main business report is the *profit and loss statement*. This report is a summary of the income and expenses of the business during a certain period. Profit and loss statements are sometimes referred to as *income statements* or *operating statements*. You may choose to prepare a profit and loss statement monthly, quarterly, or annually, depending on your particular needs. You will, at a minimum, need to have an annual profit and loss statement in order to streamline your tax return preparation.

A profit and loss statement, however, provides much more than assistance in easing your tax preparation burdens. It allows you to clearly view the performance of your business over a particular time period. As you begin to collect a series of profit and loss statements, you will be able to conduct various analyses of your business. For example, you will be able to compare monthly performances over a single year to determine which month was the best or worst for your business. Quarterly results will also be able to be contrasted. The comparison of several annual expense and revenue figures will allow you to judge the growth or shrinkage of your business over time. Numerous other comparisons are possible, depending on your particular business. How have sales been influenced by advertising expenses? Are production costs higher this quarter than last? Do seasons have an impact on sales? Are certain expenses becoming a burden on the business? The profit and loss statement is one of the key financial statements for the analysis of your business.

Generally, *income* for a business is any money that it has received or will receive during a certain period. *Expenses* are any money that it has paid or will pay out during a certain period. Simply put, if the business has more income than expenses during a certain period, it has made a profit. If it has more expenses than income, then the business has a loss for that period of time.

Income can be broken down into two basic types: service income and sales income. The difference between the two types of income lies in the need to consider inventory costs. *Service income* is income derived from performing a service for someone (cutting hair, for example). *Sales income* is revenue derived from selling a product of some type. With service income, the profit can be determined simply by deducting the expenses that are associated with making the income. With sales income, however, in addition to deducting the expenses of making the income, the cost of the product that was sold must also be taken into account. This is done through inventory costs. Thus, for sales income, the income from selling a product is actually the sales income minus the cost of the product to the seller. This inventory cost is referred to as the *cost of goods sold*.

A profit and loss statement begins with a sale. Back to the food business as an example: Smith had the following transactions during the month of July: $250.00 worth of food was sold, the wholesale cost of the food that was sold was $50.00, the cost of napkins, condiments, other supplies, and rent amounted to $100.00, and interest payments on the equipment loan were $50.00. Thus, Smith's profit and loss statement would be prepared as follows:

Gross sales income	$ 250.00
− Cost of food	$ 50.00
= Net sales income	$ 200.00
Operating expenses	$ 100.00
+ Interest payments	$ 50.00
= Net expenses	$ 150.00

Thus, for the month of July, Smith's business performed as follows:

Net sales income	$ 200.00
− Net expenses	$ 150.00
= Net profit	$ 50.00

Again, this simple setup reflects the basics of profit and loss statements for all types of businesses, no matter what their size. For a pure service business, with no inventory of any type sold to customers: income – expenses = net profit. For a sales-type business or a sales/service combined business: income – cost of goods sold – expenses = profit.

These two types of summary reports—the balance sheet and the profit and loss statement—are the basic tools for understanding the financial health of any business. The figures on them can be used for many purposes to understand the operations of a business. The balance sheet shows what proportion of a business's assets are actually owned by the business owner and what proportion is owned or owed to someone else.

Looking at Smith's balance sheet, we can see that the owner's equity is $1,670.00 of assets of $2,070.00. Thus, we can see that the owner has more than 80 percent ownership of the business, a very healthy situation. There are numerous ways to analyze the figures on these two financial statements. Understanding what these figures mean and how they represent the health of a business are keys to keeping control of the finances of any business.

Accounting Methods

There are a few more items that must be understood regarding financial recordkeeping. First is the method for recording the records. There are two basic methods for measuring transactions: the *cash method* and the *accrual method*. Cash-method accounting is a system into which income is recorded when it is received and expenses are recorded when they are paid. With cash accounting, there is no effective method to accurately reflect inventory costs. Thus, Internal Revenue Service regulations require that the cash method of accounting may only be used by those few businesses that are solely service businesses and do not sell any materials to their customers at all, even a few spare parts. If a business sells any type of product or material whatsoever, it must use the accrual method of accounting. (An exception to this general rule is allowed for any corporation or partnership with annual gross receipts of under $5 million.)

The accrual method of accounting counts income and expenses when they are due to the business. Income is recorded when the business has a right to receive the income. In other words, accounts receivable (bills owed to the business) are considered as income that has already been received by the business. Expenses are considered and recorded when they are due, even if they are not yet paid. In other words, accounts payable (bills owed by the business) are considered expenses to the business when they are received, not when they are actually paid. The vast majority of businesses will wish to use the accrual method of accounting. A business must choose to keep its records either on the accrual basis or on the cash basis. Once this decision is made, approval from the IRS must be obtained before the method can be changed. After you select the type of accounting you will use, please consult a tax professional if a change in the system must be made.

Accounting Systems

In addition, there are two basic types of recordkeeping systems: *single-entry* and *double-entry*. Both types are able to be used to keep accurate records, although the double-entry system has more ways available to double-check calculations. Double-entry recordkeeping is, however, much more difficult to master, in that each and every transaction must be entered in two separate places in the records. The system that is used in this book is a modified form of single-entry accounting. The benefits of ease of use of a single-entry system far outweigh the disadvantages of this system. The IRS recommends single-entry records for beginning small businesses, and states that this type of system can be "relatively simple...used effectively...and is adequate for income tax purposes." Many accountants will disagree with this and insist that only double-entry accounting is acceptable. For the small business owner who wishes to understand his or her own company's finances, the advantages of single-entry accounting far outweigh the disadvantages.

Accounting Periods

A final item to consider is the accounting period for your business. A business is allowed to choose between a *fiscal-year* accounting period and a *calendar-year* period. A fiscal year consists of 12 consecutive months that do not end on December 31st. A calendar year consists of 12 consecutive months that do end on December 31st. There are complex rules relating to the choice of fiscal-year accounting. Partnerships and S-corporations may generally choose to report on a fiscal-year basis only if there is a valid business purpose that supports the use of a fiscal year. This generally complicates the reporting of income and should be avoided unless there is an important reason to choose a fiscal-year accounting period. If a fiscal-year period is considered necessary, please consult a tax or accounting professional as there are complicated rules to comply with.

For the majority of small businesses, the choice of a calendar-year period is perfectly adequate and, in most cases, will simplify the tax reporting and accounting recordkeeping. In the year in which a business is either started or ended, the business year for reporting may not be a full year. Thus, even for those who choose to use a calendar year, the first year may actually start on a date other than January 1st.

The simplified small business accounting system that is explained in this book is a modified single-entry accounting system. It is presented as a system for accrual-basis accounting for small businesses. The records are designed to be used on a calendar-year basis. Within these basic parameters, the system can be individually tailored to meet the needs of most small businesses.

The backbone of the recordkeeping system is the Chart of Accounts for your business. A chart of accounts will list each of the income, expense, asset, or debt categories that you wish to keep track of. Every business transaction that you make and every financial record that you create will fit into one of these four main categories. Your transactions will either be money coming in (income) or money going out (expenses). Your records will also track things the business owns (assets) or things the business owes (debts). The chart of accounts that you create in the next chapter will allow you to itemize and track each of these four broad categories in detail.

Following is a checklist for setting up your business financial recordkeeping using this book:

Financial Recordkeeping Checklist

❏ Set up your business chart of accounts

❏ Open a business checking account

❏ Prepare a check register

❏ Set up a business petty cash fund

❏ Prepare a petty cash register

❏ Set up asset accounts

❏ Prepare current asset account records

❏ Prepare fixed asset account records

❏ Set up expense account records

❏ Set up income account records

- [ ] Set up payroll system

- [ ] Prepare payroll time sheets

- [ ] Prepare payroll depository records

- [ ] Determine proper tax forms for use in business

CHAPTER 17
Business Accounts

The financial recordkeeping system that you will set up using this book is designed to be adaptable to any type of business. Whether your business is a service business, a manufacturing business, a retail business, a wholesale distributorship, or a combination of any of these, you will be able to easily adapt this simplified system to work with your particular situation. A key to designing the most useful recordkeeping system for your particular needs is to examine your type of business in depth. After a close examination of the particular needs and operations of your type of business, you will need to set up an array of specific accounts to handle your financial records. This set of general accounts is called a *Chart of Accounts*.

A Chart of Accounts will list all of the various categories of financial transactions that you will need to track. There will be an account for each general type of expense that you want to keep track of. You will also have a separate account for each type of income your business will receive. Accounts will also be set up for your business assets and liabilities. Setting up an account for each of these categories consists of the simple task of deciding which items you will need to categorize, selecting a name for the account, and assigning a number to the account.

Before you can set up your accounts, you need to understand the reason for setting up these separate accounts. It is possible, although definitely not recommended, to run a business and merely keep track of your income and expenses without any itemization at all. However, you would be unable to analyze how the business is performing beyond a simple check to see if you have any money left after paying the expenses. You would also be unable to properly fill in the necessary information for business income tax returns. A major reason for setting up separate accounts for many business expense and income transactions is to separate and itemize the amounts spent in each category so that this information is available at tax time. This insures that a business is taking all of its allowable business deductions. The main reason, however, to set up individual accounts is to allow the business owner to have a clear view of the financial health of the business. With separate accounts for each type of transaction, a business owner can analyze the proportional costs and revenues of each aspect of the business. Is advertising costing more than labor expenses? Is the income derived from sale items worth the discount of the sale? Only by using the figures obtained from separate itemized accounts can these questions be answered.

In the following sections, you will select and number the various accounts for use in your business Chart of Accounts. You will select various income accounts, expense accounts, asset accounts, and liability accounts. You will also assign a number to each account. For ease of use, you should assign a particular number value to all accounts of one type. For example, all income accounts may be assigned #10 to 29. Sales income may be Account #11; service income may be Account #12, interest income may be Account #13. Similarly, expenses may be assigned #30 to 79. Balance Sheet accounts for assets and liabilities may be #80 to 99. Be sure to leave enough numbers for future expansion of your list of accounts. There will normally be far more expense accounts than any other type of account.

If you have income or expenses from many sources, you may wish to use a three-digit number to identify each separate category. For example, if your business consists of renting out residential houses and you have 10 properties, you may wish to set up a separate income and expense account for each property. You may wish to assign Accounts #110 to 119 to income from all properties. Thus, for example, you could then assign rental income from Property #1 to Account #111, rental income from Property #2 to Account #112, rental income from Property #3 to Account #113, and so on. Similarly, expenses can be broken down into separate accounts for individual properties. All advertising expenses could be Accounts #510 to 519; thus, advertising expenses for Property #1 could then be assigned Account #511, advertising expenses for Property #2 would be assigned Account #512, etc.

How your individual Chart of Accounts will be organized will be specific to your particular business. If you have a simple business with all income coming from one source, you will probably desire a two-digit number from, for example, 10 to 29, assigned to that income account. On the other hand, a more complex business with many sources of income and many different types of expenses may wish to use a system of three-digit numbers. Take some time to analyze your specific business to decide how you wish to set up your accounts. Ask yourself what type of information you will want to extract from your financial records. Do you need more details of your income sources? Then you should set up several income accounts for each type and possibly even each source of your income. Would you like more specific information on your expenses? Then you would most likely wish to set up clear and detailed expense accounts for each type of expense that you must pay.

Be aware that you may wish to alter your Chart of Accounts as your business grows. You may find that you have set up too many accounts and unnecessarily complicated your recordkeeping tasks. You might wish to set up more accounts once you see how your Balance Sheets and Profit and Loss Statements look. You can change, add, or delete accounts at any time. Remember, however, that any transactions that have been recorded in an account must be transferred to any new account or accounts that take the place of the old account.

Income Accounts

These are accounts that are used to track the various sources of your company's income. There may be only a few sources of income for your business or you may wish to track your income in more detail. The information which you collect in your income accounts will be used to prepare your Profit and Loss Statements periodically. Recall that a Profit and Loss Statement is also referred to as an Income and Expense Statement.

On the Chart of Accounts that is used in this book, income is separated into several categories. You can choose the income account categories which best suit your type of business. If your business is a service business, you may wish to set up accounts for labor income and for materials income. Or you may wish to set up income accounts in more detail, for example: sales income, markup income, income from separate properties, or income from separate sources in your business, etc. Nonsales income, such as bank account interest income or income on the sale of business equipment, should be placed in separate individual income accounts. You may also wish to set up separate income accounts for income from different ongoing projects or income from separate portions of your business.

Following is a list of various general income accounts. Decide how much detail you will want in your financial records regarding income and then choose the appropriate accounts. You may wish to name and create different accounts than are listed here. After you have chosen your income accounts, assign a number to each account.

Income Chart of Accounts

Account #	Account Name and Description
	Income from sale of goods
	Income from services
	Income from labor charges
	Income from sales discounts
	Income from interest revenue
	Income from consulting
	Miscellaneous income

Expense Accounts

These are the accounts that you will use to keep track of your expenses. Each separate category of expense should have its own account. Many of the types of accounts are dictated by the types of expenses which should be itemized for tax purposes. You will generally have separate accounts for advertising costs, utility expenses, rent, phone costs, etc. One or more separate accounts should also be set up to keep track of inventory expenses. These should be kept separate from other expense accounts as they must be itemized for tax purposes.

Following is a list of various general expense accounts. Please analyze your business and determine which accounts would be best suited to select for your particular situation. You will then number these accounts, as you did the income accounts. The categories presented are general categories that match most Internal Revenue Service tax forms. You may, of course, set up separate accounts that are not listed to suit your particular needs. Try not to set up too many accounts or you will have a hard time trying to remember all of them. Also note that you may add or delete accounts as you need them. If you delete an account, however, you must shift any transactions that you have recorded in that account to a new account.

Expense Chart of Accounts

Account #	Account Name and Description
	Advertising expenses
	Auto expenses
	Cleaning and maintenance expenses
	Charitable contributions
	Dues and publications
	Office equipment expenses
	Freight and shipping expenses
	Business insurance expenses
	Business interest expenses
	Legal expenses
	Business meals and lodging
	Miscellaneous expenses
	Postage expenses
	Office rent expenses
	Repair expenses
	Office supplies
	Sales taxes paid
	Federal unemployment taxes paid
	State unemployment taxes paid
	Telephone expenses
	Utility expenses
	Wages and commissions

Asset and Liability Accounts

Asset and liability accounts are collectively referred to as *Balance Sheet Chart of Accounts*. This is because the information collected on them is used to prepare your business Balance Sheets. You will set up current and fixed asset accounts and current and long-term liability accounts. Types of current asset accounts are cash, short-term notes receivable, accounts receivable, inventory, and prepaid expenses. Fixed assets may include equipment, vehicles, buildings, land, long-term notes receivable, and long-term loans receivable.

Types of current liability accounts are *short-term notes payable* (money due within one year), *short-term loans payable* (money due on a loan within one year), unpaid taxes, and unpaid wages. Long-term liability accounts may be *long-term notes payable* (money due more than one year in the future) or *long-term loans payable* (money due on a loan more than one year in the future). Finally, you will need an owner's equity account to tally the ownership value of your business.

Choose the asset and liability accounts that best suit your business and assign appropriate numbers to each account.

Balance Sheet Chart of Accounts

Account #	Account Name and Description
	Accounts receivable (current asset)
	Bank checking account (current asset)
	Bank savings account (current asset)
	Cash on hand (current asset)
	Notes receivable (current asset, if short-term)
	Loans receivable (current asset, if short-term)
	Inventory (current asset)
	Land (fixed asset)
	Buildings (fixed asset)
	Vehicles (fixed asset)
	Equipment (fixed asset)
	Machinery (fixed asset)
	Accounts payable (current debt)
	Notes payable (current, if due within 1 year)
	Loans payable (current, if due within 1 year)
	Notes payable (long-term debt, if over 1 year)
	Loans payable (long-term debt, if over 1 year)
	Mortgage payable (long-term debt, if over 1 year)
	Retained capital

Chart of Accounts

After you have selected and numbered each of your accounts, you should prepare your Chart of Accounts. Simply type the number and name of each account in a numerical list. You will refer to this chart often as you prepare your financial records. Following is a sample completed Chart of Accounts. This sample chart is set up to reflect the business operations of our sample company, Smith's Gourmet Foods. This is a company that prepares and packages food products and delivers the products directly to consumers in their homes. The chart reflects that the income will primarily come from one source: direct customer payments for the products that are sold. The expense accounts are chosen to cover most of the standard types of business expenses that a small business will encounter. The Balance Sheet accounts reflect that the business will have as assets only a bank account, some accounts receivable, inventory, and some equipment. The only liabilities that this business will have, at least initially, will be a loan for equipment and accounts payable. Although this sample Chart of Accounts is fairly brief, it covers all of the basic accounts that the business will need as it begins. There is sufficient room in the numbering system chosen to add additional accounts as the business expands.

Sample Chart of Accounts

Account #	Account Name and Description
11	Income from sale of goods
12	Miscellaneous income
31	Advertising expenses
32	Auto expenses
33	Cleaning and maintenance expenses
34	Office equipment expenses
35	Business insurance expenses
36	Business meals and lodging
37	Miscellaneous expenses
38	Postage expenses
39	Repair expenses
40	Office supplies
41	Sales taxes paid
42	Telephone expenses
43	Office rent expense
51	Cash on hand (current asset)
52	Accounts receivable (current asset)
53	Bank checking account (current asset)
54	Inventory (current asset)
61	Equipment (fixed asset)
71	Accounts payable (current debt)
81	Loans payable (long-term debt)
91	Retained capital

Tracking Business Assets

After setting up a Chart of Accounts the next financial recordkeeping task for a business will consist of preparing a method to keep track of the assets of the business. Recall that the assets of a business are everything that is owned by the business and are either current assets that can be converted to cash within a year or fixed assets that are more long-term in nature. Each of these two main categories of assets will be discussed separately.

Current Assets

Following is a list of typical current assets for a business:

- Business bank checking account
- Business bank savings account
- Cash (petty cash fund and cash on hand)
- Accounts receivable (money owed to the company)
- Inventory

A company may have other types of current assets such as notes or loans receivable, but the five listed above are the basic ones for most small businesses. In complex double-entry accounting systems, the current asset account balances are constantly being changed. In a double-entry system, each time an item of inventory is sold, for example, the account balance for the inventory account must be adjusted to reflect the sale. In single-entry systems, all asset and liability accounts are updated only when the business owner wishes to prepare a Balance Sheet. This may be done monthly, quarterly, or annually. At a minimum, this updating must take place at the end of the year in order to have the necessary figures available for tax purposes.

Current Asset Account

The main form for tracking your current business assets will be a Current Asset Account sheet. A copy of this form follows this discussion. On this form, you will periodically track the value of the current asset that you are following, except for your inventory. (For inventory, you will use specialized inventory records.) You should prepare a separate Current Asset Account sheet for each asset. For example, if your current assets consist of a business checking account, cash on hand, and accounts receivable, you will have three separate Current Asset Accounts, one for each category of asset. These forms are very simple to use. Follow the instructions on the following page:

1. Simply fill in the account number for the Current Asset Account for which you are setting up the form. You will get this number from your Chart of Accounts. Fill in also a description of the account. For example: Account #53—Business Banking Account.

2. You must then decide how often you will be preparing a Balance Sheet and updating your Balance Sheet account balances. If you wish to keep close track of your finances, you may wish to do this on a monthly basis. For many businesses, a quarterly Balance Sheet may be sufficient. All businesses, no matter how small, must prepare a Balance Sheet at least annually at the end of the year. Decide how often you wish to update the balances and enter the time period in the space provided.

3. Next, enter the date that you open the account. Under description, enter "Opening Balance." In the "Balance" column, enter the opening value. The amount to enter for an opening balance will be as follows:

    • For a bank account, this will be the opening balance of the account
    • For cash on hand, this will be the opening balance of the petty cash fund and cash on hand for sales, such as the cash used in a cash register
    • For accounts receivable, this will be the total amount due from all accounts

4. After you have entered the balances on the appropriate Current Asset Account sheet, you will transfer the balances to your Balance Sheet.

Current Asset Account

Account #:
Account Name: Period:

Date	Description of Asset	Balance	

Inventory

Any business that sells an item of merchandise to a customer must have a system in place to keep track of inventory. *Inventory* is considered any merchandise or materials that are held for sale during the normal course of your business. Inventory costs include the costs of the merchandise or products themselves and the costs of the materials and paid labor that go into creating a finished product. Inventory does not include the costs of the equipment or machinery that you need to create the finished product.

There are several reasons you will need a system of inventory control. First, if you are stocking parts or supplies to sell, you will need to keep track of what you have ordered, what is in stock, and when you will need to reorder. You will also need to keep track of the cost of your inventory for tax purposes. The amount of money that you spend on your inventory is not fully deductible in the year spent as a business deduction. The only portion of your inventory cost that will reduce your gross profit for tax purposes is the actual cost of the goods that you have sold during the tax year.

The basic method for keeping track of inventory costs for tax purposes is to determine the cost of goods sold. First, you will need to know how much inventory is on hand at the beginning of the year. To this amount, you add the cost of any additional inventory you purchased during the year. Finally, you determine how much inventory is left at the end of the year. The difference is essentially the cost (to you) of the inventory that you sold during the year. This amount is referred to as the *cost of goods sold*. Every year at tax time, you will need to figure the cost of goods sold. Additionally, you may need to determine your cost of goods sold monthly or quarterly for various business purposes.

Using our sample company, Smith's Gourmet Foods, we will start the owner's first year in business with an inventory of $0.00. When her business begins, there is no inventory. During the first year, she purchases $17,500.00 worth of products that are for selling to customers. At the end of the year, she counts all of the items that are left in her possession and determines her cost for these items. The cost of the items left unsold at the end of the year is $3,700.00.

The calculation of the cost of goods sold for the first year in business is as follows:

	Inventory at beginning of first year	$ 00.00
+	Cost of inventory added during year	$ 17,500.00
=	Cost of inventory	$ 17,500.00
−	Inventory at end of first year	$ 3,700.00
=	Cost of Goods Sold for first year	$ 13,800.00

For the second year in business, the figure for the inventory at the beginning of the year is the value of the inventory at the end of the previous year. Thus, if Smith's Gourmet Foods added $25,000.00 additional inventory during the second year of operation and the value of the inventory at the end of the second year was $4,800.00, the cost-of-goods-sold calculations for the second year would be as follows:

	Inventory at beginning of second year	$ 3,700.00
+	Cost of inventory added during year	$ 25,000.00
=	Cost of inventory	$ 28,700.00
–	Inventory at end of second year	$ 4,800.00
=	Cost of goods sold for second year	$ 23,900.00

Thus, for the second year in operation the cost of goods sold would be $23,900.00. This amount would be deducted from the gross revenues that Smith's Gourmet Foods took in for the year to determine the gross profit for the second year in business.

Physical Inventory Report

This form should be used to record the results of an actual physical counting of the inventory at the end of the year and at whatever other times during the year you decide to take a physical inventory. If you decide that you will need to track your inventory monthly or quarterly, you may need to prepare this form for those time periods. To prepare this form, take the following steps:

1. The form should be dated and signed by the person doing the inventory.

2. The quantity and description of each item of inventory should be listed, along with an item number if applicable.

3. The cost (to you) of each item should be then listed under "Unit Price." A total per item cost is then calculated by multiplying the quantity of units by the unit price. This total per item cost should be listed in the far right-hand column. You will need to extract this per item unit price from your Periodic or Perpetual Inventory Records (explained next).

4. The total inventory cost should be figured by adding all of the figures in the far right-hand column.

Physical Inventory Report

Date: Taken by:

Quantity	Description	Item #	Unit Price		Total	
				TOTAL		

Periodic Inventory Record

This is the form that you will use to keep continual track of your inventory if you have a relatively small inventory. You will use the Periodic Inventory Record for the purpose of keeping track of the costs of your inventory and of any orders of additional inventory. You will refer to this record when you need to order additional inventory, determine when an order should be received, and determine the cost of your inventory items at the end of the year or at other times if desired. If you have an extensive inventory, you will need to consult an accounting professional to assist you in setting up a perpetual-type inventory system. Or you may be able to set up a complex inventory system using commercial accounting software that is available.

1. Prepare a separate Periodic Inventory Record for each item of inventory. Identify the type of item that is being tracked by description and by item number, if applicable. You may also wish to list the supplier of the item.

2. The first entry on the Periodic Inventory Record should be the initial purchase of inventory. On the right-hand side of the record, list the following items:

   - Date purchased
   - Quantity purchased
   - Price per item
   - Total price paid
   - *Note*: Shipping charges should not be included in the prices entered. Only the actual costs of the goods should be listed.

3. When you are running low on a particular item and place an order, on the left-hand side of the record enter the following information:

   - Date of the order
   - The order number
   - The quantity ordered
   - The date the order is due to arrive

4. When the order arrives, enter the actual details about the order on the right-hand side of the page. This will allow you to keep track of your order of inventory items and also allow you to keep track of the cost of your items of inventory.

Periodic Inventory Record

Item: Item #:
Supplier:

INVENTORY ORDERED

Date	Order #	Quantity	Due

INVENTORY RECEIVED

Date	Quantity	Price	Total

Cost of Goods Sold Report

The final record for inventory control is the Cost of Goods Sold Report. It is on this report that you will determine the actual cost to your business of the goods that were sold during a particular time period. There are numerous methods to determine the value of your inventory at the end of a time period. The three most important are the specific identification method, the first-in first-out (FIFO) method, and the last-in first-out (LIFO) method. Specific identification is the easiest to use if you have only a few items of inventory, or one-of-a-kind type merchandise. With this method, you actually keep track of each specific item of inventory. You keep track of when you obtained the item, its cost, and when you sold the specific item. With the FIFO method, you keep track only of general quantities of your inventory. Your inventory costs are calculated as though the oldest inventory merchandise was sold first. The first items that you purchased are the first items that you sell. With the LIFO method, the cost values are calculated as though you sold your most-recently purchased inventory first. It is important to note that you do not necessarily have to actually sell your first item first to use the FIFO method and that you don't have to actually sell your last item first to use the LIFO method of calculation.

Although there may be significant advantages in some cases to using the LIFO method, it is also a far more complicated system than the FIFO. The specific identification method allows you to simply track each item of inventory and deduct the actual cost of the goods that you sold during the year. The FIFO method allows you to value your inventory on hand at the end of a time period based on the cost of your most recent purchases.

1. At the end of your chosen time period (monthly, quarterly, or annually), take an actual physical inventory count on your Physical Inventory Report.

2. Using the most recent purchases as listed on your Periodic Inventory Record, determine the unit price of the items left in your inventory and enter this in the Unit Price column on your Physical Inventory Report.

3. Once all of your items of inventory have been checked, counted, and a unit price determined, simply total each item and then total the value of the entire inventory. If you are conducting your final annual inventory, this figure is your inventory value at year's end.

4. On the Cost of Goods Sold Report, enter this number on the line titled "Inventory Value at End of Period." If this is your first year in business, enter "zero" as the Inventory Value at Beginning of Period. For later periods, the Inventory Value at Beginning of Period will be the Inventory Value at End of Period from the previous time period.

5. Using your Periodic Inventory Records, total the amount of orders during the period that are listed in the "Inventory Received" column. This total will be entered on the "Inventory Added During Period" line. Now simply perform the calculations. You will use the figures on this report at tax time to prepare your taxes.

Note: This type of inventory calculation is not intended for manufacturing companies that manufacture finished goods from raw materials or for those with gross annual receipts more than $10 million. For those types of companies, an additional calculation is necessary because of uniform capitalization rules. This tax rule requires that manufacturing inventory values include the overhead associated with the manufacturing process. Please consult an accounting professional if your business falls into this category.

Cost of Goods Sold Report

Period Ending:

Inventory Value at Beginning of Period		
+ Inventory Added during Period		
= Total Inventory Value		
− Inventory Value at End of Period		
= Cost of Goods Sold		

Beginning Inventory Value for Next Period
(Take from Inventory Value at End of This Period)

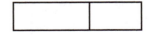

Fixed Assets

The final category of assets that you will need to track are your *fixed assets*. Fixed assets are the more permanent assets of your business, generally the assets that are not for sale to customers. The main categories of these fixed assets are:

- Buildings
- Land
- Machinery
- Tools
- Furniture and Equipment
- Vehicles

There are many more types of fixed assets, such as patents, copyrights, and goodwill. However, the six listed above are the basic ones for most small businesses. If your business includes other types of fixed assets, please consult an accounting professional. For those with basic fixed assets, you will need to keep track of the actual total costs to you to acquire them. These costs include sales taxes, transportation charges, installation costs, etc. The total cost of a fixed asset to you is referred to as the asset's *cost basis*. With a major exception explained below, the costs of fixed assets are, generally, not immediately deductible as a business expense. Rather, except for land, their costs are deductible proportionately over a period of time. This proportionate deduction is referred to as *depreciation*. Since these assets generally wear out over time (except for land), each year you are allowed to deduct a portion of the initial cost as a legitimate business expense. Each type of fixed asset is given a specific time period for dividing up the cost into proportional amounts. This time period is called the *recovery period* of the asset. Depreciation is a very complex subject and one whose rules change nearly every year. The full details of depreciation are beyond the scope of this book. What follows is only a general outline of depreciation rules. It will allow you to begin to set up your fixed asset records. However, you will need to consult either an accounting or tax professional or consult specific tax preparation manuals for details on how your specific assets should be depreciated.

The major exception to depreciation rules is that, under the rules of Internal Revenue Service Code Section 179, every year a total of $25,000.00 (beginning in the tax year 2003) of your fixed asset costs can be immediately used as a business deduction. This means that if your total purchases of equipment, tools, vehicles, etc., during a year amounted to less than $25,000.00, you can deduct all of the costs as current expenses. If your total fixed asset costs are more than $25,000.00, you can still deduct the first $25,000.00 in costs and then depreciate the remaining costs over time. Here are some basic rules relating to depreciation:

1. The depreciation rules that were in effect at the time of the purchase of the asset will be the rules that apply to that particular asset.

2. The actual cost to you of the asset is the cost basis that you use to compute your depreciation amount each year.

3. Used assets that you purchase for use in your business can be depreciated in the same manner as new assets.

4. Assets that you owned prior to going into business and that you will use in your business can be depreciated. The cost basis will be the lower of their actual market value when you begin to use them in your business or their actual cost to you. For example, you start a carpentry business and use your personal power saw in the business. It cost $150.00 new, but is now worth about $90.00. You can depreciate $90.00 (or deduct this amount as an expense if the total of your fixed asset deductions is less than $25,000.00).

5. You may depreciate proportionately those assets that you use partially for business and partially for personal use. In the above example, if you use your saw 70 percent of the time in your business and 30 percent for personal use, you may deduct or depreciate 70 percent of $90.00, which is $63.00.

The tax depreciation rules set up several categories of asset types for the purpose of deciding how long a period you must use to depreciate the asset. Cars, trucks, computer equipment, copiers, and similar equipment are referred to as five-year property. Most machinery, heavy equipment, and office furniture are referred to as seven-year property. This means that for these types of property the actual costs are spread out and depreciated over five or seven years—that is, the costs are deducted over a period of five or seven years.

There are also several different ways to compute how much of the cost can be depreciated each year. There are three basic methods: straight-line, MACRS, and ACRS. Straight-line depreciation spreads the deductible amount equally over the recovery period. Thus for the power saw that is worth $90.00 and is used 70 percent of the time in a business, the cost basis that can be depreciated is $63.00. This asset has a recovery period of seven years. Spreading the $63.00 over the seven-year period allows you to deduct a total of $9.00 per year as depreciation of the saw. After the first year, the saw will be valued on your books at $54.00. Thus, after seven years, the value of the saw on your books will be zero. It will have been fully depreciated. You will have finally been allowed to fully deduct its cost as a business expense. Of course, if you have fixed asset costs of less than $25,000.00 for the year you put the saw in service, you will be allowed to claim the entire $63.00 deduction that first year. See the glossary for an explanation of MACRS and ACRS depreciations.

Other methods of depreciation have more complicated rules that must be applied. For full details, please refer to a tax preparation manual or consult a tax or accounting professional.

Following are listed various types of property that are depreciable or deductible. Consult this list to determine which of your business purchases may be depreciated and which of them may be written off as an immediately deductible expense. Recall that up to $25,000.00 of depreciable assets may be immediately deductible as a special Section 179 deduction. Of course, also remember that tax laws are always subject to change.

DEDUCTIBLE EXPENSES

Advertising	Legal and professional fees
Bad debts	Maintenance
Bank charges	Office equipment worth less than $100
Books and periodicals	
Car and truck expenses:	Office furniture worth less than $100
Gas, repairs, licenses,	Office supplies
insurance, maintenance	Pension plans
Commissions to salespersons	Postage
Independent contractor costs	Printing costs
Donations	Property taxes
Dues to professional groups	Rent
Educational expenses	Repairs
Entertainment of clients	Refunds, returns, and allowances
Freight costs	Sales taxes collected
Improvements worth less than $100	Sales taxes paid on purchases
	Telephone
Insurance	Tools worth less than $100
Interest costs	Uniforms
Laundry and cleaning	Utilities
Licenses for business	Wages paid

DEPRECIABLE PROPERTY

Business buildings (not land)	Business machinery
Office furniture worth over $100	Tools worth over $100
Office equipment worth over $100	Vehicles used in business

Fixed Asset Account

Recall that fixed assets are business purchases that are depreciable, unless you elect to deduct fixed asset expenses up to $25,000.00 per year. For recordkeeping purposes, you will prepare a Fixed Asset Account record for each fixed asset that you have if you have acquired more than $25,000.00 in a calendar year. If you have acquired less than $25,000.00 worth in a year, you may put all of your fixed asset records on one Fixed Asset Account record.

To prepare your Fixed Asset Account record, follow these instructions:

1. List the date on which you acquired the property. If the property was formerly personal property, list the date on which you converted it to business property.

2. Then list the property by description. Enter the actual cost of the property. If the property is used, enter the lower amount of the cost of the property or the actual market value of the property. If the property is part business and part personal, enter the value of the business portion of the property.

3. If you will have more than $25,000.00 worth of depreciable business property during the year, you will additionally need to enter information in the next three columns on the record. First, you will need to enter the recovery period for each asset. For most property other than buildings, this will be either five or seven years. Please consult a tax manual or tax professional.

4. You will need to enter the method of depreciation. Again, check a tax manual or tax professional.

5. Finally, you will need to determine the amount of the deduction for the first year (*Hint:* consult a tax manual or tax professional).

6. Once you have set up a method for each fixed asset, each year you will determine the additional deduction and update the balance. You will then use that figure on your business tax return and in the preparation of your Balance Sheet.

Fixed Asset Account

Date	Item	Cost		Years	Method	Annual	Balance	

Tracking Business Debts

Business debts are also referred to as *business liabilities*. However, technically, business liabilities also include the value of the owner's equity in the business. Business debts can be divided into two general categories. First are *current debts*, those that will normally be paid within one year. The second general category is *long-term debts*. These are generally debts that will not be paid off within one year. Current debts for most small businesses consist primarily of accounts payable and taxes that are due during the year. For small businesses, the taxes that are due during a year fall into three main categories: estimated income tax payments, payment of collected sales taxes, and payroll taxes. Since the collection and payment of sales taxes are handled differently in virtually every state, you will need to contact your state's department of revenue or similar body to determine the specific necessary recordkeeping requirements for that business debt. Payroll taxes will be explained in the next chapter and estimated taxes will be dealt with in Chapter 19.

That leaves us only with accounts payable to track as a current debt. You will have only one simple form to use to keep track of this important category. *Accounts payable* are the current bills that your business owes. They may be for equipment or supplies that you have purchased on credit or for items that you have ordered on account. Regardless of the source of the debt, you will need a clear system to record the debt and keep track of how much you still owe on the debt.

Long-term debts are, generally, debts based on business loans for equipment, inventory, business-owned vehicles, or business property. In the accounting system outlined in this book, you will only keep track of the current principal and interest for these debts. For long-term debts of your business, you will fill in the Long-Term Debt Record, that is explained later in this chapter. You will find an Accounts Payable Record on the following form. You will enter any bills or short-term debts that you do not pay immediately on this record. If you pay the bill off upon receipt of the bill, you need not enter the amount on this record. Your records for expenses will take care of the necessary documentation for those particular debts. If your business has many accounts payable that must be tracked, it may be a good idea to prepare an individual Accounts Payable Record for each account.

Accounts Payable Record

Follow these instructions to prepare and fill in this particular form:

1. For those debts that you do not pay off immediately, you will need to record the following information in the left-hand column of the record:

   - The date the debt was incurred
   - To whom you owe the money
   - Payment terms (for instance: due within 30, 60, or 90 days)
   - The amount of the debt

2. In the right-hand column of the Accounts Payable Record, you will record the following information:

   - The date of any payments
   - To whom the payments were made
   - The amount of any payments made

3. By periodically totaling the left- and right-hand columns, you will be able to take a look at the total amount of your unpaid accounts payable. You may wish to do this weekly, monthly, or quarterly. You will also need this figure for your total unpaid accounts payable for the preparation of your Balance Sheet.

4. When you have totaled your accounts payable at the end of your chosen periodic interval, you should start a new record and carry the unpaid accounts over to it. Using this simple record, you will be able to check your accounts payable at a glance and also have enough information available to use in preparing a Balance Sheet for your business.

Accounts Payable Record

Period from: to:

UNPAID ACCOUNTS

Date	Due to	Terms	Amount	
		TOTAL		

PAYMENTS

Date	Paid to	Amount	
	TOTAL		

Total Unpaid Accounts

− Total Payments

= Total Accounts Payable

Long-Term Debt Record

If your business has any outstanding loans that will not be paid off within one year, you will prepare a Long-Term Debt Record for each loan. You will track the principal and interest paid on each long-term debt of your business. This information will enable you to have long-term debt figures for use in preparing your Balance Sheet and interest-paid figures for use in preparing your Profit and Loss Statements. On the following page, you will find a Long-Term Debt Record to be used for this purpose. In order to fill in this record, follow these directions:

1. You will need to enter the following information for each company to whom a loan is outstanding:

    *   Company name
    *   Address
    *   Contact person
    *   Phone number
    *   Loan account number
    *   Loan interest rate
    *   Original principal amount of the loan
    *   Term of the loan

2. You will need a loan payment book or amortization schedule in order to obtain the necessary information regarding the portions of each of your payments that are principal and interest. As you make a payment, enter the following information:

    *   Date of payment
    *   Total payment made
    *   Amount of principal paid
    *   Amount of interest paid
    *   Balance due (the previous balance minus principal)

3. Total the balance due after each payment. Using this method of tracking accounts payable will allow you to always have a running total of your long-term liability for each long-term debt.

4. To prepare a Balance Sheet entry for long-term debts, you will simply need to total all of the various account balances for all of your long-term debts.

5. You should also periodically total all of the columns on your Long-Term Debt Record. You will need the totals of the interest paid for your Annual Expense Summaries.

Long-Term Debt Record

Company:
Address:
Contact Person
Loan Account #:
Original Loan Amount:

Phone:
Loan Interest Rate:
Term:

Date	Payment		Principal		Interest		Balance	
TOTALS								

Tracking Business Expenses

The expenses of a business are all of the transactions of the business where money is paid out of the business, with one general exception. Money paid out of the business to pay off the principal of a loan is not considered an expense of a business. Because of the tax deductibility of the cost of most business expenses, it is crucial for a business to keep careful records of what has been spent to operate the business. But even beyond the need for detailed expense records for tax purposes, a small business needs a clear system that will allow a quick examination of where money is being spent. The tracking of business expenses will allow you to quickly see where your money is flowing.

In order to track your business expenses, you will use a Weekly Expense Record and a Monthly Expense Summary. You may also need to use a number of additional specialized forms if your business needs dictate their use. There is also an Annual Expense Summary for totaling your expense payments.

On your Weekly Expense Record, you will record all of your business expenses in chronological order. The expense transactions will generally come from three main sources: your business bank account check register, your monthly business credit card statements, and your petty cash register. You will transfer all of the expenses from these three sources to the main expense record. This will provide you with a central listing of all of the expenditures for your business.

From this record, you will transfer your expenses to a Monthly Expense Summary. On the Monthly Expense Summary, you will enter a line for each expense type that you have listed on your business Chart of Accounts. You will then go through your Weekly Expense Records for each month and total the expenses for each account. You will enter this total in the column for the specific type of expense.

Finally, on a monthly basis, you will transfer the totals for your various expense categories to the Annual Expense Summary record. On this record, you collect and record the total monthly expenses. With these figures, you will be able to easily total your expense amounts to ascertain your quarterly and annual expenses.

By recording your business expenses in this manner, you should have little difficulty being able to keep track of the money flowing out of your business on a daily, weekly, monthly, quarterly, and annual basis. You will have all of the information that you will need to easily provide the necessary expenditure figures for preparing a Profit and Loss Statement. Remember that you must tailor the forms to fit your particular business.

Weekly Expense Record

1. Fill in the date or dates that the form will cover where indicated at the top.

2. Beginning with your bank account check register, transfer the following information from the register to the Weekly Expense Record:

   - The date of the transaction
   - The check number
   - To whom the amount was paid
   - The expense account number (from your Chart of Accounts)
   - The amount of the transaction

3. Next, transfer the following information from your records that you have kept regarding your petty cash to the expense record:

   - The date of the transaction
   - In the "Check #" column, put "PC" indicating it was a petty cash expense
   - To whom the amount was paid
   - The expense account number (off your Chart of Accounts)
   - The amount of the transaction
   - *Note*: Do not list the checks that you make out to "Petty Cash" as an expense

4. For credit card transactions, follow these rules:

   - Do not list payment to a credit card company as an expense
   - List the monthly amount on the credit card bill for interest as an interest expense
   - Individually, list each business purchase on the credit card as a separate expense item, assigning an account number to each separate business charge. Make a notation for the date, to whom the expense was paid, and the amount. In the "Check #" column, provide the type of credit card, for example, "V" for Visa
   - Do not list any personal charge items as business expenses
   - If a charged item is used partially for business and partially for personal reasons, list only that portion that is used for business reasons as a business expense

5. At the end of the period, total the Amount column. You will use this weekly total expense amount to cross-check your later calculations.

6. It is a good idea to keep all of your various business expense receipts for at least three years after the tax period to which they relate. You may wish to buy envelopes for each weekly period, label each appropriately, and file your weekly business expense receipts in them. This will make it easy to find each specific receipt, if necessary.

Weekly Expense Record

Week of:

Date	Check #	To Whom Paid	Account #	Amount	
			TOTALS		

Monthly Expense Summary

Using this record, you will compile and transfer the total expense amount for each expense category. In this way, you will be able to keep a monthly total of all of the expenses, broken down by category of expense. To fill in this form, do the following:

1. Indicate the month that the Monthly Expense Summary will cover where shown.

2. In the first column on the left-hand side, list all of your expense account names and numbers from your business Chart of Accounts.

3. In the next column, using your Weekly Expense Records, transfer the amounts for each expense. If you have more than four expense amounts for any account, use a second Monthly Expense Summary to record additional amounts.

4. In the Total column, list the total expenses in each category for the month.

5. At the bottom of the page, total the amount for all of the categories for the month. Don't forget to include any amounts from any additional records in your totals.

6. To double-check your transfers and your calculations, total all of your Weekly Expense Record total amounts. This figure should equal your Monthly Expense Summary total for that month. If there is a discrepancy, check each of your figures until you discover the error.

Monthly Expense Summary

Month of:

Account Name/#	Amount		Amount		Amount		Amount		Total	
								TOTAL		

Annual Expense Summary

1. Fill in the year. Fill in your account numbers from your Chart of Accounts across the top row. If you have more than nine expense accounts, use a second and third page, if necessary.

2. On a monthly basis, carry the totals from all of the rows on your Monthly Expense Summaries to the appropriate column of the Annual Expense Summary.

3. At the end of each quarter, total all of the monthly entries to arrive at your quarterly totals for each category.

4. To double-check your monthly calculations, total your categories across each month and put this total in the final column. Compare this total with the total on your Monthly Expense Records. If there is a discrepancy, check each of your figures until you discover the error. Don't forget to include your extra records if you have more than nine expense accounts to list.

5. To double-check your quarterly calculations, total your monthly totals in the final quarterly column. This figure should equal the total of the quarterly category totals across the quarterly row. If there is a discrepancy, check each of your figures until you discover the error.

6. Finally, total each of your quarterly amounts to arrive at the annual totals. To cross-check your calculations, total the quarterly totals in the final column. This figure should equal the total for all of the annual totals in each category across the Annual Total row. If there is a discrepancy, check each of your figures until you discover the error.

Annual Expense Summary

Year of:

Account # ⇨														Total
January														
February														
March														
1st Quarter														
April														
May														
June														
2nd Quarter														
July														
August														
September														
3rd Quarter														
October														
November														
December														
4th Quarter														
Annual TOTAL														

Tracking Business Income

The careful tracking of your business income is one of the most important accounting activities you will perform. It is essential for your business that you know intimately where your income comes from. Failure to accurately track income and cash is one of the most frequent causes of business failure. You must have in place a clear and easily understood system to track your business income. There are three separate features of tracking business income that must be incorporated into your accounting system. You will need a system in place to handle cash, a system to track all of your sales and service income, and a system to handle credit sales.

The first system you will need is a clear method for handling cash on a weekly basis. This is true no matter how large or small your business may be and regardless of how much or how little cash is actually handled. You must have a clear record of how much cash is on hand and how much cash is taken in during a particular time period. You will also need to have a method to tally this cash flow on a monthly basis. For these purposes, two forms are provided: a Weekly Cash Report and a Monthly Cash Report Summary.

The second feature of your business income tracking system should be a method to track your actual income from sales or services. This differs from your cash tracking. With these records you will track taxable and nontaxable income whether the income is in the form of cash, check, credit card payment, or payment on an account. Please note that when *nontaxable income* is referred to, it means only that income which is not subject to any state or local sales tax (generally, this will be income from the performance of a service). These records will also track your intake of sales taxes, if applicable. For this segment of your income tracking, you will have a Weekly Income Record. You will also track your income on income summaries that will provide you with monthly, quarterly, and annual reports of your taxable income, nontaxable income, and sales tax collection.

The third feature of your business income tracking consists of a method to track and bill credit sales. With this portion of income tracking, you will list and track all of your sales to customers that are made on account or on credit. The accounts that owe you money are referred to as your *accounts receivable*. These are the accounts from whom you hope to receive payment. The tracking of these credit sales will take place on a Monthly Credit Sales Record. You will also use a Credit Sales Aging Report to see how your customers are doing over time. The actual billing of these credit sales will require you to prepare and incorporate an invoice, statement, and past due statement, all of which are explained at the end of this chapter.

Tracking Cash

Most businesses will have to handle cash in some form. Here we are not talking about the use of petty cash. *Petty cash* is the cash that a business has on hand for the payment of minor expenses that may crop up and for which the use of a business check is not convenient. The cash handling discussed in this section is the daily handling of cash used to take money in from customers or clients and the use of a cash drawer or some equivalent. You must have some method to accurately account for the cash used in your business in this regard.

Weekly Cash Report

1. You must decide how much cash you will need to begin each period with sufficient cash to meet your needs and make change for cash sales. Usually $100.00 should be sufficient for most needs. Choose a figure and begin each period with that amount in your cash drawer. Excess cash that has been collected should be deposited in your business bank account. Each period, fill in the date and the cash on hand on your Weekly Cash Report.

2. As you take in cash and checks throughout the period, record each item of cash taken in, checks taken in, and any instances of cash paid out. Cash out does not mean change that has been made, but rather cash paid out for business purposes (for example, a refund).

3. Your business may have so much daily cash flow that it will be burdensome to record each item of cash flow on your sheet. In that case, you will need a cash register of some type. Simply total the cash register at the end of the day and record the total cash in, checks in, and cash out in the appropriate places on the Weekly Cash Report.

4. At the end of each period, total your Cash In and Checks In. Add these two amounts to your Cash on Hand at the beginning of the period. This equals your Total Receipts for the period. Subtract any Cash Out from this amount for the Balance on Hand. Make a bank deposit for all of the checks and for all of the cash in excess of the amount that you will need to begin the next period. Subtract the Bank Deposit from the Balance. This figure should equal your actual cash on hand at the end of the period.

5. In the space for deposits, note the following: a deposit number, if applicable; the date of the deposit; the deposit amount; and the name and signature of the person who made the deposit. Don't forget to also record your deposit in your business bank account check register.

Weekly Cash Report

Week of: _____   Cash on Hand Beginning: _____

Week	CASH IN Name	Amount		CHECKS IN Name	Amount		CASH OUT Name	Amount	
1									
2									
3									
4									
5									
6									
7									
8									
9									
10									
11									
12									
TOTAL									

Deposit #:	
Deposit Date:	
Deposit Amount:	
Deposited by:	
Signed:	

Total Cash in

+ Total Checks in

+ Cash on Hand Beginning

= Total Receipts

– Total Cash Out

= Balance on Hand

– Bank Deposit

= Cash on Hand Ending

225

Monthly Cash Report Summary

This form will be used to keep a monthly record of your Weekly Cash Reports. It serves as a monthly listing of your cash flow and of your business bank account deposits. You will, of course, also record your bank deposits in your business bank account check register. To use this form, follow these instructions:

1. On a weekly basis, collect your Weekly Cash Reports. From each Report, record the following information on the monthly summary:

    *   Cash on hand at the beginning of the period
    *   Cash taken in
    *   Checks taken in
    *   Cash paid out
    *   The amount of the weekly bank deposit
    *   Cash on hand at the end of the period and after the bank deposit

2. You can total the Deposit column as a cross-check against your bank account check register record of deposits.

Monthly Cash Report Summary

Month:

Date	On Hand		Cash in		Checks in		Cash out		Deposit		On Hand	
1												
2												
3												
4												
5												
6												
7												
8												
9												
10												
11												
12												
13												
14												
15												
16												
17												
18												
19												
20												
21												
22												
23												
24												
25												
26												
27												
28												
29												

Tracking Income

The second feature of your business income tracking system should be a method to keep track of your actual income. This portion of the system will provide you with a list of all taxable and nontaxable income and of any sales taxes collected, if applicable. For sales tax information, please contact your state's sales tax revenue collection agency. If your state has a sales tax on the product or service that you provide, you will need accurate records to determine your total taxable and nontaxable income and the amount of sales tax that is due. For this purpose and for the purpose of tracking all of your income for your own business analysis, you should prepare a Weekly Income Record. The information from these reports will then be used to prepare Monthly and Annual Income Summaries.

Weekly Income Record

1. You will need to contact your state taxing agency for information on how to determine if a sale or the provision of a service is taxable or nontaxable. You will also need to determine the appropriate rates for sales tax collection.

2. For each item, record the following information:

   - Invoice number
   - Taxable income amount
   - Sales tax amount
   - Nontaxable income amount
   - Total income (Taxable, sales tax, and nontaxable amounts combined)

3. On a weekly basis, total the amounts in each column to determine the totals for the particular time period. These figures will be carried over to the Monthly and Annual Income Summaries, that will be explained next.

Weekly Income Record

Week of:

Invoice #	Taxable Income		Sales Tax		Nontaxable Income		Total Income	
Weekly TOTAL								

Monthly Income Summary

1. Fill in the appropriate month.

2. Using your Weekly Income Records, record the following information for each week:

   • Invoice number
   • Total taxable income amount
   • Total sales tax amount
   • Total nontaxable income amount
   • Total income (taxable, sales tax, and nontaxable amounts combined)

3. On a monthly basis, total the amounts in each column to determine the totals for the particular month. These figures will be carried over to the Annual Income Summary, that will be explained next.

Monthly Income Summary

Month of:

Invoice #	Taxable Income		Sales Tax		Nontaxable Income		Total Income	
Monthly TOTAL								

Annual Income Summary

1. On a monthly basis, carry the totals from all of the columns on your Monthly Income Summary to the appropriate columns of the Annual Income Summary.

2. At the end of each quarter, total all of the monthly entries to arrive at your quarterly totals for each category.

3. To double-check your monthly calculations, total your categories across each month and put this total in the final column. Compare this total with the total on your Monthly Income Summaries. If there is a discrepancy, check each of your figures until you discover the error.

4. To double-check your quarterly calculations, total your monthly totals in the final column. This figure should equal the total of the quarterly category totals across the quarterly row. If there is a discrepancy, check each of your figures until you discover the error.

5. Finally, total your quarterly amounts to arrive at the annual totals. To cross-check your calculations, total the quarterly totals in the final column. This figure should equal the total for all of the annual totals across the Annual Total row. If there is a discrepancy, check each of your figures until you discover the error.

Annual Income Summary

Year of:

Date	Taxable Income		Sales Tax		Nontaxable Income		Total Income	
January								
February								
March								
1st Quarter								
April								
May								
June								
2nd Quarter								
July								
August								
September								
3rd Quarter								
October								
November								
December								
4th Quarter								
Annual TOTAL								

Tracking Credit Sales

The final component of your business income tracking system will be a logical method to track your credit sales. You will use a Monthly Credit Sales Record to track the actual sales on credit, and Credit Sales Aging Report to track the payment on these sales. In addition, several forms are provided for the billing of these credit sales: an Invoice, Statement, Past Due Statement, and Credit Memo.

Monthly Credit Sales Record
1. Fill in the appropriate date or time period.

2. For each sale that is made on credit, fill in the following information from the customer Invoice (see Invoice instructions later in this chapter):

   - Invoice number
   - Date of the sale
   - Customer name
   - Total sale amount

3. The final column is for recording the date that the credit sale has been paid in full.

4. The information from your Monthly Credit Sales Record will also be used to prepare your Credit Sales Aging Report on a monthly basis.

Monthly Credit Sales Record

Month of:

Invoice #	Sale Date	Customer	Sale Total		Date Paid

Credit Sales Aging Report

This report is used to track the current status of your credit sales or accounts receivables. Through the use of this form you will be able to track whether or not the people or companies that owe you money are falling behind on their payments. With this information, you will be able to determine how to handle these accounts: sending past due notices, halting sales to them, turning them over to a collection agency, etc. To use this form, do the following:

1. Decide on which day of the month you would like to perform your credit sales aging calculations.

2. For each credit sales account, enter the name of the account from your Monthly Credit Sales Record.

3. In the "Total" column, enter the total current amount that is owed to you. If this figure is based on credit sales during the current month, enter this figure again in the "Current" column. Do this for each credit account.

4. Each month you will prepare a new Credit Sales Aging Report on a new sheet. On the same date in the next month, determine how much of the originally owed balance has been paid off. Enter the amount of the unpaid balance from the previous month in the "30–60 days" column. Enter any new credit sales for the month under the "Current" column. The figure in the "Total" column should be the total of all of the columns to the right of the "Total" column.

5. Each month, determine how much was paid on the account, deduct that amount from the oldest amount due, and shift the amounts due over one column to the right. Add any new credit sales to the "Current" column and put the total of the amounts in the "Total" column.

6. After entering the information for each month, total each of the columns across the "Total" line at the bottom of the report. The "Total" column is 100 percent of the amount due. Calculate the percentage for each of the other columns to determine how much of your accounts receivable are 30, 60, 90, or more than 90 days overdue.

Credit Sales Aging Report

Account Name	Total		Current		30–60 Days		60–90 Days		90 Days +	
TOTALS										
PERCENT	100%									

Invoices and Statements

For credit sales, you will need to provide each customer with a current Invoice. You will also need to send a Statement if the balance is not paid within the first 30 days. In addition, you will need to send a Past Due Statement if the balance becomes overdue. Finally, a Credit Memo form is provided to record instances when a customer is given credit for a returned item. You will need to produce two copies of each of these forms: one for your records and one for the customer.

Invoice

The invoice is your key credit sales document. To prepare and track invoices, follow these directions:

1. Make a number of copies of the Invoice form. You can insert your business card in the upper-left corner before copying. Number each form consecutively. Make a photocopy of the form when the form is sent out to the customer or print two copies if using the Forms-on-CD.

2. For each order, fill in the following information:

    *   Date
    *   Invoice number
    *   Name and address of who will be billed for the order
    *   Name and address where the order will be shipped
    *   Item number of the product or service sold
    *   Quantity ordered
    *   Description of the item
    *   Per unit price of the item
    *   Total amount billed (quantity times per unit price)

3. Subtotal all of the items where shown. Add any sales taxes and shipping costs and total the balance.

4. Record the pertinent information from the Invoice on the Monthly Credit Sales Record.

5. Record the pertinent information from the Invoice on the Monthly Income Summary.

6. Send one copy of the Invoice to the customer with the order and file the other copy in a file for your invoices.

Invoice

Date:

Invoice No.:

Bill to:

Ship to:

Item #	Qty.	Description	Price Each		Total	

Subtotal		
Tax		
Shipping		
BALANCE		

Statement and Past Due Statement

Statements are used to send your credit customers a notice of the amount that is currently due. Statements are generally sent at 30-day intervals, beginning either 30 days after the invoice is sent, at the beginning of the next month, or at the next cycle for sending statements. Follow these instructions for preparing your statements:

1. You should decide on a statement billing cycle. Generally, this is a specific date each month (for example: the 1st, 10th, or 15th of each month).

2. Make a copy of the Statement form using your business card in the upper-left corner. Fill in the date and the account name and address in the "Account" box.

3. In the body of the form, enter information from any Invoice that is still unpaid as of the date you are completing the Statement. You should enter the following items for each unpaid Invoice:

    *   The date of the Invoice
    *   A description of the Invoice (including Invoice number)
    *   Any payments received since the last statement or since the sale
    *   The amount still owed on that Invoice

4. When all of the invoice information for all the customer's invoices has been entered, total the "Amount Due" column and enter the balance at the bottom. The information on the Statement can then be used to enter information on your Credit Sales Aging Report.

5. The Past Due Statement is simply a version of the basic Statement that includes a notice that the account is past due. This Past Due Statement should be sent when the account becomes overdue. Fill it out in the same manner used for statements.

Statement

Date:

Account:

Date	Description	Payment		Amount Due	

Please pay this BALANCE

Past Due Statement

Date:

Account:

This account is now past due. Please pay upon receipt to avoid collection costs

Date	Description	Payment		Amount Due	

Please pay this BALANCE

Credit Memo

The final form for tracking your business income is the Credit Memo. This form is used to provide you and your customer with a written record of any credit given for goods that have been returned by the customer. You will need to set a policy regarding when such credit will be given (for example, for only a certain time period after the sale, for defects, or for other limitations). To use the Credit Memo, follow these instructions:

1. Fill in the date, the number of the original Invoice, and the customer's name and address in the "Credit" box.

2. Fill in the following information in the body of the Credit Memo:

    • Item number of item returned
    • Quantity of items returned
    • Description of item returned
    • Per unit price of item returned
    • Total amount of credit (quantity x per unit price)

3. Subtotal the credit for all items. Add any appropriate sales tax credit and total those amounts for the credit. This is the amount that will be credited or refunded to the customer.

4. In the lower left corner of the form, indicate the reason for the return, any necessary approval, and the date of the approval.

5. Handle the Credit Memo like a negative Invoice. Record the amount of credit as a negative on the Weekly Income Record.

6. Record the pertinent information from the Credit Memo as a negative amount on the appropriate Monthly Credit Sales Record, if the Credit Memo applies to a previous sale on credit that was recorded on a Monthly Credit Sales Record.

Credit Memo

Date:

Invoice #:

Credit to:

GOODS RETURNED

Item #	Qty.	Description	Price Each		Total	

Reason for return: Subtotal

Approved by: Tax

Date: CREDIT

CHAPTER 18

Business Payroll

One of the most difficult and complex accounting functions that small businesses face is their payroll. Because of the various state and Federal taxes that must be applied and the myriad government forms that must be prepared, the handling of a business payroll often causes accounting nightmares. Even if there is only one employee, there is a potential for problems.

First, let's examine the basics. If your business is a corporation, all pay must be handled as payroll, even if you are the only employee. The corporation is a separate entity and the corporation itself will be the employer. You and any other people that you hire will be the employees. A business payroll entails a great deal of paperwork and has numerous government tax filing deadlines. You will be required to make payroll tax deposits, file various quarterly payroll tax returns, and make additional end-of-the-year reports.

Initially, you must take certain steps to set up your payroll and official status as an employer. The following information contains the instructions only for meeting Federal requirements. Please check with your particular state and local governments for information regarding any additional payroll tax, state unemployment insurance, or workers' compensation requirements.

Setting up Your Payroll

1. The first step in becoming an employer is to file Internal Revenue Service Form SS-4: *Application for Employer Identification Number*. This will officially register your business with the Federal government as an employer. This form and instructions are included on the Forms-on-CD.

2. Next, each employee must fill in an IRS Form W-4: *Employee's Withholding Allowance Certificate*. This will provide you with the necessary information regarding withholding allowances to enable you to prepare your payroll.

3. You must then determine the gross salary or wage that each employee will earn. For each employee, complete an Employee Payroll Record and prepare a Quarterly Payroll Time Sheet as explained later in this chapter.

4. You will then need to consult the tables in IRS Circular E: *Employer's Tax Guide*. From the tables in this publication, you will be able to determine the proper deductions for each employee for each pay period. If your employees are paid on an hourly basis and the number of hours worked is different each pay period, you will have to perform these calculations for each pay period.

5. Before you pay your employee, you should open a separate business bank account for handling your business payroll tax deductions and payments. This will allow you to immediately deposit all taxes due into this separate account and help prevent the lack of sufficient money available when the taxes are due.

6. Next you will pay your employee and record the deduction information on the Employee Payroll Record.

7. When you have completed paying all of your employees for the pay period, you will write a separate check for the total amount of all of your employees' deductions and any employer's share of taxes. You will then deposit this check into your business payroll tax bank account that you set up following the instructions above.

8. At the end of every month, you will need to transfer the information regarding employee deductions to your Payroll Depository Record and Annual Payroll Summary. Copies of these forms and instructions are included later in this chapter. You will then calculate your employer share of Social Security and Medicare taxes. Each month (or quarter if your tax liability is less than $500.00 per quarter), you will need to deposit the correct amount of taxes due to the Federal government. This is done either by making a monthly payment to your bank for the taxes due using IRS Form 8109: *Federal Tax Deposit Coupon* or by making the payment on a quarterly basis when you file IRS Form 941: *Employer's Quarterly Federal Tax Return*. Copies of these forms are contained on the Forms-on-CD.

9. On a quarterly or annual basis, you will also need to make a tax payment for Federal Unemployment Tax, using IRS Form 940 or IRS Form 940-EZ: *Employer's Annual Federal Unemployment (FUTA) Tax Return*. This tax is solely the responsibility of the employer and is not deducted from the employee's pay. Also on a quarterly basis, you will need to file IRS Form 941: *Employer's Quarterly Federal Tax Return*. If you have made monthly deposits of your taxes due, there will be no quarterly taxes to pay, but you will still need to file these forms quarterly.

10. Finally, to complete your payroll, at the end of the year you must do the following:

- Prepare IRS Form W-2: *Wage and Tax Statement* for each employee
- File IRS Form W-3: *Transmittal of Wage and Tax Statements*

Remember that your state and local tax authorities will generally have additional requirements and taxes that will need to be paid. In many jurisdictions, these requirements are tailored after the Federal requirements and the procedures and due dates are similar.

Quarterly Payroll Time Sheet

On the following page is a Quarterly Payroll Time Sheet. If your employees are paid an hourly wage, you will prepare a sheet like this for each employee for each quarter during the year. On this sheet you will keep track of the following information:

- Number of hours worked (daily, weekly, and quarterly)
- Number of regular and overtime hours worked

The information from this Quarterly Payroll Time Sheet will be transferred to your individual Employee Payroll Record in order to calculate the employee's paycheck amounts. This is explained following the Quarterly Payroll Time Sheet.

Quarterly Payroll Time Sheet

Employee:

Week of	Sun	Mon	Tue	Wed	Thu	Fri	Sat	Reg	OT	Total
Quarterly TOTAL										

Employee Payroll Record

You will use this form to track each employee's payroll information.

1. For each employee, fill in the following information at the top of the form:

    *   Name and address of employee
    *   Employee's Social Security number
    *   Number of exemptions claimed by employee on Form W-4
    *   Regular and overtime wage rates
    *   Pay period (ie., weekly, biweekly, monthly, etc.)
    *   Date check is written
    *   Payroll check number

2. For each pay period, fill in the number of regular and overtime ("OT") hours worked by the employee from his or her Quarterly Payroll Time Sheet. Multiply this amount by the employee's wage rate to determine the *gross pay*. For example: 40 hours at the regular wage of $8.00/hour = $320.00; plus five hours at the overtime wage rate of $12.00/hour = $60.00. Gross pay for the period is $320.00 + $60.00 = $380.00.

3. Determine the Federal withholding tax deduction for the pay amount by consulting the withholding tax tables in IRS Circular E: *Employer's Tax Guide*. Enter this figure on the form in the "Fed. W/H" column.

4. Determine the employee's share of Social Security and Medicare deductions. As of 2000, the employee's Social Security share rate is 6.2 percent and the employee's Medicare share rate is 1.45 percent. Multiply these rates times the employee's gross wages and enter the figures in the appropriate places; the "S/S Ded." and "Medic. Ded." columns. For example: for $380.00, the Social Security deduction would be $380.00 x .062 = $23.56 and the Medicare deduction would be $380.00 x .0145 = $5.51.

5. Determine any state taxes and enter in the appropriate column.

6. Subtract all of the deductions from the employee's gross wages to determine the employee's *net pay*. Enter this figure in the final column and prepare the employee's paycheck using the deduction information from this sheet. Also prepare a check to your payroll tax bank account for a total of the Federal withholding amount and two times the Social Security and Medicare amounts. This includes your employer share of these taxes. The employer's share of Social Security and Medicare taxes is equal to the employee's share.

Employee Payroll Record

Employee:

Address:

Social Security #:

Number of Exemptions:

Rate of Pay: Overtime Rate:

Pay Period:

Date	Check #	Pay Period	Reg. Hours	OT Hours	Gross Pay		Fed. W/H		S/S Ded.		Medic. Ded.		State Taxes		Net Pay	
Pay Period TOTAL																

Payroll Depository Record

You will be required to deposit taxes with the IRS on a monthly or quarterly basis (unless your total employment taxes totaled more than $50,000.00 for the previous year, in which case you should obviously consult an accountant). If your employment taxes total less than $500.00 per quarter, you may pay your payroll tax liability when you quarterly file your Federal Form 941: *Employer's Quarterly Federal Tax Return*. If your payroll tax liability is more than $500.00 per quarter, you must deposit your payroll taxes on a monthly basis with a bank using IRS Form 8109: *Federal Tax Deposit Coupon*. Copies of these two Federal forms are contained on the Forms-on-CD. To track your payroll tax liability, use the Payroll Depository Record which follows these instructions:

1. On a monthly basis, total each column on all of your Employee Payroll Records. This will give you a figure for each employee's Federal withholding, Social Security, and Medicare taxes for the month.

2. Total all of the Federal withholding taxes for all employees for the month and enter this figure in the appropriate column on the Payroll Depository Record.

3. Total Social Security and Medicare taxes for all of your employees for the entire month and enter this figure in the appropriate columns on the Payroll Depository Record. Note that "SS/EE" refers to Social Security/Employee's Share and that "MC/EE" refers to Medicare/Employee's Share.

4. Enter identical amounts in the SS/ER and MC/ER columns as you have entered in the SS/EE and MC/EE columns. "ER" refers to the employer's share. The employer's share of Social Security and Medicare is the same as the employee's share, but is not deducted from the employee's pay.

5. Total all of the deductions for the month. This is the amount of your total monthly Federal payroll tax liability. If necessary, write a check to your local bank for this amount and deposit it using IRS Form 8109: *Federal Tax Deposit Coupon*.

6. If you must file only quarterly, total all three of your monthly amounts on a quarterly basis and pay this amount when you file your IRS Form 941: *Employer's Quarterly Federal Tax Return*. On a yearly basis, total all of the quarterly columns to arrive at your total annual Federal payroll tax liability.

Payroll Depository Record

Month	Fed. W/H	SS/EE	SS/ER	MC/EE	MC/ER	Total
January						
February						
March						
1st Quarter						

1st Quarter Total Number of Employees: Total Wages Paid:

Month	Fed. W/H	SS/EE	SS/ER	MC/EE	MC/ER	Total
April						
May						
June						
2nd Quarter						

2nd Quarter Total Number of Employees: Total Wages Paid:

Month	Fed. W/H	SS/EE	SS/ER	MC/EE	MC/ER	Total
July						
August						
September						
3rd Quarter						

3rd Quarter Total Number of Employees: Total Wages Paid:

Month	Fed. W/H	SS/EE	SS/ER	MC/EE	MC/ER	Total
October						
November						
December						
4th Quarter						

4th Quarter Total Number of Employees: Total Wages Paid:

Yearly TOTAL						

Yearly Total Number of Employees: Total Wages Paid:

Annual Payroll Summary

The final payroll form is used to total all of the payroll amounts for all employees on a monthly, quarterly, and annual basis. Much of the information on this form is similar to the information that you compiled for the Payroll Depository Record. However, the purpose of this form is to provide you with a record of all of your payroll costs, including the payroll deduction costs. This form will be useful for both tax and planning purposes as you examine your business profitability on a quarterly and annual basis. Follow these directions to prepare this form:

1. For each month, total all of your employees' gross and net pay amounts from their individual Employee Payroll Records and transfer these totals to this form.

2. For each month, transfer the amounts for Federal withholding from the Payroll Depository Record to this form.

3   For each month, total both columns on your Payroll Depository Record for SS/EE ("Social Security/Employee") and SS/ER ("Social Security/Employer") and transfer this total to the "S/S Taxes" column on this summary. Total the MC/EE ("Medicare/Employee") and MC/ER ("Medicare/Employer") columns also and enter the total in the "Medicare Taxes" column on this form.

4. On a quarterly basis, total the columns to determine your quarterly payroll costs. Annually, total the quarterly amounts to determine your annual costs.

Annual Payroll Summary

	Gross Pay		Federal W/H		S/S Taxes		Medicare Taxes		State Taxes		Net Pay	
January												
February												
March												
1st Quarter Total												
April												
May												
June												
2nd Quarter Total												
July												
August												
September												
3rd Quarter Total												
October												
November												
December												
4th Quarter Total												
Yearly TOTAL												

Payroll Checklist

❏ File IRS Form SS-4: *Application for Employer Identification Number* and obtain Federal Employer Identification Number (FEIN)

❏ Obtain IRS Form W-4: *Employee's Withholding Allowance Certificate* for each employee

❏ Set up Quarterly Payroll Time Sheets and Employee Payroll Records for employees

❏ Open separate business payroll tax bank account

❏ Consult IRS Circular E: *Employer's Tax Guide* and use tables to determine withholding tax amounts

❏ Obtain information on any applicable state or local taxes

❏ List Federal withholding, Social Security, Medicare, and any state or local deductions on Employee Payroll Record

❏ Pay employees and deposit appropriate taxes in payroll tax bank account

❏ Fill in Payroll Depository Record and Annual Payroll Summary

❏ Pay payroll taxes

> ❏ Monthly, using IRS Form 8109: *Federal Tax Deposit Coupon*, if your payroll tax liability is more than $500 per quarter

> ❏ Quarterly, using IRS Form 941: *Employer's Quarterly Federal Tax Return*, if your payroll tax liability is less than $500 per quarter

> ❏ Annually, file IRS Form 940 or 940-EZ: *Employer's Annual Federal Unemployment (FUTA) Tax Return*

❏ Annually, prepare and file IRS Form W-2: *Wage and Tax Statement* and IRS Form W-3: *Transmittal of Wage and Tax Statement* for each employee

CHAPTER 19
Taxation of S-Corporations

Corporations are a separate entity under the law and as such are subject to taxation at both the state and Federal levels. As noted earlier, there are two types of corporations: C-corporations and S-corporations. The difference between the two is in the area of taxation. In general, C-corporations are subject to Federal income tax on the annual profits in many ways similar to the tax on individual income. However, there are significant differences. The most important aspect is the "double" taxation on corporate income if it is distributed to the shareholders in the form of dividends. At the corporate level, corporate net income is subject to tax at the corporate level. Corporate funds that are distributed to officers or directors in the form of salaries, expense reimbursements, or employee benefits may be used by a corporation as a legitimate business deduction against the income of the corporation. Corporate surplus funds that are paid out to shareholders in the form of dividends on their ownership of stock in the corporation, however, are not allowed to be used as a corporate deduction. Thus, any funds used in this manner have been subject to corporate income tax prior to distribution to the shareholders. The dividends are then also subject to taxation as income to the individual shareholder and so are subject to a "double" taxation.

S-corporations are taxed similarly to partnerships, with the corporation acting only as a conduit and all of the deductions and income passing to the individual shareholders where they are subject to income tax. The S-corporation does not pay a corporate tax and files a different type of tax return than does a standard corporation. Taxation of the profits of the S-corporation falls to the individuals who own shares in the corporation. This also allows for each individual shareholder to personally deduct their share of any corporate losses. Corporations in general, however, may be used by businesses in many ways to actually lessen the Federal and state income tax burdens. A competent tax professional should be consulted. A brief study of the Federal tax forms your business will use will provide you with an overview of the method by which corporations are taxed. The financial records that you will compile using the forms in this book will make your tax preparation much easier, whether you handle this yourself or it is handled by a tax professional. A basic comprehension of the information required on Federal tax forms will help you understand why certain financial records are necessary. Understanding tax reporting will also assist you as you decide how to organize your business financial records.

A chart of tax forms is provided detailing which IRS forms may be necessary. In addition, a schedule of tax filing is also provided to assist you in keeping your tax reporting timely. Finally, a sample of each IRS tax form mentioned is included on the enclosed Forms-on-CD.

S-Corporation Tax Forms Checklist

❏ IRS Form 1040: *U.S. Individual Income Tax Return*. Must be filed by all S-corporation shareholders. Do not use IRS Form 1040-A or IRS Form 1040-EZ

❏ IRS Form 2553: *Election by a Small Business Corporation*. Must be filed by all S-corporations

❏ IRS Form 1120 S: *U.S. Income Tax Return for an S Corporation*. Must be filed by all S-corporations

❏ IRS Schedule K-1 (Form 1120S): *Shareholder's Share of Income, Credits, Deductions, etc.* Must be completed by all S-corporations

❏ IRS Form 1040-ES: *Estimated Tax for Individuals*. Must be used by all S-corporation shareholders who have a profit requiring estimated taxes

❏ IRS Form SS-4: *Application for Employer Identification Number*. Must be filed by all S-corporations

❏ IRS Form W-2: *Wage and Tax Statement*. Must be filed by all S-corporations

❏ IRS Form W-3: *Transmittal of Wage and Tax Statements*. Must be filed by all S-corporations

❏ IRS Form W-4: *Employee's Withholding Allowance Certificate*. Must be provided to employees of S-corporations. It is not filed with the IRS

❏ IRS Form 940 or IRS Form 940-EZ: *Employer's Annual Federal Unemployment (FUTA) Tax Return*. Must be filed by all S-corporations

❑ IRS Form 941: *Employer's Quarterly Federal Tax Return*. Must be filed by all S-corporations

❑ IRS Form 8109: *Federal Tax Deposit Coupon*. Must be filed by all S-corporations with a monthly tax liability over $500

❑ Any required state and local income and sales tax forms. Please check with the appropriate tax authority for more information

S-Corporation Tax Schedules

S-Corporation Monthly Tax Schedule

❑ If corporate payroll tax liability is over $1000 monthly, the corporation must make monthly tax payments using IRS Form 8109: *Federal Tax Deposit Coupon*

❑ If required: file and pay any necessary state or local sales tax

S-Corporation Quarterly Tax Schedule

❑ Pay any required estimated taxes using vouchers from IRS Form 1040-ES: *Estimated Tax for Individuals*

❑ File IRS Form 941: *Employer's Quarterly Federal Tax Return* and make any required payments of FICA and withholding taxes

❑ If corporate unpaid FUTA tax liability is over $100, make FUTA deposit using IRS Form 8109: *Federal Tax Deposit Coupon*

❑ If required: file and pay any necessary state or local sales tax

S-Corporation Annual Tax Schedule

❏ Prepare IRS Form W-2: *Wage and Tax Statement* and provide to each employee by January 31st. Also file IRS Form W-3: *Transmittal of Wage and Tax Statements* for each employee and copies of all W-2 forms with IRS by January 31st

❏ If corporation has paid any independent contractors over $600 annually, prepare IRS Form 1099-MISC: *Miscellaneous Income* and provide to recipients by January 31. Also file IRS Form 1096: *Annual Summary and Transmittal of U.S. Information Returns* and copies of all 1099 forms with IRS by January 31

❏ Make required unemployment tax payment and file IRS Form 940 or IRS Form 940-EZ: *Employer's Annual Federal Unemployment (FUTA) Tax Return*

❏ File IRS Form 1120 S: *U.S. Income Tax Return for an S Corporation* and IRS Schedule K-1 (Form 1120S): *Shareholder's Share of Income, Credits, Deductions, etc.*

❏ If required: file and pay any necessary state or local sales, income, or unemployment tax

Appendix: State Incorporation Information

On the following pages are state listings containing relevant information regarding incorporation. You are advised to check your state's listing carefully to determine the particular requirements for incorporation in your jurisdiction. Virtually every state has some differing conditions for incorporation. You are also advised to write to the state corporation department (or visit their website) for information on incorporation. They will provide you with any necessary updates on the information contained in this appendix. Following is an explanation of the listings:

Address of state corporation department: This listing provides the street address of each state's department that handles the registration of corporations.

State web address: This listing notes the internet web address of each state's online website. For most state sites, you will arrive at the main index for the state and will need to locate the specific site for the state's statute/legislative information by using the references in the listing below, *State law reference*. These websites were current at the time of this book's publication.

Download state forms: This listing provides a direct link to the state website from which you should be able to download any specific state forms. Generally, this is the Secretary of State's office website in a state.

State law reference: Should you wish to research the law in your state, this lists the name and chapter of the state statute in which the corporation laws are found in each state.

Title of filing: This listing specifies the name of the document that is filed with the state for incorporation. In this book, the document has always been referred to as "Articles of Incorporation." A number of states, however, use different titles. Please substitute the correct title on your form before filing it.

Availability of forms: This listing provides the name of the forms that are available from each state.

Filing fees: The cost of filing the Articles of Incorporation with the state. In some states, the fee is variable based on the amount of capital stock of the corporation.

Other fees: Details any other fees that are due at the time of filing or soon thereafter. These can be franchise taxes, organizational taxes, or various other required fees.

Name reservation: All states allow a proposed corporation to register its corporate name prior to filing in order to reserve the corporation's name. The cost and time limits, however, differ widely.

Name requirements: Specifies the corporate designation that is required in each state. Most states allow "corporation," "incorporated," "limited," "company," or some abbreviation of these. However, many states have variations on what designation is allowed.

Incorporator requirements: This listing specifies the number, age, and residency requirements for the person(s) acting as the incorporator(s) of the corporation.

Corporate purpose requirements: This specifies what must be put in the Articles of Incorporation regarding the business purpose of the enterprise. If the listing states: "General 'all-purpose' clause;" you should include the clause that is in the basic Articles of Incorporation form in this book. If a specific business purpose is required, replace this general clause with a statement of the actual business purpose.

Director requirements: Most states allow a corporation to have only one director, who may, generally, be a non-resident. However, several states have a requirement that the corporation have three directors, unless there are fewer than three shareholders. In these states, if there are fewer than three shareholders, the number of directors can equal the number of shareholders (ie., a one-shareholder corporation can have one director).

Paid-in-capital requirements: Most states have no requirement for paid-in-capital. A few, however, require that the corporation has $1,000.00 in actual paid-in-capital prior to commencing business. These states also require that you state this fact in the Articles of Incorporation.

Publication requirements: A few states require that you publish either your intention to incorporate or the actual fact of incorporation in a newspaper. Most states, however, do not have this requirement.

Other provisions: This listing details any other special incorporation requirements of each state. These range from additional items that must be added to the Articles of Incorporation to the use of different terminology. Check this listing carefully to determine the situation in your state.

Alabama

Address of state corporation department:
Alabama Secretary of State
Corporation Section
Box 5616
Montgomery AL 36103
State web address: http://www.alabama.gov/
Download state forms: http://www.sos.state.al.us/downloads/dl1.cfm
State law reference: Code of Alabama, Section 10-2B.
Title of filing: Articles of Incorporation.
Availability of forms: Domestic for-Profit Corporation Articles of Incorporation Guidelines.
Filing fees: $35 to the Judge of Probate in the county in which the corporation's registered office will be located and $40 to Secretary of State.
Other fees: Tax, $10 per $1,000 of stock, minimum $50; Permit, minimum $10.
Name reservation: Reservable for 120 days for $10 fee (required).
Name requirements: Corporation, Incorporated, or abbreviation.
Incorporator requirements: One or more persons, partnerships, or corporations. Need not be residents.
Corporate purpose requirements: General "all purpose" clause (see instructions).
Director requirements: One or more (may be nonresidents).
Paid-in capital requirements: None.
Publication requirements: None.
Other provisions: None.

Alaska

Address of state corporation department:
Alaska Department of Commerce and Economic Development
Corporations Section
Post Office Box 110808
Juneau AK 99811-0808
State web address: http://www.state.ak.us/
Download state forms: http://www.dced.state.ak.us/bsc/cforms.htm
State law reference: Alaska Statutes, Title 10, Section 10.06.
Availability of forms: Articles of Incorporation (Domestic for Profit Corporation).
Title of filing: Articles of Incorporation.
Filing fees: $250.
Other fees: Biennial corporation tax at filing, $100.
Name reservation: Reservable for 120 days for $25 fee.

Name requirements: Corporation, Incorporated, Company, Limited, or abbreviation.
Incorporator requirements: One or more persons, 18 years or older. Need not be resident.
Corporate purpose requirements: General "all purpose" clause (see instructions).
Director requirements: Three required, unless the Articles of Incorporation state otherwise. Then, there may be one or more (may be nonresidents).
Paid-in capital requirements: None.
Publication requirements: None.
Other provisions: Articles must include a statement of codes from the Alaska Standard Industrial Classification Code List describing business type.

Arizona

Address of state corporation department:
Arizona Corporation Commission
Corporation Filing Section
1300 West Washington Street
Phoenix AZ 85007-2927
State web address: http://www.azleg.state.az.us/
Download state forms: http://www.cc.state.az.us/corp/filings/forms/index.htm
State law reference: Arizona Revised Statutes, Section 10.
Title of filing: Articles of Incorporation.
Availability of forms: General Filing Instructions for Arizona Business Corporations, Articles of Incorporation for Domestic Corporations.
Filing fees: $60.
Other fees: None.
Name reservation: Reservable for 120 days for $10 fee.
Name requirements: Corporation, Incorporated, Company, Limited, or abbreviation.
Incorporator requirements: One or more persons.
Corporate purpose requirements: General "all purpose" clause (see instructions).
Director requirements: One or more.
Paid-in capital requirements: None.
Publication requirements: Articles must be published within 60 days of filing.
Other provisions: Articles must specify ending of corporation's fiscal year.

Arkansas

Address of state corporation department:
Arkansas Secretary of State
Corporation Division
State Capitol
Little Rock AR 72201-1095

State web address: http://www.arkleg.state.ar.us/
Download state forms:
http://www.sosweb.state.ar.us/corp_ucc_forms.html
State law reference: Arkansas Code, Section 4-27.
Title of filing: Articles of Incorporation.
Availability of forms: Articles of Incorporation.
Filing fees: Online, $45; Paper, $50.
Other fees: Initial corporation franchise tax due upon filing, minimum $50.
Name reservation: Reservable for 120 days.
Name requirements: Corporation, Incorporated, Company, Limited, or abbreviation.
Incorporator requirements: One or more persons.
Corporate purpose requirements: A specific primary purpose must be stated.
Director requirements: One or more (may be nonresidents).
Paid-in capital requirements: None.
Publication requirements: None.
Other provisions: There are no preemptive rights unless granted in the Articles.

California

Address of state corporation department:
Business Programs Division
1500 11th Street
Sacramento, CA 95814
Attention: Document Filing Support Unit
State web address: http://www.state.ca.us/
Download state forms: http:www.ss.ca.gov/business/corp/corp_formsfees.htm
State law reference: California Corporations Code, Section 100+.
Title of filing: Articles of Incorporation.
Availability of forms: Articles of Incorporation (Stock): General stock corporation.
Filing fees: $100.
Other fees: Franchise tax upon filing, $800; Annual filing agent statement, $10.
Name reservation: Reservable for 60 days for $10 fee.
Name requirements: Corporation, Incorporated, Limited, or abbreviation.
Incorporator requirements: One or more persons.
Corporate purpose requirements: General "all purpose" clause (see instructions).
Director requirements: Three (unless fewer than three shareholders, then same amount).
Paid-in capital requirements: None.
Publication requirements: None.

Other provisions: If initial directors are named in the Articles, they must sign the Articles of Incorporation. No preemptive rights unless granted in Articles.

Colorado

Address of state corporation department:
Colorado Secretary of State
Corporations Section
1560 Broadway, Suite 200
Denver CO 80202-5169
State web address: http://www.leg.state.co.us/
Download state forms: http://www.sos.state.co.us/pubs/business/doc/forms.html
State law reference: Colorado Revised Statutes, Section 7.
Title of filing: Articles of Incorporation.
Availability of forms: Form 200: Articles of Incorporation.
Filing fees: $50.
Other fees: None.
Name reservation: Reservable for 120 days for $10 fee (renewable).
Name requirements: Corporation, Incorporated, Company, Limited, or abbreviation.
Incorporator requirements: One or more persons, 18 years or older.
Corporate purpose requirements: General "all purpose" clause (see instructions).
Director requirements: One or more, 18 years or older. Need not be a state resident.
Paid-in capital requirements: None.
Publication requirements: None.
Other provisions: None.

Connecticut

Address of state corporation department:
Connecticut Secretary of State
Corporation Division
30 Trinity Street #104
Hartford CT 06106-1629
State web address: http://www.cga.state.ct.us/lco/
Download state forms: http://www.sots.state.ct.us/Forms/forms.html
State law reference: General Statutes of Connecticut, Section 33.
Title of filing: Certificate of Incorporation.
Availability of forms: Certificate of Incorporation.
Filing fees: $50.
Other fees: Initial tax upon filing, minimum $150; Biennial or annual report $75.
Name reservation: Reservable for 120 days for a $30 fee.

Name requirements: Corporation, Incorporated, Company, Limited, or abbreviation.

Incorporator requirements: One or more persons.

Corporate purpose requirements: General "all purpose" clause (see instructions).

Director requirements: One or more. Need not be a state resident.

Paid-in capital requirements: Articles must state minimum of $1,000.

Publication requirements: None.

Other provisions: First corporate report due within 30 days of first organizational meeting.

Delaware

Address of state corporation department:
Division of Corporations
PO Box 898
Dover, DE 19903

State web address: http://www.delaware.gov/

Download state forms: http://www.state.de.us/corp/corpforms.shtml

State law reference: Delaware Code, Chapter 1, Title 8.

Title of filing: Certificate of Incorporation.

Availability of forms: Stock Certificate of Incorporation.

Filing fees: $89.

Other fees: State tax, minimum $15; Indexing, $25; Annual report, $15; Franchise, tax $20.

Name reservation: Reservable for 30 days for $10 fee.

Name requirements: Corporation, Incorporated, Company, Limited, or abbreviation.

Incorporator requirements: One or more persons, partnerships, or corporations.

Corporate purpose requirements: General "all purpose" clause (see instructions).

Director requirements: One or more (may be nonresidents).

Paid-in capital requirements: None.

Publication requirements: None.

Other provisions: None.

District of Columbia (Washington D.C.)

Address of state corporation department:
Department of Consumer and Regulatory Affairs
Business and Professional Licensing
Administration
Corporations Division
941 North Capitol Street, NE
Washington, DC 20002

State web address: http://dccouncil.washington.dc.us/

Download state forms: http://dcra.dc.gov/information/build_pla/business_services/coporations_division.shtm

State law reference: District of Columbia Code, Section 29.

Title of filing: Articles of Incorporation.

Availability of forms: Articles of Incorporation Instruction Sheet, Articles of Incorporation Sample Guidelines.

Filing fees: $150.

Other fees: Initial license fee, minimum $35.

Name reservation: Reservable for 60 days for $25 fee.

Name requirements: Corporation, Incorporated, Company, Limited, or abbreviation.

Incorporator requirements: One or more persons, 18 years or older.

Corporate purpose requirements: A specific primary purpose must be stated.

Director requirements: One or more.

Paid-in capital requirements: Articles must state minimum of $1,000.

Publication requirements: None.

Other provisions: Corporation's name must not indicate that the corporation is organized under an Act of Congress.

Florida

Address of state corporation department:
Department of State
Division of Corporations
PO Box 6327
Tallahassee, FL 32314

State web address: http://www.leg.state.fl.us/

Download state forms: http://www.dos.state.fl.us/doc/form_download.html

State law reference: Florida Statutes, Section 607+.

Title of filing: Articles of Incorporation.

Availability of forms: Profit Articles of Incorporation

Filing fees: $35.

Other fees: Registered agent designation, $35; Annual report filing fee, $61.25.

Name reservation: Reservable for 120 days.

Name requirements: Corporation, Incorporated, Company, or abbreviation.

Incorporator requirements: One or more persons.

Corporate purpose requirements: General "all purpose" clause (see instructions).

Director requirements: One or more (may be nonresidents).

Paid-in capital requirements: None.

Publication requirements: None.

Other provisions: A Certificate of Designation of Registered Agent must be filed at the time of filing for incorporation.

Georgia

Address of state corporation department:
Georgia Secretary of State
Corporation Division
Suite 315 West Tower
2 Martin Luther King Drive SW
Atlanta GA 30334-9000

State web address: http://www.legis.state.ga.us/

Download state forms: http://www.sos.state.ga.us/corporations/filing_procedures.htm

State law reference: Official Code of Georgia Annotated, Title 14, Chapter 2.

Title of filing: Articles of Incorporation.

Availability of forms: Corporations: Profit and Nonprofit.

Filing fees: $100.

Other fees: Publication of Notice of Intent to file for incorporation, $40.

Name reservation: Reservable for 90 days for no fee.

Name requirements: Corporation, Incorporated, Company, Limited, or abbreviation.

Incorporator requirements: One or more persons or corporations.

Corporate purpose requirements: General "all purpose" clause (see instructions).

Director requirements: One or more (may be nonresidents).

Paid-in capital requirements: None.

Publication requirements: Must publish Notice of Intent to File to incorporate.

Other provisions: None.

Hawaii

Address of state corporation department:
State of Hawaii
Department of Commerce And Consumer Affairs
Business Registration Division
1010 Richards Street
Mailing Address: PO Box 40, Honolulu, Hawaii 96810

State web address: http://www.capitol.hawaii.gov

Download state forms: http://www.businessregistrations.com/registration/index.htm

State law reference: Hawaii Revised Statutes, Title 23, Chapter 415.

Title of filing: Articles of Incorporation.

Availability of forms: Articles of Incorporation (Domestic Profit) Form DC-1 with Instructions.

Filing fees: $100.

Other fees: Expedited service fee, $40; Annual report, $25.

Name reservation: Reservable for 120 days for $20 fee.

Name requirements: Corporation, Incorporated, Limited, or abbreviation.

Incorporator requirements: One or more persons or corporations.

Corporate purpose requirements: A specific primary purpose must be stated.

Director requirements: One or more.

Paid-in capital requirements: None.

Publication requirements: None.

Other provisions: At least one director must be state resident.

Idaho

Address of state corporation department:
Idaho Secretary of State
Corporation Division
700 W. Jefferson Street
Boise ID 83720

State web address: http://www.state.id.us/

Download state forms: http://www.idsos.state.id.us/corp/corindex.htm

State law reference: Idaho Code, Title 30.

Title of filing: Articles of Incorporation.

Availability of forms: Articles of Incorporation (General Business).

Filing fees: $100 typed; $120 not typed.

Other fees: $20 special handling fee if Certificate is to be returned within eight hours.

Name reservation: Reservable for four months for $20 fee.

Name requirements: Corporation, Incorporated, Company, Limited, or abbreviation.

Incorporator requirements: One or more persons.

Corporate purpose requirements: A specific primary purpose must be stated.

Director requirements: One or more (may be nonresidents).

Paid-in capital requirements: None.

Publication requirements: None.

Other provisions: None.

Illinois

Address of state corporation department:
Illinois Secretary of State
Corporation Division
Michael J. Howlett Bldg.
501 S. 2nd St., Rm. 328
Springfield, IL 62756

State web address: http://www.legis.state.il.us/

Download state forms: http://www.cyberdriveillinois.com/publications/businesspub.html

State law reference: Illinois Annotated Statutes, Chapter 805.

Title of filing: Articles of Incorporation.

Availability of forms: Form BCA-2.10 Articles of Incorporation.

Filing fees: $150.

Other fees: Initial franchise tax, minimum $25; Filing annual report, $25.

Name reservation: Reservable 90 days for $25 fee.

Name requirements: Corporation, Incorporated, Company, Limited, or abbreviation.

Incorporator requirements: One or more persons 18 years or older or corporations.

Corporate purpose requirements: General "all purpose" clause (see instructions).

Director requirements: One or more (may be nonresidents).

Paid-in capital requirements: None.

Publication requirements: None.

Other provisions: Illinois requires the use of state-provided forms for all corporate filings.

Indiana

Address of state corporation department:
Secretary of State
Corporations Division
302 W. Washington St., Rm. E018
Indianapolis, IN 46204

State web address: http://www.state.in.us/

Download state forms: http://www.ai.org/sos/forms/index.html

State law reference: Indiana Business Corporation Law, Section 23-1.

Title of filing: Articles of Incorporation.

Availability of forms: State Form 4159, Articles of Incorporation.

Filing fees: $90.

Other fees: Biennial report, $15 per year.

Name reservation: Reservable for 120 days for $20 fee (reservation is renewable).

Name requirements: Corporation, Incorporated, Company, Limited, or abbreviation.

Incorporator requirements: One or more persons.

Corporate purpose requirements: General "all purpose" clause (see instructions).

Director requirements: One or more (may be nonresidents).

Paid-in capital requirements: None.

Publication requirements: None.

Other provisions: No preemptive rights unless granted by the Articles of Incorporation.

Iowa

Address of state corporation department:
Iowa Secretary of State
Business Services
First Floor, Lucas Building
Des Moines, IA 50319

State web address: www.legis.state.ia.us/

Download state forms: http://www.sos.state.ia.us/business/form.html

State law reference: Iowa Code Annotated, Chapter 490.

Title of filing: Articles of Incorporation.

Availability of forms: Articles of Incorporation.

Filing fees: $50.

Other fees: None.

Name reservation: Reservable for 120 days for $10 fee.

Name requirements: Corporation, Incorporated, Company, Limited, or abbreviation.

Incorporator requirements: One or more persons or corporations.

Corporate purpose requirements: General "all purpose" clause (see instructions).

Director requirements: One or more (may be non-residents).

Paid-in capital requirements: None.

Publication requirements: None.

Other provisions: No preemptive rights unless granted in the Articles. Names of the initial board of directors must be given in the Articles.

Kansas

Address of state corporation department:
Kansas Secretary of State
Business Services
Memorial Hall, 1st Floor
120 SW 10th Avenue
Topeka, KS 66612-1594

State web address: http://www.accesskansas.org/
Download state forms: http://www.kssos.org/business/business.html
State law reference: Kansas Statutes Annotated, Section 17.
Title of filing: Articles of Incorporation.
Availability of forms: For Profit Articles of Incorporation.
Filing fees: $90.
Other fees: None.
Name reservation: Reservable for 120 days for $20 fee.
Name requirements: Many business designation names allowed.
Incorporator requirements: One or more persons, partnerships, or corporations.
Corporate purpose requirements: General "all purpose" clause (see instructions).
Director requirements: One or more (may be nonresidents).
Paid-in capital requirements: None.
Publication requirements: None.
Other provisions: Names and addresses of initial directors must be given in Articles of Incorporation.

Kentucky

Address of state corporation department:
Secretary of State
PO Box 718
Frankfort, KY 40602-0718
State web address: http://www.lrc.state.ky.us/
Download state forms: http://www.kysos.com/BUSSER/BUSFIL/forms.asp
State law reference: Kentucky Revised Statutes, Title 23, Chapter 271B.
Title of filing: Articles of Incorporation.
Availability of forms: Domestic Corporations: Articles of Incorporation—Business Corporation (SOS PAOI) with instruction sheet.
Filing fees: $40.
Other fees: Organization tax, minimum $10 (paid to State Treasurer).
Name reservation: Reservable for 120 days for $15 fee (renewable).
Name requirements: Corporation, Incorporated, Company, Limited, or abbreviation.
Incorporator requirements: One or more persons or corporations.
Corporate purpose requirements: General "all purpose" clause (see instructions).
Director requirements: One or more (may be nonresidents).
Paid-in capital requirements: None.

Publication requirements: None.
Other provisions: Number of initial directors must be stated in Articles.

Louisiana

Address of state corporation department:
Louisiana Secretary of State
Commercial Division
PO Box 94125
Baton Rouge, LA 70804-9125
State web address: www.legis.state.la.us/
Download state forms: http://www.sos.louisiana.gov/comm/corp/corp-index.htm
State law reference: Louisiana Revised Statutes, Section 12+.
Title of filing: Articles of Incorporation.
Availability of forms: #399: Articles of Incorporation—Louisiana Business and instruction sheet.
Filing fees: $60.
Other fees: Notary fee in Orleans parish, $25; Recording of articles, variable.
Name reservation: Reservable for 60 days for $10 fee.
Name requirements: Corporation, Incorporated, Company, Limited, or abbreviation.
Incorporator requirements: One or more persons or corporations.
Corporate purpose requirements: General "all purpose" clause (see instructions).
Director requirements: Not less than one.
Paid-in capital requirements: None.
Publication requirements: None.
Other provisions: Corporate name using "Company" cannot be preceded by "and" or "&." No preemptive rights unless granted by Articles.

Maine

Address of state corporation department:
Maine Secretary of State
Bureau of Corporations
Corporate Examining Section
101 State House Station
Augusta ME 04333-0148
State web address: http://janus.state.me.us/legis/
Download state forms: http://www.maine.gov/sos/cec/corp/formsnew/busforms.htm
State law reference: Maine Revised Statutes, Title 13A.
Title of filing: Articles of Incorporation.
Availability of forms: Form MBCA-6: Articles of Incorporation (Revised).
Filing fees: $125.

Other fees: Capital stock fee, minimum $30.

Name reservation: Reservable for 120 days for $20 fee.

Name requirements: No requirements.

Incorporator requirements: One or more persons or corporations.

Corporate purpose requirements: General "all purpose" clause (see instructions).

Director requirements: Three (unless less than three shareholders, then same amount).

Paid-in capital requirements: None.

Publication requirements: None.

Other provisions: Number of initial board of directors must be stated in Articles. Registered Agent is referred to as "Clerk" in Maine.

Maryland

Address of state corporation department:
State Department of Assessments and Taxation
Charter Division
301 W. Preston St., Room 801
Baltimore, MD 21201-2395

State web address: www.mlis.state.md.us/index.html

Download state forms: http://www.dat.state.md.us/sdatweb/charter.html

State law reference: Annotated Code of Maryland, Corp. and Assoc. Articles, Title 2.

Title of filing: Articles of Incorporation.

Availability of forms: Stock Corporation Form and Instructions.

Filing fees: $100.

Other fees: None.

Name reservation: Reservable for 30 days for $7 fee.

Name requirements: Corporation, Incorporated, Company, Limited, or abbreviation.

Incorporator requirements: One or more persons.

Corporate purpose requirements: General "all purpose" clause (see instructions).

Director requirements: Three (unless less than three shareholders, then same amount).

Paid-in capital requirements: None.

Publication requirements: None.

Other provisions: If name includes "Company," may not be preceded by "and" or "&." Names of initial directors must be stated in Articles.

Massachusetts

Address of state corporation department:
Secretary of the Commonwealth
One Ashburton Place, 17th floor
Boston, MA 02108

State web address: www.mass.gov/

Download state forms: http://www.state.ma.us/sec/cor/coridx.htm

State law reference: Massachusetts Business Corporation Law, Chapter 156B.

Title of filing: Articles of Organization.

Availability of forms: Domestic Profit Corporations Guidelines.

Filing fees: Contact Secretary of State.

Other fees: None.

Name reservation: Reservable for 30 days, renewable once.

Name requirements: Any name that indicates that business is incorporated.

Incorporator requirements: One or more persons, over 18 years old.

Corporate purpose requirements: A specific primary purpose must be stated.

Director requirements: Three (unless fewer than three shareholders, then same amount).

Paid-in capital requirements: None.

Publication requirements: None.

Other provisions: Name of initial directors and officers must be stated in Articles of Organization. Secretary is referred to as "Clerk" in Massachusetts. End date of fiscal year is required in Articles of Organization.

Michigan

Address of state corporation department:
Michigan Department of Commerce
Corporation Bureau
Box 30054
Lansing MI 48909

State web address: www.michiganlegislature.org

Download state forms: http://www.michigan.gov/businessstartup/0,1607,7-152-9738---,00.html

State law reference: Michigan Compiled Laws, Section 450.

Title of filing: Articles of Incorporation.

Availability of forms: Articles of Incorporation with Instructions.

Filing fees: $10.

Other fees: Organization fee, minimum $50.

Name reservation: Reservable for six months for $10 fee, renewable.

Name requirements: Corporation, Incorporated, Company, Limited, or abbreviation.

Incorporator requirements: One or more persons, partnerships, or corporations.

Corporate purpose requirements: General "all purpose" clause (see instructions).

Director requirements: One or more (may be nonresidents).

Paid-in capital requirements: None.

Publication requirements: None.

Other provisions: Mandatory filing with Michigan Treasury for various tax licenses is required (sales, use, income withholding, and single business tax).

Minnesota

Address of state corporation department:
Secretary of State
Business Services Division
180 State Office Bldg.
100 Rev. Dr. Martin Luther King Jr. Blvd.
St. Paul, MN 55155-1299

State web address: http://www.leg.state.mn.us/

Download state forms: http://www.sos.state.mn.us/business/forms.html

State law reference: Minnesota Statutes, Section 302A.

Title of filing: Articles of Incorporation.

Availability of forms: Articles of Incorporation (Business and Non-Profit) [same form].

Filing fees: $135.

Other fees: None.

Name reservation: Reservable for 12 months, renewable.

Name requirements: Corporation, Incorporated, Company, Limited, or abbreviation.

Incorporator requirements: One or more persons.

Corporate purpose requirements: General "all purpose" clause (see instructions).

Director requirements: One or more.

Paid-in capital requirements: None.

Publication requirements: None.

Other provisions: If name includes "Company," cannot be preceded with "and" or "&." Cumulative voting allowed unless stated in Articles.

Mississippi

Address of state corporation department:
Mississippi Corporation Registration
PO Box 136
301 North President Street
Jackson, Mississippi 39201

State web address: http://www.mscode.com/

Download state forms: http://www.sos.state.ms.us/forms/forms.asp?Unit=Corporations

State law reference: Mississippi Code Annotated, Title 79, Chapter 4.

Title of filing: Articles of Incorporation.

Availability of forms: Form F0001: Articles of Incorporation with instructions.

Filing fees: $50.

Other fees: Annual report, $25.

Name reservation: Reservable for 180 days for $25 fee.

Name requirements: Corporation, Incorporated, Company, Limited, or abbreviation.

Incorporator requirements: One or more persons.

Corporate purpose requirements: General "all purpose" clause (see instructions).

Director requirements: One or more (may be nonresidents).

Paid-in capital requirements: None.

Publication requirements: None.

Other provisions: Initial directors must be named in Articles. Within 60 days of incorporation, must file for Franchise Tax Registration with State Tax Commission.

Missouri

Address of state corporation department:
Corporations Division
PO Box 778
600 W. Main Street, Rm. 322
Jefferson City, MO 65102

State web address: www.moga.state.mo.us/

Download state forms: http://sos.state.mo.us/forms.asp

State law reference: Revised Statutes of Missouri, Chapter 351.

Title of filing: Articles of Incorporation.

Availability of forms: Articles of Incorporation of a For Profit Corporation (Corp. 41).

Filing fees: Organization tax, minimum $58, based on amount of stock.

Other fees: None.

Name reservation: Reservable for 60 days for $20 fee.

Name requirements: Corporation, Incorporated, Company, Limited, or abbreviation.

Incorporator requirements: One or more persons, 18 years or older.

Corporate purpose requirements: A specific primary purpose must be stated.

Director requirements: Three (unless less than three shareholders, then same amount).

Paid-in capital requirements: None.

Publication requirements: None.

Other provisions: Number of initial directors must be stated in the Articles of Incorporation.

Montana

Address of state corporation department:
Secretary of State
PO Box 202801
Helena, MT 59620-2801
State web address: http://leg.state.mt.us/
Download state forms: http://sos.state.mt.us/css/BSB/Filing_Forms.asp#CORPORATIONS
State law reference: Montana Code Annotated, Title 35.
Title of filing: Articles of Incorporation.
Availability of forms: Articles of Incorporation for Domestic Profit Corporation.
Filing fees: $70
Other fees: License fee, minimum $50; priority filing, add $20.
Name reservation: Reservable for 120 days for $10 fee.
Name requirements: Corporation, Incorporated, Company, Limited, or abbreviation.
Incorporator requirements: One or more persons or corporations.
Corporate purpose requirements: General "all purpose" clause (see instructions).
Director requirements: One or more (may be nonresidents).
Paid-in capital requirements: None.
Publication requirements: None.
Other provisions: Number of directors must be specified in the Articles of Incorporation.

Nebraska

Address of state corporation department:
Nebraska Secretary of State
Corporation Division
Box 94608
Lincoln NE 68509
State web address: http://www.unicam.state.ne.us/
Download state forms: http://www.sos.state.ne.us/corps/corpform.htm
State law reference: Revised Statutes of Nebraska, Chapter 21.
Title of filing: Articles of Incorporation.
Availability of forms: Filing Articles of Incorporation for Business Corporations Instructions.
Filing fees: Variable fee based on amount of stock, $60 minimum.
Other fees: Recording, $5 per page.
Name reservation: Reservable for 120 days for $25 fee.
Name requirements: Corporation, Incorporated, Company, Limited, or abbreviation.
Incorporator requirements: One or more persons.
Corporate purpose requirements: General "all purpose" clause (see instructions).
Director requirements: One or more (may be nonresidents).
Paid-in capital requirements: None.
Publication requirements: Notice of incorporation must be published for three consecutive weeks.
Other provisions: None.

Nevada

Address of state corporation department:
Secretary of State
New Filings Division
206 N. Carson Street
Carson City, NV 89701-4299
State web address: http://www.leg.state.nv.us/
Download state forms: http://sos.state.nv.us/comm_rec/crforms/domestic_index.htm
State law reference: Nevada Revised Statutes, Chapter 78.
Title of filing: Articles of Incorporation.
Availability of forms: Domestic Corporations Filing Packet (NRS 78) [complete packet includes instructions, Articles of Incorporation, fee schedules, and credit card checklist to file Articles of Incorporation].
Filing fees: Variable fee based on amount of stock, minimum $125.
Other fees: Filing of list of officers and directors, $85.
Name reservation: Reservable for 90 days for $20 fee, nonrenewable.
Name requirements: Corporation, Incorporated, Company, Limited, or abbreviation.
Incorporator requirements: One or more persons.
Corporate purpose requirements: General "all purpose" clause (see instructions).
Director requirements: One or more (may be nonresidents).
Paid-in capital requirements: None.
Publication requirements: None.
Other provisions: No given names may be used in corporate name. A list of officers and directors must be filed with the state.

New Hampshire

Address of state corporation department:
Secretary of State
Corporation Division, Department of State
107 N. Main St.
Concord, NH 03301-4989

State web address: http://www.nh.gov/
Download state forms: http://www.sos.nh.gov/corporate/Forms.html
State law reference: New Hampshire Revised Statutes Annotated, Chapter 293A.
Title of filing: Articles of Incorporation.
Availability of forms: Form 11: Articles of Incorporation.
Filing fees: $35.
Other fees: Filing of addendum, $50; License fee, minimum $75, variable.
Name reservation: Reservable for 120 days for $15 fee.
Name requirements: Corporation, Incorporated, Limited, or abbreviation.
Incorporator requirements: One or more persons or corporations.
Corporate purpose requirements: A specific primary purpose must be stated.
Director requirements: One or more (may be nonresidents).
Paid-in capital requirements: None.
Publication requirements: None.
Other provisions: An Addendum to the Articles must be filed stating that the stock of the corporation is either exempt or has been registered with the state.

New Jersey

Address of state corporation department:
NJ Division of Revenue
Corporate Filings Unit
PO Box 302
Trenton, NJ 08625
State web address: www.njleg.state.nj.us
Download state forms: http://www.state.nj.us/treasury/revenue/
State law reference: New Jersey Statutes, Title 14A.
Title of filing: Certificate of Incorporation.
Availability of forms: Complete Business Registration Packet
Filing fees: $100.
Other fees: Annual report, $40.
Name reservation: Reservable for 120 days for $50 fee.
Name requirements: Corporation, Incorporated, or abbreviation.
Incorporator requirements: One or more persons or corporations.
Corporate purpose requirements: General "all purpose" clause (see instructions).
Director requirements: One or more (may be nonresidents).

Paid-in capital requirements: None.
Publication requirements: None.
Other provisions: Number of directors on initial board must be stated in Certificate of Incorporation.

New Mexico

Address of state corporation department:
Public Regulation Commission
Corporations Bureau
Chartered Documents Division
PO Box 1269
Santa Fe, New Mexico 87504-1269
State web address: http://legis.state.nm.us
Download state forms: http://www.nmprc.state.nm.us/corporations/corpsforms.htm
State law reference: New Mexico Statutes Annotated, Section 53.
Title of filing: Articles of Incorporation.
Availability of forms: Domestic Profit Corporations: Requirements, Instructions, & Forms
Filing fees: Variable fee based on amount of stock, minimum $100.
Other fees: Initial corporate report filing fee, $20 (filed within 20 days).
Name reservation: Reservable for 120 days for a $20 fee.
Name requirements: Corporation, Incorporated, Company, Limited, or abbreviation.
Incorporator requirements: One or more persons or corporations.
Corporate purpose requirements: A specific primary purpose must be stated.
Director requirements: One or more (may be nonresidents).
Paid-in capital requirements: None.
Publication requirements: None.
Other provisions: None.

New York

Address of state corporation department:
New York State
Department of State
Division of Corporations
Albany, NY 12231
State web address: http://assembly.state.ny.us/
Download state forms: http://www.dos.state.ny.us/corp/corpwww.html
State law reference: New York Business Corporation Law.
Title of filing: Certificate of Incorporation.
Availability of forms: Certificate of Incorporation.
Filing fees: $125.

Other fees: Organization tax, minimum $10, variable based on stock.

Name reservation: Reservable for 60 days for $20 fee, renewable twice.

Name requirements: Corporation, Incorporated, Limited, or abbreviation.

Incorporator requirements: One or more persons.

Corporate purpose requirements: General "all purpose" clause (but see *Other Provisions* below).

Director requirements: One or more.

Paid-in capital requirements: None.

Publication requirements: None.

Other provisions: Purpose must state that corporation needs no approval of any state body. Articles must appoint N.Y. Secretary of State as registered agent.

North Carolina

Address of state corporation department:
Corporations Division
PO Box 29622
Raleigh, NC 27626-0622

State web address: www.ncga.state.nc.us/

Download state forms: http://www.secretary.state.nc.us/corporations/indxfees.asp

State law reference: General Statutes of North Carolina, Chapter 55.

Title of filing: Articles of Incorporation.

Availability of forms: Articles of Incorporation for Business.

Filing fees: $125.

Other fees: Filing annual report, $10.

Name reservation: Reservable for 120 days for $10 fee.

Name requirements: Corporation, Incorporated, Company, Limited, or abbreviation.

Incorporator requirements: One or more persons.

Corporate purpose requirements: General "all purpose" clause (see instructions).

Director requirements: One or more (may be nonresidents).

Paid-in capital requirements: None.

Publication requirements: None.

Other provisions: None.

North Dakota

Address of state corporation department:
Secretary of State
State of North Dakota
600 E Boulevard Ave Dept 108
Bismarck ND 58505-0500

State web address: http://www.state.nd.us/

Download state forms: http://www.state.nd.us/sec/businessserv/registrations/index.html

State law reference: North Dakota Century Code, Title 10-19.1.

Title of filing: Articles of Incorporation.

Availability of forms: North Dakota Business or Farming Corporation Articles of Incorporation and Registered Agent Consent.

Filing fees: $30.

Other fees: Initial franchise fee, minimum $50, variable (see below also).

Name reservation: Reservable for 12 months for $10 fee.

Name requirements: Corporation, Incorporated, Company, Limited, or abbreviation.

Incorporator requirements: One or more persons.

Corporate purpose requirements: General "all purpose" clause (see instructions).

Director requirements: One or more.

Paid-in capital requirements: None.

Publication requirements: None.

Other provisions: If "Company" is in corporate name, may not be preceded by "and" or "&." Consent to be Registered Agent must be filed with a $10 fee.

Ohio

Address of state corporation department:
Ohio Secretary of State
Corporation Division
30 East Broad Street, 14th Floor
Columbus OH 43215-3463

State web address: http://www.ohio.gov/

Download state forms: http://serform.sos.state.oh.us/sos/busiServ/formRef.htm

State law reference: Ohio Revised Code, Title 17, Chapter 1701.

Title of filing: Articles of Incorporation.

Availability of forms: Guide to Organizing a Business and Form 532: Initial Articles of Incorporation.

Filing fees: Minimum $125.

Other fees: None.

Name reservation: Reservable for 60 days for $5 fee.

Name requirements: Corporation, Incorporated, Company, or abbreviation.

Incorporator requirements: One or more persons.

Corporate purpose requirements: General "all purpose" clause (see instructions).

Director requirements: Three (unless fewer than three shareholders, then same amount).

Paid-in capital requirements: None.

Publication requirements: None.
Other provisions: Corporate Bylaws are referred to as the corporate "Code of Regulations" in Ohio. Must also file Appointment of Statutory Agent form.

Oklahoma

Address of state corporation department:
Secretary of State
2300 N Lincoln Blvd., Room 101
Oklahoma City, OK 73105-4897
State web address: http://www.oklahoma.gov/
Download state forms: http://www.state.ok.us/~sos/forms/forms.htm
State law reference: Oklahoma Statutes, Title 18.
Title of filing: Certificate of Incorporation.
Availability of forms: Certificate of Incorporation Procedures (profit) and Certificate of Incorporation Form (profit).
Filing fees: Minimum $50, variable fee based on amount of stock.
Other fees: None.
Name reservation: Reservable for 60 days for $10 fee.
Name requirements: May contain various business designations.
Incorporator requirements: One or more persons, partnerships, or corporations.
Corporate purpose requirements: General "all purpose" clause (see instructions).
Director requirements: One or more (may be nonresidents).
Paid-in capital requirements: None.
Publication requirements: None.
Other provisions: None.

Oregon

Address of state corporation department:
State of Oregon
Corporation Division
255 Capitol Street NE, Suite 151
Salem, Oregon 97310-1327
State web address: http://www.leg.state.or.us/
Download state forms: http://www.filinginoregon.com/forms/index.htm
State law reference: Oregon Revised Statutes, Chapter 60.
Title of filing: Articles of Incorporation.
Availability of forms: Articles of Incorporation.
Filing fees: $50.
Other fees: Annual report, $30.
Name reservation: Reservable for 120 days for $10 fee.

Name requirements: Corporation, Incorporated, Company, Limited, or abbreviation.
Incorporator requirements: One or more persons, partnerships, or corporations.
Corporate purpose requirements: General "all purpose" clause (see instructions).
Director requirements: One or more.
Paid-in capital requirements: None.
Publication requirements: None.
Other provisions: None.

Pennsylvania

Address of state corporation department:
Department of State
Corporation Bureau
PO Box 8722
Harrisburg, PA 17105-8722
State web address: http://www.state.pa.us/
Download state forms: http://www.dos.state.pa.us/corps/cwp/view.asp?a=1093&Q=431210&corpsNav=|
State law reference: Pennsylvania Consolidated Statutes, Title 15.
Title of filing: Articles of Incorporation.
Availability of forms: Articles of Incorporation.
Filing fees: $125.
Other fees: None.
Name reservation: Reservable for 120 days for $52 fee.
Name requirements: May use various business designations.
Incorporator requirements: One or more persons or corporations.
Corporate purpose requirements: General "all purpose" clause (see instructions).
Director requirements: One or more (may be nonresidents).
Paid-in capital requirements: None.
Publication requirements: Must publish intent to file or filing of Articles with Department of State.
Other provisions: Must file Docketing Statement at time of filing Articles.

Rhode Island

Address of state corporation department:
Office of the Secretary of State
Corporations Division
100 North Main Street
Providence, Rhode Island 02903-1335
State web address: http://www.state.ri.us/
Download state forms: http://www2.corps.state.ri.us/corporations/

State law reference: General Laws of Rhode Island, Title 7, Chapter 7-1.1.
Title of filing: Articles of Incorporation.
Availability of forms: Articles of Incorporation.
Filing fees: $230.
Other fees: License fee, minimum $100, variable based on stock amount.
Name reservation: Reservable for 120 days for $50 fee.
Name requirements: Corporation, Incorporated, Company, Limited, or abbreviation.
Incorporator requirements: One or more persons.
Corporate purpose requirements: General.
Director requirements: One or more (may be nonresidents).
Paid-in capital requirements: None.
Publication requirements: None.
Other provisions: Registered Agent must sign Articles of Incorporation.

South Carolina

Address of state corporation department:
South Carolina Secretary of State
PO Box 11350
Columbia, SC 29211
State web address: http://www.myscgov.com/
Download state forms: http://www.scsos.com/Forms.htm
State law reference: Code of Laws of South Carolina, Title 33.
Title of filing: Articles of Incorporation.
Availability of forms: Articles of Incorporation for a Domestic Corporation.
Filing fees: $135.
Other fees: Incorporation tax, $100; License fee and report fee, minimum $25.
Name reservation: Reservable for 120 days for $10 fee.
Name requirements: Corporation, Incorporated, Company, Limited, or abbreviation.
Incorporator requirements: One or more persons, partnerships, or corporations.
Corporate purpose requirements: General "all purpose" clause (see instructions).
Director requirements: One or more (may be nonresidents).
Paid-in capital requirements: None.
Publication requirements: None.
Other provisions: Certificate of Attorney must be signed by a South Carolina lawyer. Initial Corporate Report must state specific business purpose.

South Dakota

Address of state corporation department:
South Dakota Secretary of State
Corporation Division
500 E. Capitol Avenue #204
Pierre SD 57501-0570
State web address: http://www.state.sd.us/
Download state forms: http://www.sdsos.gov/Corporations/corpcover.htm
State law reference: South Dakota Compiled Laws, Title 47.
Title of filing: Articles of Incorporation.
Availability of forms: Domestic Business Corporations Booklet and Articles of Incorporation.
Filing fees: Minimum $100 variable fee based on amount of stock.
Other fees: Annual report, $25.
Name reservation: Reservable for 120 days for $15 fee.
Name requirements: Corporation, Incorporated, Company, Limited, or abbreviation.
Incorporator requirements: One or more persons, 18 years or older.
Corporate purpose requirements: General "all purpose" clause (see instructions).
Director requirements: One or more.
Paid-in capital requirements: Must have paid-in capital of at least $1,000.
Publication requirements: None.
Other provisions: Articles of Incorporation must state number, names, and addresses of initial directors.

Tennessee

Address of state corporation department:
State of Tennessee
Department of State
Division of Business Services
312 Eighth Avenue North
6th Floor, William Snodgrass Tower
Nashville TN 37243
State web address: http://state.tn.us/
Download state forms: http://www.state.tn.us/sos/forms.htm
State law reference: Tennessee Code Annotated, Title 48.
Title of filing: Charter.
Availability of forms: Corporate Filing and Information Services, Filing Guide For-Profit Corporations, and Charter.
Filing fees: $100.

Other fees: Register of deeds filing fee, $5/page if office is in Tennessee.

Name reservation: Reservable for four months for $20 fee.

Name requirements: Corporation, Incorporated, or abbreviation.

Incorporator requirements: One or more persons, partnerships, or corporations.

Corporate purpose requirements: General "all purpose" clause (see instructions).

Director requirements: One or more (may be nonresidents).

Paid-in capital requirements: None.

Publication requirements: None.

Other provisions: Articles of Incorporation also referred to as the Corporate Charter in Tennessee.

Texas

Address of state corporation department:
Secretary of State
PO Box 13697
Austin, TX 78711-3697

State web address: http://www.state.tx.us/

Download state forms: http://www.sos.state.tx.us/corp/index.shtml

State law reference: Texas Business Corporation Act.

Title of filing: Articles of Incorporation.

Availability of forms: Form 201: Articles of Incorporation for a Business Corporation.

Filing fees: $300.

Other fees: Initial franchise tax, $100 minimum.

Name reservation: Reservable for 120 days for $40 fee.

Name requirements: Corporation, Incorporated, or abbreviation.

Incorporator requirements: One or more persons, partnerships, or corporations.

Corporate purpose requirements: General "all purpose" clause (see instructions).

Director requirements: One or more (may be nonresidents).

Paid-in capital requirements: Paid-in capital must be at least $1,000.

Publication requirements: None.

Other provisions: Number, names, and addresses of initial directors must be stated in Articles.

Utah

Address of state corporation department:
State of Utah
Division of Corporations & Commercial Code

In person: 160 East 300 South, Main Floor
Mail in: 160 East 300 South, 2nd Floor, Box 146705
Salt Lake City, UT 84114-6705

State web address: http://www.utah.gov/

Download state forms: http://www.commerce.state.ut.us/corporat/corpforms.htm

State law reference: Utah Code Annotated, Title 16-100.

Title of filing: Articles of Incorporation.

Availability of forms: Information on Incorporating a Business Corporation, Preparing Articles for Profit Corporation.

Filing fees: $50.

Other fees: Annual report fee, $12.

Name reservation: Reservable 120 days for a fee.

Name requirements: Corporation, Incorporated, Company, or abbreviation.

Incorporator requirements: One or more persons, 18 years or older.

Corporate purpose requirements: General.

Director requirements: Three (unless fewer than three shareholders, then same amount).

Paid-in capital requirements: None.

Publication requirements: None.

Other provisions: Names and addresses of the initial directors must be stated in the Articles of Incorporation. Registered agent must sign Articles.

Vermont

Address of state corporation department:
Vermont Secretary of State
81 River Street, Drawer 09
Montpelier, VT 05609

State web address: www.leg.state.vt.us/

Download state forms: http://www.sec.state.vt.us/tutor/dobiz/dobizdoc.htm#forms

State law reference: Vermont Statutes Annotated, Title 11A.

Title of filing: Articles of Incorporation.

Availability of forms: Articles of Incorporation.

Filing fees: Minimum $75, variable fee based on amount of stock.

Other fees: Annual report, $25.

Name reservation: Reservable for 120 days for $20 fee.

Name requirements: Corporation, Incorporated, Company, Limited, or abbreviation.

Incorporator requirements: One or more persons, 18 years or older.

Corporate purpose requirements: General.

Director requirements: Three (unless fewer than three shareholders, then same amount).

Paid-in capital requirements: None.

Publication requirements: None.

Other provisions: Number, names, and addresses of the initial directors must be stated in the Articles of Association.

Virginia

Address of state corporation department:
Virginia State Corporation Commission
1300 E. Main Street
Richmond VA 23219-3630

State web address: http://www.virginia.gov/

Download state forms: http://www.state.va.us/scc/division/clk/fee_bus.htm

State law reference: Code of Virginia, Title 13.1, Chapter 9.

Title of filing: Articles of Incorporation.

Availability of forms: SCC Form 619: Articles of Incorporation—Stock Corporation.

Filing fees: $25.

Other fees: Charter fee, minimum $50, variable fee based on stock amount.

Name reservation: Reservable for 120 days for $10 fee.

Name requirements: Corporation, Incorporated, Company, Limited, or abbreviation.

Incorporator requirements: One or more persons.

Corporate purpose requirements: General "all purpose" clause (see instructions).

Director requirements: One or more (may be nonresidents).

Paid-in capital requirements: None.

Publication requirements: None.

Other provisions: None.

Washington

Address of state corporation department:
Washington Secretary of State
Corporations Division
Box 40234
Olympia WA 98504

State web address: http://www.leg.wa.gov/

Download state forms: http://www.secstate.wa.gov/corps/registration_forms.aspx

State law reference: Revised Code of Washington, Title 23B.

Title of filing: Articles of Incorporation.

Availability of forms: Application to Form a Profit Corporation.

Filing fees: $175.

Other fees: None.

Name reservation: Reservable for 180 days for a fee.

Name requirements: Corporation, Incorporated, Company, Limited, or abbreviation.

Incorporator requirements: One or more persons or corporations.

Corporate purpose requirements: General "all purpose" clause (see instructions).

Director requirements: One or more (may be nonresidents).

Paid-in capital requirements: None.

Publication requirements: None.

Other provisions: Must state official Washington State Unified Business Identifier in Articles, if issued. Registered agent must sign Articles.

West Virginia

Address of state corporation department:
West Virginia Secretary of State
Corporation Division
1900 Kanawha Blvd #157
Charleston WV 25305-0770

State web address: www.legis.state.wv.us/

Download state forms: www.wvsos.com/business/services/formindex.htm

State law reference: West Virginia Code, Chapter 31, Article 1.

Title of filing: Articles of Incorporation.

Availability of forms: Form CD-1: Articles of Incorporation.

Filing fees: $50.

Other fees: Annual license tax, minimum $75, variable fee based on stock.

Name reservation: Reservable for 120 days for $15 fee.

Name requirements: Corporation, Incorporated, Company, Limited, or abbreviation.

Incorporator requirements: One or more persons or corporations.

Corporate purpose requirements: General "all purpose" clause (see instructions).

Director requirements: One or more (may be nonresidents).

Paid-in capital requirements: None.

Publication requirements: None.

Other provisions: Number of initial directors must be stated in the Articles of Incorporation.

Wisconsin

Address of state corporation department:
Wisconsin Department of Financial Institutions
Corporation Division
345 W. Washington Avenue
Madison WI 53703-2701

State web address: www.legis.state.wi.us/

Download state forms: http://www.wdfi.org/corporations/

State law reference: Wisconsin Statutes Annotated, Chapter 180.

Title of filing: Articles of Incorporation.

Availability of forms: Form 2: Articles of Incorporation—Stock For-Profit Corporation.

Filing fees: Minimum $100 variable fee based on amount of stock.

Other fees: Annual report, $25.

Name reservation: Reservable for 120 days for $15 fee.

Name requirements: Corporation, Incorporated, Company, Limited, or abbreviation.

Incorporator requirements: One or more persons.

Corporate purpose requirements: General "all purpose" clause (see instructions).

Director requirements: One or more (may be nonresidents).

Paid-in capital requirements: None.

Publication requirements: None.

Other provisions: None.

Wyoming

Address of state corporation department:
Wyoming Secretary of State
Corporation Division
200 W. 24th Street #106
Cheyenne WY 82001-3642

State web address: http://legisweb.state.wy.us/

Download state forms: http://soswy.state.wy.us/corporat/corporat.htm

State law reference: Wyoming Statutes, Chapter 16.

Title of filing: Articles of Incorporation.

Availability of forms: Articles of Incorporation.

Filing fees: $100.

Other fees: Annual report, $25.

Name reservation: Reservable for 120 days for a minimum fee.

Name requirements: No statutory requirements.

Incorporator requirements: One or more persons or corporations.

Corporate purpose requirements: A specific primary purpose must be stated.

Director requirements: One or more (may be nonresidents).

Paid-in capital requirements: None.

Publication requirements: None.

Other provisions: Written Consent to Appointment as Registered Agent must accompany filing of Articles of Incorporation.

Glossary of Business, Legal, and Accounting Terms

Account: A separate record of an asset, liability, income, or expense of a business.

Accounting: The process for recording, summarizing, and interpreting business financial records.

Accounting method: The method of recording income and expenses for a business; can be either accrual method or cash method.

Accounting period: A specific time period covered by the financial statements of a business.

Accounting system: The specific system of record-keeping used to set up the accounting records of a business. See also *single-entry accounting* or *double-entry accounting*.

Accounts payable: Money owed by a business to another for goods or services purchased on credit. Money that the business intends to pay to another.

Accounts receivable: Money owed to the business by another for goods or services sold on credit. Money that the business expects to receive.

Accrual method: Accounting method in which all income and expenses are counted when earned or incurred regardless of when the actual cash is received or paid.

Accrued expenses: Expenses that have been incurred but have not yet been paid.

Accrued income: Income that has been earned but has not yet been received.

ACRS: Accelerated Cost Recovery System. Generally, a method of depreciation used for assets purchased between 1980 and 1987.

Agent: A person who is authorized to act on behalf of another. A corporation acts only through its agents, whether they are directors, employees, or officers.

Aging: The method used to determine how long accounts receivable have been owed to a business.

Articles of Incorporation: The charter of the corporation, the public filing with a state that requests that the corporation be allowed to exist. Along with the Corporate Bylaws, they provide details of the organization and structure of the business. They must be consistent with the laws of the state of incorporation.

Assets: Everything a business owns, including amounts of money that are owed to the business.

Assumed name: A name, other than the corporation's legal name as shown on the Articles of Incorporation, under which a corporation will conduct business. Most states require registration of the fictitious name if a company desires to conduct business under an assumed name. The corporation's legal name is not an assumed name.

Authorized stock: The number of shares of stock that a corporation is allowed to issue as stated in the Articles of Incorporation. All authorized shares need not be issued.

Balance sheet: The business financial statement that depicts the financial status of the business on a specific date by summarizing the assets and liabilities of the business.

Balance sheet accounts: Asset and liability accounts used to prepare business balance sheets.

Balance sheet equation: Assets = Liabilities + Equity, or Equity = Assets − Liabilities.

Board of directors: The group with control of the general supervision of the corporation. They are elected by the shareholders and the directors, in turn, appoint the officers of the corporation.

Bookkeeping: The actual process of recording the figures in accounting records.

Business corporation laws: For each individual state, these provide the legal framework for the operation of corporations. The Articles of Incorporation and the Bylaws of a corporation must adhere to the specifics of state law.

Business liabilities: Business debts. Also the value of the owner's equity in his or her business.

Bylaws: The internal rules that govern the management of the corporation. They contain the procedures for holding meetings, appointments, elections and other management matters. If these conflict with the Articles of Incorporation, the provision in the Articles will be controlling.

C-corporation: A business entity owned by shareholders that is not an S-corporation. Subject to double taxation, unlike S-corporations.

Calendar year: Year consisting of 12 consecutive months ending on December 31st.

Capital: Initially, the actual money or property that shareholders transfer to the corporation to allow it to operate. Once in operation, capital also consists of accumulated profits. The net worth of the corporation, the owner's equity in a business, and/or the ownership value of the business.

Capital expense: An expense for the purchase of a fixed asset; an asset with a useful life of over one year. Generally, must be depreciated rather than deducted as a business expense.

Capital stock: See *authorized stock*.

Capital surplus: Corporation owner's equity. See also *retained capital*.

Cash: All currency, coins, and checks that a business has on hand or in a bank account.

Cash method: Accounting method in which income and expenses are not counted until the actual cash is received or paid.

Certificate of Incorporation: See *Articles of Incorporation*. Note, however, that some states will issue a Certificate of Incorporation after the filing of the Articles of Incorporation.

Chart of Accounts: A listing of the types and numbers of the various accounts that a business uses for its accounting records.

Check register: A running record of checks written, deposits made, and other transactions for a bank account.

Close corporation: Corporation with less than 50 shareholders that has elected to be treated as a close corporation. Not all states have close corporation statutes. (For information regarding close corporations, please consult a competent attorney.)

Closely held corporation: Not a specific state-sanctioned type of corporation, but rather a designation of any corporation in which the stock is held by a small group of people or entities and is not publicly traded.

Common stock: The standard stock of a corporation that includes the right to vote the shares and the right to proportionate dividends. See also *preferred stock*.

Consent Resolution: Any resolution signed by all of the directors or shareholders of a corporation authorizing an action, without the necessity of a meeting.

Corporate record book: Contains all the corporate records (except accounting records).

Corporate stock transfer book: Record of the issuance and transfer of stock certificates.

Corporation: A business entity owned by shareholders; can be a C-corporation or an S-corporation.

Cost basis: Total cost to a business of a fixed asset.

Cost of goods sold: The amount that a business has paid for the inventory that it has sold during a specific period. Calculated by adding beginning inventory and additions to inventory and then deducting the ending inventory value.

Credit: In double-entry accounting, an increase in liability or income accounts or a decrease in asset or expense accounts.

Cumulative voting: A voting right of shareholders that allows votes for directors to be spread among the various nominees. This right protects the voting strength of minority shareholders. The amount of votes in cumulative voting is based on the number of shares held times the number of director positions to be voted on. The shareholder can then allocate the total cumulative votes in any manner.

Current assets: Cash and any other assets that can be converted to cash or consumed by the business within one year.

Current debt: Debt that will normally be paid within one year.

Current liabilities: Debts of a business that must be paid within one year.

Current ratio: A method of determining the liquidity of a business. Calculated by dividing current assets by current liabilities.

Debit: In double-entry accounting, a decrease in liability or income accounts or an increase in asset or expense accounts.

Debt: The amount that a business owes to another. Also known as "liability."

Debt ratio: A method of determining the indebtedness of a business. Calculated by dividing total liabilities by total assets.

Depreciation: Cost of fixed asset deductible proportionately over time.

Dissolution: Methods by which a corporation concludes its business and liquidates. Dissolutions may be involuntary because of bankruptcy or credit problems or voluntary on the initiation of the directors or shareholders of a corporation.

Dividend: A distribution of money or property paid by the corporation to a shareholder based on the amount of shares held. A proportionate share of the net profits of a business that the board of directors has determined should be paid out to shareholders, rather than held as retained earnings. Dividends must be paid out of the corporation's net earnings and profits. The board of directors has the authority to declare or withhold dividends based on sound business discretion.

Domestic corporation: A corporation is a domestic corporation in the state in which it is incorporated. See also *foreign corporation.*

Double-entry accounting: An accounting system under which each transaction is recorded twice: as a credit and as a debit. A very difficult system of accounting to learn and understand.

Equity: Any debt that a business owes. It is owner's equity if owed to the business owners and liabilities if owed to others.

Expenses: The costs to a business of producing its income. Any money that it has paid or will pay out during a certain period

FEIN: Federal Identification Number, used for tax purposes.

FICA: Federal Insurance Contributions Act. Taxes withheld from employees and paid by employers for Social Security and Medicare.

Fictitious name: See *assumed name.*

FIFO: First-in, first-out method of accounting for inventory. The inventory value is based on the cost of the latest items purchased.

Financial statements: Reports that summarize the finances of a business; generally a profit and loss statement and a balance sheet.

Fiscal year: A 12-month accounting period used by a business.

Fiscal-year reporting: For income tax purposes, reporting business taxes for any 12-month period that does not end on December 31 of each year.

Fixed assets: Assets of a business that will not be sold or consumed within one year. Generally, fixed assets (other than land) must be depreciated.

Foreign corporation: A corporation is referred to as a foreign corporation in all states other than the one in which it is actually incorporated. In order to conduct active business affairs in a different state, a foreign corporation must be registered with the other state for the authority to transact business and it must pay an annual fee for this privilege.

FUTA: Federal Unemployment Tax Act. Federal business unemployment taxes.

General journal: In double-entry accounting, used to record all of the transactions of a business in chronological order. Transactions are then posted (or transferred) to the appropriate accounts in the general ledger.

General ledger: In double-entry accounting, the central listing of all accounts of a business.

Gross pay: The total amount of an employee's compensation before the deduction of any taxes or benefits.

Gross profit: Gross sales minus the cost of goods sold.

Gross sales: The total amount received for goods and services during an accounting period.

Income: Any money that a business has received or will receive during a certain period.

Income statement: Financial statement that shows the income and expenses for a business. Also referred to as an "operating statement" or "profit and loss statement."

Incorporator: The person who signs the Articles of Incorporation. Usually a person, but some states allow a corporation or partnership to be an incorporator.

Indemnify: To reimburse or compensate. Directors and officers of corporations are often reimbursed or indemnified for all the expenses they may have incurred in incorporating.

Initial capital: The money or property that an owner or owners contribute to starting a business.

Intangible personal property: Generally, property not attached to land that you cannot hold or touch (for example: copyrights, business goodwill, etc.).

Inventory: Goods that are held by a business for sale to customers.

Invoice: A bill for the sale of goods or services that is sent to the buyer.

Issued shares: The number of authorized shares of stock that are actually transferred to shareholders of the corporation. Also referred to as outstanding shares. See also *treasury shares*.

Ledgers: The accounting books for a business. Generally, refers to the entire set of accounts for a business.

Liabilities: The debts of a business.

LIFO: Last-in, first-out method of valuing inventory. Total value is based on the cost of the earliest items purchased.

Liquidity: The ability of a company to convert its assets to cash and meet its obligations with that cash.

Long-term assets: The assets of a business that will be held for over one year. Those assets of a business that are subject to depreciation (except for land).

Long-term debts: Debts that will not be paid off in one year.

Long-term liabilities: The debts of a business that will not be due for over one year.

Long-term loans payable: Money due on a loan more than one year in the future.

Long-term notes payable: Money due more than one year in the future.

MACRS: Modified accelerated cost recovery system. A method of depreciation for use with assets purchased after January 1, 1987.

Managers: In a limited liabiility company, those persons selected by the members of the company to handle the management functions of the company. Managers of limited liability companies may or may not be members/owners of the company. Managers are roughly analogous to the officers of a corporation.

Members: In a limited liability company, those persons who have ownership interests (equivalent to shareholders in a corporation). Most states allow single-member limited liability companies.

Minutes: A written record of the activities of a meeting.

Net income: The amount of money that a business has after deducting the cost of goods sold and the cost of all expenses. Also referred to as "net profit."

Net loss: The amount by which a business has expenses and costs of goods sold greater than income.

Net pay: The amount of compensation that an employee actually will be paid after the deductions for taxes and benefits.

Net profit: The amount by which a business has income greater than expenses and cost of goods sold. Also referred to as "net income."

Net sales: The value of sales after deducting the cost of goods sold from gross sales.

Net worth: The value of the owner's share in a business. The value of a business determined by deducting the debts of a business from the assets of a business. Also referred to as "owner's equity."

No-par value: Shares of stock that have no specific face value. The board of directors can assign a value to the shares for sale and can then allocate a portion of the sales price to the paid-in-capital account.

Nontaxable income: Income that is not subject to any state or local sales tax.

Not-for-profit corporation: A corporation formed under state law that exists for a socially worthwhile purpose. Profits are not distributed but retained and used for corporate purposes. May be tax-exempt. Also referred to as "nonprofit."

Officers: Manage the daily operations of a corporation. Generally consists of a president, vice president, secretary, and treasurer. Appointed by the board of directors.

Operating margin: Net sales divided by gross sales. The actual profit on goods sold, before deductions for expenses.

Operating statement: Financial statement that shows the income and expenses for a business. Also referred to as "income statement" or "profit and loss statement."

Owner's equity: The value of an owner's share in a business. Also referred to as "capital."

Par value: The face value assigned to shares of stock. Par-value stock must be sold for at least the stated value, but can be sold for more than the par value.

Partnership: An unincorporated business entity that is owed by two or more persons.

Payee: Person or business to whom a payment is made.

Payor: Person or business that makes a payment.

Perpetual duration: Existence of a corporation forever.

Personal property: All business property other than land and the buildings that are attached to the land.

Petty cash: Cash that a business has on hand for payment of minor expenses when use of a business check is not convenient. Not to be used for handling sales revenue.

Petty cash fund: A cash fund. Considered part of cash on hand.

Petty cash register: The sheet for recording petty cash transactions.

Physical inventory: The actual process of counting and valuing the inventory on hand at the end of an accounting period.

Piercing the corporate veil: A legal decision that allows a court to ignore the corporate entity and reach the assets of the shareholders, directors, or officers.

Plant assets: Long-term assets of a business. Those business assets that are subject to depreciation (other than land).

Posting: In double-entry accounting, the process of transferring data from journals to ledgers.

Pre-paid expenses: Expenses that are paid for before they are used (for example: insurance, rent, etc.).

Preemptive rights: A shareholder right that allows shareholders the opportunity to maintain their percentage of ownership of the corporation in the event that additional shares are offered for sale.

Preferred stock: Generally, stock that provides the shareholder with a preferential payment of dividends, but does not carry voting rights.

Profit and loss statement: Financial statement that shows the income and expenses for a business. Also referred to as an "income statement" or "operating statement."

Proxy: A written shareholder authorization to vote shares on behalf of another. Directors may never vote by proxy (except in some close corporations).

Quorum: The required number of persons necessary to officially conduct business at a meeting. Generally, a majority of the shareholders or directors constitutes a quorum.

Real property: Land and any buildings or improvements that are attached to the land.

Reconciliation: The process of bringing a bank statement into agreement with the business check register.

Recovery period: Specific time period for dividing up the cost into proportionate amounts.

Registered agent: The person designated in the Articles of Incorporation who will be available to receive service of process (summons, subpoena, etc.) on behalf of the corporation. A corporation must always have a registered agent.

Registered office: The actual physical location of the registered agent. Need not be the actual principal place of business of the corporation.

Resolution: A formal decision that has been adopted by either the shareholders or the board of directors of a corporation.

Retail price: The price for which a product is sold to the public.

Retained capital: Corporation owner's equity. See also *capital surplus*.

Retained earnings: In a corporation, the portion of the annual profits of a business that are kept and reinvested in the business, rather than paid to shareholders in the form of dividends.

Revenue: Income that a business brings in from the sale of goods or services or from investments.

S-corporation: A type of business corporation in which all of the expenses and profits are passed through to its shareholders to be accounted for at tax time individually in the manner of partnerships. A specific IRS designation that allows a corporation to be taxed similarly to a partnership, yet retain limited liability for its shareholders.

Salary: Fixed weekly, monthly, or annual compensation for an employee.

Sales: Money brought into a business from the sale of goods or services.

Sales income: Revenue derived from selling a product of some type

Salvage value: The value of an asset after it has been fully depreciated.

Service income: Income derived from performing a service for someone.

Service of process: To accept subpoenas or summonses for a corporation.

Shareholder's equity: In a corporation, the owner's equity of a business divided by the number of outstanding shares.

Shareholders: Owners of issued stock of a corporation and, therefore, owners of an interest in the corporation. They elect the board of directors and vote on major corporate issues.

Short-term loans payable: Money due on a loan within one year.

Short-term notes payable: Money due within one year.

Single-entry accounting: A business recordkeeping system that generally tracks only income and expense accounts. Used generally by small businesses, it is much easier to use and understand than double-entry accounting.

Sole proprietorship: An unincorporated business entity in which one person owns the entire company.

Stock transfer book: The ledger book (or sheets) in which the registered owners of shares in the corporation are recorded.

Straight-line depreciation: Spreads the deductible amount equally over the recovery period.

Supplies: Materials used in conducting the day-to-day affairs of a business (as opposed to raw materials used in manufacturing).

Tangible personal property: Property not attached to land that you can hold and touch (for example: machinery, furniture, equipment).

Taxes payable: Total of all taxes due but not yet paid.

Treasury shares: Shares of stock that were issued, but later reacquired by the corporation and not canceled. May be issued as dividends to shareholders. They are issued, but not outstanding for terms of voting and quorums.

Trial balance: In double-entry accounting, a listing of all the balances in the general ledger in order to show that debits and credits balance.

Wages: Hourly compensation paid to employees, as opposed to salary.

Wages payable: Total of all wages and salaries due to employees but not yet paid out.

Wholesale price: The cost to a business of goods purchased for later sale to the public.

Working capital: The money available for immediate business operations. Current assets minus current liabilities.

Index

⭐ Nova Publishing Company ⭐
Small Business and Consumer Legal Books and Software

Law Made Simple Series

Basic Wills Simplified

ISBN 0-935755-90-X	Book only	$22.95
ISBN 0-935755-89-6	Book w/Forms-on-CD	$28.95

Divorce Agreements Simplified

ISBN 0-935755-87-X	Book only	$24.95
ISBN 0-935755-86-1	Book w/Forms-on-CD	$29.95

Living Trusts Simplified

ISBN 0-935755-53-5	Book only	$22.95
ISBN 0-935755-51-9	Book w/Forms-on-CD	$28.95

Living Wills Simplified

ISBN 0-935755-52-7	Book only	$22.95
ISBN 0-935755-50-0	Book w/Forms-on-CD	$28.95

Personal Bankruptcy Simplified (3rd Edition)

ISBN 1-892949-01-6	Book only	$22.95
ISBN 1-892949-02-4	Book w/Forms-on-CD	$28.95

Personal Legal Forms Simplified (3rd Edition)

ISBN 0-935755-97-7	Book w/Forms-on-CD	$28.95

Small Business Made Simple Series

C-Corporations: Small Business Start-up Kit

ISBN 0-935755-78-0	Book w/Forms-on-CD	$24.95

The Complete Book of Small Business Management Forms

ISBN 0-935755-56-X	Book w/Forms-on-CD	$24.95

Limited Liability Company: Small Business Start-up Kit (2nd Edition)

ISBN 1-892949-04-0	Book w/Forms-on-CD	$29.95

Partnerships: Small Business Start-up Kit

ISBN 0-935755-75-6	Book w/Forms-on-CD	$24.95

S-Corporation: Small Business Start-up Kit (2nd Edition)

ISBN 1-892949-05-9	Book w/Forms-on-CD	$29.95

Small Business Accounting Simplified (3rd Edition)

ISBN 0-935755-91-8	Book only	$22.95

Small Business Bookkeeping Systems Simplified

ISBN 0-935755-74-8	Book only	$14.95

Small Business Legal Forms Simplified (4th Edition)

ISBN 0-935755-98-5	Book w/Forms-on-CD	$29.95

Small Business Payroll Systems Simplified

ISBN 0-935755-55-1	Book only	$14.95

Sole Proprietorship: Small Business Start-up Kit

ISBN 0-935755-79-9	Book w/Forms-on-CD	$24.95

Legal Self-Help Series

Divorce Yourself: The National No-Fault Divorce Kit (5th Edition)

ISBN 0-935755-93-4	Book only	$24.95
ISBN 0-935755-94-2	Book w/Forms-on-CD	$34.95

Incorporate Now!: The National Corporation Kit (4th Edition)

ISBN 1-892949-00-8	Book w/Forms-on-CD	$29.95

Prepare Your Own Will: The National Will Kit (5th Edition)

ISBN 0-935755-72-1	Book only	$17.95
ISBN 0-935755-73-X	Book w/Forms-on-CD	$27.95

National Legal Kits

Simplified Bankruptcy Kit

ISBN 0-935755-83-7	Book only	$17.95

Simplified Divorce Kit

ISBN 0-935755-81-0	Book only	$19.95

Simplified Will Kit

ISBN 0-935755-96-9	Book only	$16.95

⭐ Ordering Information ⭐

Distributed by:
National Book Network
4501 Forbes Blvd. Suite 200
Lanham MD 20706

Shipping: $4.50 for first & $.75 for each additional
Phone orders with Visa/MC: (800) 462-6420
Fax orders with Visa/MC: (800) 338-4550
Internet: www.novapublishing.com